Frédéric Ozanam

Letters

Frédéric Ozanam
Letters
ISBN/EAN: 9783337105129
Printed in Europe, USA, Canada, Australia, Japan
Cover: Foto ©ninafisch / pixelio.de

More available books at **www.hansebooks.com**

OF

FREDERIC OZANAM,

*PROFESSOR OF FOREIGN LITERATURE
IN THE SORBONNE.*

Translated from the French,
WITH A CONNECTING SKETCH OF HIS LIFE,
BY
AINSLIE COATES.

"It is the doctrine of progress by Christianity that I attempt to bring back as consolation in these unquiet days."
FREDERIC OZANAM—*Civilization in the Fifth Century.*

NEW YORK, CINCINNATI, AND ST. LOUIS:
BENZIGER BROTHERS,
Printers to the Holy Apostolic See.
LONDON: ELLIOT STOCK.
1886.

CONTENTS.

CHAPTER		PAGE
I.	INTRODUCTORY—HIS FAMILY AND EARLY LIFE	1
II.	LAWYER'S OFFICE—PLANS FOR FUTURE WRITING—LITERARY OCCUPATIONS	17
III.	EARLY RESIDENCE IN PARIS—MM. AMPÈRE AND CHATEAUBRIAND—LETTERS	34
IV.	CHOLERA—SOCIAL PRESENTIMENTS—VARIED OCCUPATIONS AND ACQUAINTANCES	58
V.	CHRISTIAN ACTIVITY—PRACTICAL WORK—INWARD QUESTIONINGS	76
VI.	MORE QUESTIONINGS—CONFERENCE OF NOTRE DAME—HOME RECOLLECTIONS—ABBÉ MARDUEL—POLITICAL OPINIONS	84
VII.	VACATIONS—LAMARTINE—SELF-DISGUST—ANXIETY ABOUT HIS MOTHER—THE GRANDE CHARTREUSE—ASSOCIATION OF CHRISTIAN ARTISTS	111
VIII.	LEAVES PARIS FOR LYONS—ABSENCE OF VOCATION—ITALY—DANTE—SOCIETY OF ST. V. DE PAUL—ENDEAVOUR MADE TO OBTAIN A CHAIR OF COMMERCIAL LAW AT LYONS, AND TO HAVE OZANAM NOMINATED TO IT—RECONCILIATION OF THE TWO CLASSES, THE RICH AND THE POOR, BY CHRISTIAN CHARITY—LAW OCCUPATIONS	159

Contents.

CHAPTER	PAGE

IX. DEATH OF HIS FATHER—HIS MOTHER'S DECLINING HEALTH—PERPLEXITY AND DISTRESS OF ALL KINDS—ENDEAVOURS TO OBTAIN THE CHAIR OF LAW — DISGUST WITH THE BAR — ENERGETIC PLEADINGS—VIEWS ON MARRIAGE—SOCIETY OF ST. VINCENT DE PAUL—STUDIES ON DANTE - 188

X. VISIT TO PARIS — INCREASED ILLNESS OF HIS MOTHER—LACORDAIRE—SILVIO PELLICO—HIS MOTHER'S DEATH—OPENS HIS COURSE AS PROFESSOR OF COMMERCIAL LAW—THE CHAIR OF M. QUINET—M. COUSIN - - - - - 238

XI. OPENING LECTURE OF THE COURSE OF COMMERCIAL LAW—NOTES OF THE COURSE BY M. FOISSET— WEDDING POEM—M. COUSIN'S DESIRE—SOCIETY OF ST. VINCENT DE PAUL—LITERARY CONTEST AND SUCCESS—ENTRANCE INTO THE SORBONNE —HIS FRIENDS' EFFORTS FOR HIS MARRIAGE— HIS OWN THOUGHTS ON IT—AMELIE SOULACROIX —VISITS GERMANY - - - - - - 257

XII. RETURN HOME—ENTRANCE ON HIS DUTIES AT THE SORBONNE—MARRIAGE - - - - - 299

LETTERS

OF

FREDERIC OZANAM.

CHAPTER I.

INTRODUCTORY—HIS FAMILY AND EARLY LIFE.

A LITTLE more than thirty years ago, a young Frenchman (comparatively young, at least, for he had only passed his fortieth birthday) died at Marseilles. After his death, his wife consoled herself by collecting, arranging, and putting through the press his literary remains—so much as it was practicable to publish—in nine volumes. His friends showed their appreciation of his amiable character, intellectual endowments, and earnest life by rendering their aid in this enterprise, and his all but native city, Lyons, thought the best monument they could raise to his memory was an edition of his works. This man was Antoine-Frederic Ozanam, Professor of Foreign Literature in the Sorbonne. To him M. Guizot, speaking in the Academy after his death, referred as "model of a Christian man of letters: dignified and humble; ardent friend of science, and firm champion of the faith; tasting with tenderness the pure joys of life, and submitting with gentleness to the long expectation of death; carried away from the holiest affections and from the noblest labours, too soon according to the world, but already ripe for heaven and for glory." And of him M. Renan, who had perhaps listened to his lectures, is reported to have exclaimed: "Ah, how we loved him! What a beautiful soul!" After the publication of his Works which spread over a period of twelve or fourteen years —his literary remains were very numerous, and many of them quite unfinished—his friends, apparently with considerable hesitation, resolved upon putting a biography of him into the hands of the public, by publishing two volumes of letters. These remarkable letters are worthy of being widely known and read. Ozanam calls himself loquacious and prolix. One of his friends says of him that he not only possessed the art of loving his friends, but that of telling them so. Certainly some of these letters—written, perhaps, at rare intervals— are of a very unusual length. Whole pages are taken up in reasoning of things around him, persuading and exhorting, opening out his troubles and perplexities, sometimes in descriptions of country or of manner of life; lastly, in laying out in detail large plans of work to be done, both in action and writing, both by himself and any of his friends who would assist him. As they date from his eighteenth year, they are many of them written at a time when both heart and hand are apt to be diffuse and flowing. One of his friends, indeed, said that Ozanam never was young; but while this may be descriptive of the subjects, the scope, and the reasoning of his letters, there is plenty of the artlessness and freshness and ready flow of youth about them. Some of these letters might easily, however, be divested of the epistolary form altogether, and appear by themselves as dissertations, reports, etc. But there is no end of the short sentences or brief passages which might at the same time be culled for profit and interest from almost all. Twenty or twenty-five years after his death, his elder brother completed the monument of affection and esteem by publishing a "Life," in which a detailed account of his youth up to the time when the letters commence, and much which could not be drawn from the letters, is found, together with extracts from the letters themselves, and from his works.

These letters are translated and reproduced in the following pages. Not, indeed, wholly; there is much in them which may trench on Protestant feeling, or offend Protestant sympathies; and although it would not be well to exclude all these passages, simply upon this account, yet as by reason of the length of the letters much must be omitted, it seemed preferable to omit first some of those parts which from any cause might be presumed to lack interest to the present reader. Of the accompanying sketch of the life perhaps the same may be said.

Frederic Ozanam, though he might be styled a native of Lyons, was born in Milan. In the early part of the present century, his father, John Antoine Ozanam, with his wife and two children, had settled here. The family were said to be anciently of Jewish origin, and the name to be derived from the plural form of the word "Hosanna.' John Antoine, a man of forty years old at this time, and his wife Marie, eight years younger, each had a history behind them. The husband was a medical man at the time Frederic's life opens, having passed his examinations at Pavia since coming to Milan. Early in life he had felt the desire of practising what in later years he considered "a kind of priesthood," of which he often repeated that to fulfil its functions worthily one must be ready, if necessary, to give one's life for one's patients. In this he joined example to precept. When, in 1813, the typhus made terrible ravages in Milan, it is said that he established himself in the military hospital, and alone—for two doctors had just succumbed to the terrible plague—took under his charge three hundred sick, until the danger was past. For this devotion, "the decoration of the Iron Crown" was sent him. Later on, for many years he gave gratuitous aid to the poor, and his son Frederic chronicles that, after his death, when he had to inspect his affairs, he found that a large share of his visits were made to the poor, to those from whom he had no expectation of payment. His father, falling into the error which he himself somewhat singularly repeated in later years, desired to bring him up for the law, and to this desire he had deferred. He was, however, compelled to take arms at the beginning of the Revolution in 1793. In this time of terror his father was imprisoned and threatened with death; the fall of Robespierre intervened, after the young soldier had, by a desperately bold stroke, risked his own life to save his father's. He was at some of the most celebrated battles of the campaign— among others, Lodi and Pavia—passed through various adventures, and received various wounds, and was presented to Bonaparte, who promised to remember him.

He did not, however, desire to be remembered with martial honours; after six years' service, he obtained with some trouble his dismission, and in the following year married. A reverse of fortune drove him in a year or two to Milan, and there, wanting resources for his family, his mind fell back upon its early idea, and he entered the profession for which Nature seemed to have destined him.

His wife Marie, born at Lyons, where her father was a silk merchant, was still a child there, when, amid the other horrors of the Revolution, its siege took place. The little girl was hidden in the cellar, that she might be sheltered from the bombs; she saw her father and mother dragged to prison, together with a brother who was afterwards massacred. The parents escaped death, and were after joined by their child in Switzerland. In a village near Lausanne they took up their abode for a while, and there little Marie made her first Communion, instructed by a good Swiss curé, who was accustomed to repeat to his little catechumen with great gentleness some sweet words, which she in her turn repeated to her children when they were round her knees—whether they were the refrain of a hymn or not we know not: "We will go both of us, we will go both of us into Paradise." The miseries of her childhood, her later misfortunes—in especial the frequent loss of children—and her own somewhat delicate health, had made her nervous and prone "to look on the dark side of things." "The least thing excited her uneasiness," and the scrupulosity of her own conscience added to this. Probably, however, these developments came later on more into view; and in spite of all she was gentle and lively, making joyful songs for her children in their family feasts, and, adds her eldest son, in sketching her life, as an evident proof of her great goodness, "she kept during all her life the same servant." She herself, notwithstanding her many hindrances, was very active in her domestic life, rising at seven, dressing quickly, and forthwith "looking well to the ways of her household, occupying herself continually with her young children, teaching them to walk, to read, to write; her happiness, above all, was to give them their earliest lessons of piety and religion." She saw them put to bed, taught them to turn their little hearts to God, and spoke to them at the last a few words "of God, the Holy Virgin, the good Angel, or the Saints, mingling her gentle words with those mother's kisses which penetrated to the depth of the soul, and which embalmed them for ever." She watched over all their little works, taught them how to study; and the time was ruled for study, for play, for eating, and for sleeping, with regularity, and her watchfulness grew rather than lessened with their increasing years. Father and mother were earnest-minded Christians, having, indeed, as it would appear, no idea of forsaking the form of faith in which they had been brought up, but having certainly as little of abandoning the faith, or attempting to substitute for it the sceptical forms of their day. "In the midst of an age of scepticism," says Frederic, writing many years later, "God gave me the grace of being born in the faith. As a child He set me on the knees of a Christian father and of a holy mother."

While yet very young, John Antoine Ozanam had read the Bible of Calmet from beginning to end. Family prayer was had each evening; sometimes pious reading followed the prayer. Two children formed this family at the time our history opens—Elisa, a girl of twelve, lively and intelligent, "with a remarkable memory and a great aptitude for the sciences," and Alphonse, nine years old, who, later on, writes his mother's memoirs. The servant, Marie Croziat, must also be introduced here, as being in reality one of the family and a very valuable member. She must now have been about thirty years in the service of either parents or grandparents, of an honesty above proof, and a "fabulous economy," labouring with all her might, and gifted by nature with a good deal of originality, and also, what was perhaps better still, a very good judgment. She had passed the dark days of the Revolution with her masters or mistresses, and though she was not exempt from defects of temper and manner, her employers would as little have thought of separating from her as she from them. She died in the family many years later. "Seventy-two years in the service of our family," says Alphonse Ozanam. Here, then, and in this manner, had this family been living for four years, watching the *dénouement* of the "gigantic drama" which was working a complete revolution in the history of their country. "The brilliant star of Napoleon began to pale," the Russian war drew to its disastrous end, and the Milan hospitals were filled with sick and wounded, while typhus made frightful ravages.

It was at this time that, on one spring day, another babe came into the family (April 23rd, 1813), Antoine Frederic, who was baptized in a church since destroyed and rebuilt, Santa Maria dei Servi. He was a delicate child, and as he grew out of his first days, showed a nervous temperament from which he was destined to suffer greatly in future life, and an intellect decidedly in advance of his physical powers. He spoke early, and before he was able to walk they used to set him on the table whilst his brother and sister repeated their lessons; among other things, the fables of La Fontaine. He paid a serious attention to them, retained without difficulty entire passages whose poetry enticed him and favoured his infant memory. He also learned to make use of and apply them, and was hardly two years old when, his father playing with him, he quoted appositely a portion of one of them in answer to him.

His sister, Elisa, then fourteen or fifteen, was delighted with the cleverness of her little brother, and undertook carefully to develop his intelligence. She became his instructress in his early years, and taught him the elements of sacred history, geography, and some little fables. This gentle instructress, of whom Frederic, many years later, said that she was "pious and intelligent as the angels whom she went to rejoin," died after a short illness, when her little pupil was six or seven years old. When Frederic was four the family had returned to Lyons, where he was brought up, "becoming Lyonnese by heart." Dr. Ozanam removed when Milan came under Austrian rule, and when Frederic was ten years old he began to attend the Royal College at Lyons. The director of the College at that time was the Abbé Rousseau, and the child was happy in his teachers. One of them—M. Legeay—says that "he was of the small number of those of whom a prudent master ought to restrain the ardour."

Several Latin poems, preserved by M. Legeay, are given. One is put into the mouth of the unfortunate

Marie Antoinette, addressed to Madame Elizabeth in her last moments; one is addressed to the Virgin Mary; and there are various others. Of two of these the age is given—thirteen. One of these two last is "Of the Shortness of Life." A rough translation of this is added:

OF THE SHORTNESS OF LIFE.

As the swift eagle like a flash of light
From thundercloud comes down with rapid flight,
From the high heaven the little birds upon,
Snatches with quick claw and again is gone;

Or as in Grecian games the flying steed,
When first the trumpet gives the signal shrill,
From post to goal darts on with breathless speed,
And in a moment at the end stands still;

So, O my friends! the years are flying on
Not to return: so swiftly life is gone,
Youth's laughter dies away, and Time hath brought
With speedy foot old age with pensive thought.

The course of nature no delay can hold,
Not virtue's self—not prayers though humbly told;
No hundred victims with their dying breath
Can keep from us indomitable Death.

As from the snowy heights the mountain stream
Rushes in torrents o'er the stony ground,
O'erwhelms, effaces, like a passing dream,
Houses and trees which in its path are found;

So our sweet life departs with hasty flight;
Hardly the morning's dawn is o'er the land
When Vesper beams from heaven with evening light,
And following darkness cometh close at hand.

Hardly has man, unhappy, left the bed,
A cradled infant where he feebly lay,
He presses on the tomb with trembling tread ;
Just born he seeks the tomb—another stay !

In vain we deck our temples with a crown,
In vain among the fragrant rose we twine
The violet, and our troubles seek to drown,
Our rugged cares, with draughts of honeyed wine.

In vain, triumphant in the martial field
When death is all around, the hero stands,
And, joyful, bears the trophies war can yield—
Crops of bright laurels—to his native land ;

In vain the poet with his speaking song
Earns for himself from all a poet's name ;
And in his joy, the coming years along,
Deems he has gained an ever-flowing fame.

Earth, fame, and life must all behind be left ;
Wife and beloved children, friends so dear ;
While in one darksome kingdom we bereft
Abide, the land of shadows dark and drear.

Why not then seek the inmost rest of soul ?
The mind's repose, with virtue's constant powers,
Use Heaven's brief gift, the flying years control,
And with good deeds adorn the passing hours ?

Alas ! O friends ! believe, believe !
Time flies along, the minutes will not stay ;
And we our short career must quickly leave :
They draw, they snatch us with themselves away.

Here are a few more of his early poems as specimens. The translation in French prose of this and the preceding is given by M. Legeay, who deemed it well worth his while to preserve these compositions of his pupil.

THE ASCENSION OF CHRIST.

Who is this rising through the radiant skies
With shining vesture and with countenance,
As upward to the distant stars He flies,
    Of brilliant glance?

Light flowing from His brow divine,
And majesty o'er all doth shine;
And with sweet incense doth His floating hair
    Fill the soft air.

O day for ever placed 'mid days on high!
O shining grace of His all-conquering breath!
In which our Lord, returning to the sky,
    Trampled on Death!

Already rising swift, He leaves our earth,
Our earth unhappy as it lies adown:
He looketh back, then tendeth toward the mirth
    Of His Father's throne.

So He o'ercomes the darkness of the tomb,
And snaps death's bonds with all-victorious strife:
He comes with spoils from Hades' deepest gloom
    To the shores of life.

Not so much beauty follows the first birth,
When the sweet sun comes forth with radiance bright,
And in his brilliant course the joyful earth
    Recreates with light.

Why ragest thou, O Satan, still in vain?
Why sighs the gulf of darkness from beneath?
Behold, He triumphs who hath burst the reign
    And gates of Death!

Behold, the happy souls are in His train,
Following their Saviour, and with joy they sing,
They chant His praises; in full choir again
    They lead their King.

When about fifteen, Frederic gathered together a few of his Latin poems into a little book, which, with all modesty and affection, he dedicated to his father and his mother. An epistle in Latin verse to his father ends with the words, "Do not disdain these firstfruits of my labour; be for me not a judge, but a father." Here is the dedication—in French apparently—to his "dear mamma:" "It is again this giddy scholar who comes to break your head with his Latin. Take him to your indulgence; you have accustomed him to believe that all that he does for you may be agreeable to you. Besides, he pays you with what money he has. It is the only present which his purse permits him to offer you. Receive it with the wishes your son forms for you, Frederic Ozanam." A little later he composed a French poem, "Jeremiah on the Ruins of Jerusalem," from which are translated roughly a few extracts of the close; and a very different little thing—a translation into Latin verse from the Italian of Tasso, of Tasso's sonnet to his cats.

    Liban's proud cedar which into the sky
        Carried its head on high,
    Is fallen; now its trunk must lowly lie.
        Its boughs are dead and dry,
    Which rose aloft erewhile to touch the skies,
    And seemed to dare the fiercest storm to rise.

    Bethlehem's lily droops, its dazzling white
    Has gone, the rose no longer blooms in light:
    And thou thyself shalt see thy youth decay,
    Shalt see eclipsed thy vigour and thy power;
        And all thy beauty only is a flower
    Which soon in years shall wither and decay.

      o   o   o   o   o

All feel the burden of their conquering foe,
    And Zion weeps her widowhood :
Where I heard solemn hymns before,
I only hear the silence round,
And on these altars where of yore
The Ark of Covenant was found,
I only see dumb monsters lie
Who, gorged with blood and carnage past,
Still feed them on some new repast ;
Where are the monarchs of a sinful race?
Where are the kings of Israel found,
Whom yesterday in stately grace
I saw within their palace ground?

Then comes the prophet's parting address to Zorobabel :

With clearest voices let these ruins call,
And be they graven deep within thy soul,
That Zion's wail be king's untimely fall ;
That Babel, drunken, with her blood and dole,
May teach thee at what price man may the Lord
        Insult with deed or word.

But lo! upon my eyelid what new star
Sends down its ray?—a veil is torn aside,
The secret future opens from afar,
And brilliant day pours light as in a tide :
My heart is drunk with joy, reborn of pain,
        Destiny unfolds again.

Where go these warriors? O'er the desert sands
I see them marching towards our gloomy hills ;
As the proud eagle, so their conquering bands
Have come to lift up Sion from her ills ;
The temple rises and the walls once more
        They now restore.

But what new sun before them beaming light,
Illumines with its shining Israel?
It speaks already of the tempest's flight—

'Tis thou, my blessed son, Zorobabel!
These faithful hosts back to their land who brings;
    Winds lend your wings.

Console thyself, O Sion! wipe thy tears.
I see the incense on thine altars rise;
Thy land hath laid aside her woes and fears,
And in the temple now her songs arise;
She brings to God her firstfruits once again
    With joyful strain.

And thou, proud Queen—thou, haughty Babylon!
Where shall we seek thy state, thy ruins where?
The Lord in wrath hath overturned thy throne,
Thy crown is broken, answered is our prayer;
But thou, Jerusalem, forget no more
    Thy Saviour Lord to adore.

He speaks. Zorobabel with heart-relief
Hastes to o'ertake his people in their grief,
And with the blessing of the prophet's hand
Takes up his chains and quits his native land.

TASSO'S SONNET TO HIS CATS.

As when the tempest on a cloudy night
Covers the heavens and lifts with thunder hoarse
The watery deep, with terror and affright
The trembling sailor seeks to guide his course
By stars he dimly sees through clouds alight
With fiery vengeance, so to me whom force
Of stern misfortune in this dungeon drear
Hath cast adown, I seek my only cheer
In thy bright eyes, O cat! and thus it seems
Their sparkling glance brings comfort to my dreams.
As polar star gives hope amid the storm,
So I see them; and yet another form—
A little cat—my straining eyes descry,
And then still more uplighteneth my care.
I think I have, as in the starry sky
Beside the Pole, a great and little Bear!
O cats who lighten up my toilsome day—

Oh cats, how much I love you, who shall say!
May kindly Fortune keep you safe from blows,
And bring of meat and milk in full supplies!
Only enlighten me, my verse to close,
With the bright sparkle of your glancing eyes!

Frederic was rapidly approaching a less serene time of life, so far as outward things were concerned; and indeed even now, before he went out into the world, and before it might have been expected, a trial fell upon him—a trial which comes in some form or other, at some time or other, to many, not to all—a trial from which neither his Christian education, his upright simple-heartedness, neither father, nor mother, nor brother, though they might help, could entirely save him. Distressing doubts found their way into his mind—sceptical doubts. "The noises of a world which believed not," he says, "came even to me. I knew all the horror of those doubts which consume the heart by day, and which one finds again at night on a pillow moistened by tears. The uncertainty of my eternal destiny left me no repose." It was given to a "priest philosopher"—M. Noirot, professor of philosophy for twenty years in the College at Lyons—to come to his effectual aid, and to put 'into his thoughts order and light,' so that 'he believed henceforward with a faith reassured and touched with so rare a benefit he promised to God to devote his days to the service of the truth which gave him peace." M. Noirot was a highly intelligent and benevolent-hearted man. He took his young pupil Frederic with him in his walks about the rugged borders of the Saone and in the environs of Lyons, and there conversed with him without note of time on whatever he wished to consult him; and it was he who re-opened "the windows of his soul to the day," who dusted out from them and from the corners of his soul the cobwebs which too much thought of many things had engendered. "To him eternal gratitude," said Frederic later on. This desolating time passed over at last, leaving, as one result, a kindlier consideration for those with whom in later years he had to do. "Oh," said he to his brother often then, "they accuse me sometimes of treating with too much indulgence and gentleness those who have not faith. When one has passed through the sufferings of doubt, one would feel it a crime to treat harshly those unhappy ones to whom God has not yet granted the grace of believing."

In the midst almost of his troubles, or perhaps directly after—after the promise which he had made to God—the thought rose up in his mind which left it no more, which remained with him always, forming his life-work—or the greater part of his life-work—the thought of a work which he would execute, to which he would devote himself—a written book which should undertake the proof and illustration of the truth of Christianity by history. He was then sixteen. Title and plan altered and developed as years passed on, but to the day of his death the elaboration and development of this idea occupied his mind.

CHAPTER II.

LAWYER'S OFFICE—PLANS FOR FUTURE WRITING—
LITERARY OCCUPATIONS.

FREDERIC OZANAM left college at sixteen or seventeen as Bachelor of Letters, and, by his father's desire, entered as clerk in the study of M. Coulet, a distinguished lawyer of the bar of Lyons. Dr. Ozanam had set his heart on his son's entering the magistracy. He wished, he said, in some memoirs which he left behind, to make him an advocate, or rather a counsellor, a judge, in some Royal Court. " He has delicate sentiments," added the father, " pure and generous, and he will be an enlightened and upright magistrate. I dare to hope he will be our consolation in our old age." When Frederic entered the office of M. Coulet, his father gave him, apparently as a *douceur*, a master in drawing and also in German, to relieve the dryness of his law occupations. But his mind was surging with all manner of thoughts outside his apparent career; and, as letters of this date show, his work which he intended to write never ceased to occupy him.

To M. Hippolyte Fortoul and to M. H——,
Students-in-Law.

Lyons, January 15th, 1831.

My good Friends,

*   *   *   *   *

As for me, my part is taken, my task is traced for life; and, in character of friend, I ought to let you share it.

As you, I feel that the past is falling, that the foundations of the old building are shaken, and that a terrible shock has changed the face of the earth. But what will rise out of the ruins? Will society remain buried under the rubbish of overturned thrones, or will she re-appear more brilliant, younger, and more beautiful? Shall we see "*Novos cœlos et novam terram*"? There is the great question. I, who believe in Providence, and who do not despair of my country as Charles Nodier, I believe in a sort of palingenesis. But what will be the form of it? What will be the law of the new society? I do not undertake to decide it.

Nevertheless, that which I believe to be certain is, that there is a Providence, and that this Providence could never abandon during six thousand years reasonable creatures, naturally desirous of the true, the good, and the beautiful, to the evil genius of ill and of error; that, consequently, all the beliefs of the human kind cannot be extravagances, and that there are truths all over the world. These truths, the point is to find again, to disengage them from the error which envelops them. We must search in the ruins of the old world for the cornerstone on which to reconstruct the new. This would be almost like the columns which, according to historians, were raised before the deluge to transmit the deposit of traditions to those who should survive as the ark floated over the waters, carrying with her the fathers of the human race.

But this stone of hope, this column of traditions, this barque of safety, where must we seek it? Among all the ideas of antiquity, where shall we disinter the only true, the only legitimate ones? Where shall we begin, where finish?

Here I pause, and I reflect: the first need of man, the first need of society, are the religious ideas; the heart thirsts for the infinite. Besides, if there is a God, and if there are men, there must be relations between them; from thence a religion; consequently a primitive revelation; consequently, again, it is a primitive religion, ancient in its origin, essentially divine, and by that even essentially true.

It is this heritage, transmitted from on high to the first man, and from the first man to his descendants, that I am eager to search out. I wander away, then, across the countries and the ages, stirring the dust on all the tombs, rummaging the *débris* of all the temples, digging up all the myths, from the savages of Koock until the Egypt of Sesostris, from the Indians of Vishnu to the Scandinavians of Odin. I examine the traditions of each people. I ask myself the origin, the reason of them; and, aided by the lights of geography and history, I acknowledge in all religion two elements sufficiently distinct: an element variable, particular, secondary, which has its origin in the circumstances of time and of place in which each people was found, and an element immutable, universal, primitive, inexplicable by history and geography. And as this element is found in all religious beliefs, and appears so much more entire, so much purer, as one returns to the most ancient times, I conclude that it is it alone which reigns in the earliest days, and which constitutes the primitive religion. I conclude, consequently, that religious truth is that which, spread over all the earth, is found again among all nations, transmitted by the first man to his posterity, afterwards corrupted, mingled with all fables and with all errors.

Here is the need which I have felt in society; in myself I have felt one altogether analogous: I must have something solid to which I may attach myself and take root to resist the torrent of doubt. And then, O my friends! my soul is filled with joy and consolation; for see! by the strength of her reason, she has found again precisely this Catholicism* which was formerly taught me by the mouth of an excellent mother, which was so dear to my childhood, and which nourished so often my mind and my heart with its beautiful memories and its hopes yet more beautiful—Catholicism with all its grandeurs, with all its delights! Shaken some. time by doubt, I felt an invincible need to attach myself with all my strength to the column of the temple, even should it crush me in its fall; and now, behold to-day I find it again, this column, resting upon knowledge, luminous with the rays of wisdom, glory, and beauty! I find it again; I embrace it with enthusiasm, with love. I will abide beside it, and from it I will stretch out my arm. I will show it as a pharos of deliverance to those who are

---

* It must be remembered that this word is used by Ozanam to a great extent as a synonym for Christianity.

floating on the sea of life, happy if some friends will group themselves around me! Then we would join our efforts, we would create a work together; others should unite themselves to us, and perhaps one day society would gather altogether under this protecting shadow. Catholicism, full of youth and force, should rise all at once upon the world; it should put itself at the head of the new-born century to conduct it to civilization, to happiness! O my friends! I feel myself moved in speaking to you, I am filled with intellectual enjoyment; for the work is magnificent, and I am young. I have much hope; and I believe that the time will come when I shall have nourished, strengthened my thought, when I shall be able to express it worthily. Yes, preliminary labours have already discovered to me the vast perspective which I have just opened out, and over which my imagination hovers with transport. But it is little to contemplate the road which I have to run. I must put myself in the way, for the hour has come; and if I wish to make a book at thirty-five, I must begin at eighteen the preliminary labours, which are in great number.

In effect, to know a dozen languages, to consult sources and documents, to know tolerably well geology and astronomy, to be able to discuss the chronologic and cosmogonic systems of peoples and of learned men; to study, in a word, universal history in all its extent, and the history of religious beliefs in all its depth—that is what I have to do to attain to the expression of my idea. You will exclaim, without doubt; you will mak merry over the temerity of this poor Ozanam; you will think of the frog of La Fontaine, and of the *ridiculus mus* of Horace. As you please! I also have been astonished at my boldness; but what is to be done? When an idea has seized upon you for two years, and taken the first place in your thought, impatient as it is to spread itself without, are you master to hold it back? When a voice cries to you without ceasing, *Do this, I will it!* can you tell it to keep silence?

For the rest, I have communicated my thought to M. Noirot, who has encouraged me much to accomplish my plan. And as I showed him that I feared to find the charge too heavy for me, he has assured me that I should find many studious young people ready to help me with their counsels and their labours: then I have thought of you, my good friends.

I would tell you yet many things, but the departure of the bearer of the letter does not leave me the time. Another time I will speak to you of my manner of thinking on Saint-Simonism: it does not take here, and it is not generally thought of in a favourable manner.

My little brother Charlot has written to H——, but I have not his letter here to send it.

Adieu! many things to the friends at Paris; and to you, dear friends, the sincere friendship of your college companion.

To M. Hippolyte Fortoul and M. H——.

Lyons, February 21st, 1831.

My good Friends,

It is my turn to scold. You had promised to my next letter a prompt reply; I have written, more than a month has passed, and I have not yet heard from you. And yet the months now are centuries, the weeks are epochs. All these vast spectacles ought to stir young souls; all this ought to make young hearts gush out, and feel their need of overflowing to those around by sweet and familiar intercourse. Why, then, do you thus leave your poor friends of the province in a complete emptiness of ideas and of documents?

As to myself, many things pass in my mind; and certainly, if I had the leisure to reflect, I should have in myself wherewith to make a good course in psychology. When my eyes turn towards society, the prodigious variety of events excites in me the most different sentiments: by turns my heart is inundated with joy or steeped in bitterness; my mind dreams a future of glory and of happiness, or fancies it sees in the distance barbarism and desolation approaching with rapid steps. . . . I tell myself that the spectacle to which we are called is grand; that it is great to assist at so solemn an epoch; that the mission of a young man in society is to-day very grave and very important. Far from me the thoughts of discouragement! Dangers are an aliment for a soul which feels in itself an immense and undefined want which nothing can satisfy. I rejoice at being born at an epoch when perhaps I shall have to do much good, and then I feel a new ardour for work.

I pursue my researches as much as possible, I prepare myself for my work; for, denuded as I am of scientific resources, all that I can do is to give myself up to preliminary studies. I endeavour to embrace in one general glance the subject which must one day take up all my faculties; I measure the course, and the more I survey it, the more satisfaction I feel, because my presentiments on the issue of my researches take more force and consistency, and I see more clearly for the last result the great principle which at first appeared to me through so many clouds—the perpetuity, the *catholicism* of religious ideas, the truth, the excellence, the beauty of Christianity.

I needed, my good friends, to open my heart a little, separated as I am almost continually from my dear M—— and my other old companions. I have seen M. Noirot. He is better: his indisposition has lessened, but his goodness is always the same. He received us very well; he has explained to us thy two letters, my dear Fortoul: he little approves that thou shouldst give thyself up exclusively to metaphysical speculations. He always loves thee much, and begs thee much to write to him, to tell him of all thy philosophical designs. What a friend is this good M. Noirot! To him eternal gratitude,—to you inviolable attachment, and the constant memory of your friend and companion-in-arms.

It will be seen by the date that Frederic was not eighteen when these letters were written. He had arranged the plan and foreseen the reasons for his work, the way of executing it, and the numerous studies necessary for it. He walked the streets reading old books as he went along, absorbed in his own thoughts and occupations; and, being very short-sighted, striking sometimes against the people he happened to meet, although he hastened to excuse himself earnestly when such misadventures happened. The next letter is to a dear cousin and companion:

To M. Ernest Falconnet.

Lyons, September 4th, 1831.

My dear Ernest,

*   *   *   *   *

. . . Since I have reflected on the fate of humanity, one principal idea has always struck me: in the same way as a flower contains in its bosom the innumerable germs of flowers which must succeed it, in the same way the present, which comes from the past, contains the future. If, then, it is true that humanity is to undergo a new recomposition at the end of the revolutions which she experiences, we must acknowledge that the elements of this definitive synthesis are to be found again in the past; for we must not admit that Providence has left the human race sitting during six thousand years in the shadow of error and of death, without light and without support.

In applying this formula to religion we will say that, man being a being essentially religious, and religion being absolutely necessary to his development, intellectual and moral, it is impossible that he should remain a century even, in ignorance or in error on a subject so grave. On the other side, could he, by his own forces, arrive quickly at religious truth? No, since at the end of four thousand years, Aristotle and Plato, the two greatest geniuses which have ever existed, were yet very far from possessing pure ideas; and that which is best in Plato are the traditions which he has copied. Besides, physical wants absorbing the attention, left little time for philosophic reflection. And it is proved that without education man remains shut up in the material world; that to education alone it belongs to raise him to moral ideas. This education transmitted from father to son, from whom did the first father receive it? There is the proof of a primitive revelation. Then this question of right, *What is the religious future of humanity?* develops, clears up, and gives place to this question of fact, *What was the primitive religion?*

Nunc animis opus, Ænea, nunc pectore firmo. Here we must arm ourselves with courage and resolution for immense researches; for here we are about to make the tour of the world. It is a question of describing all the religions of the peoples of antiquity, and of the savage peoples (who are also from our point of view, *ancient primitive*); it is a question of bringing together in one vast tableau all the beliefs and their phases. I call this first labour *Hierography*.

We have acquired the knowledge of facts, we must determine their relations, we must understand the genealogy, the parentage of the diverse religions. Now, the *parent beliefs* are divided into sects, into multiplied branches. This work I name *Symbolic*.

Now, it remains to discover the causes of this innumerable variety. We must explain each myth to discover its spirit and meaning: to discover under the veil of allegory the fact, or the mystery, which is hidden there; and, putting on one side all the secondary, variable elements, those which relate to times, places, circumstances, to gather up, as the gold from the bottom of the crucible, the primitive, universal element—Christianity; this is *Hermeneutic*.

And these three sciences—the one of facts, the second of relations, the third of causes—are brought together in a single one, which I name *Mythology*.

Elaborated thus, in an order analytic and rational, this science brought to its term may be presented under the form of synthesis or history.

Then would be offered to our attention, upon the first plan, the creation of man and the primitive revelation; after that, sin and the corruption of belief; lastly, the developments and the subdivisions of each of these adulterated sources and the permanence of the tradition of the Mosaic law till the day of Christ.

And there, if death or old age have not yet arrested us, there, rises up the grand figure of Christianity in all its splendour: the Christ, the philosophy of His doctrine presented as the definitive law of humanity; afterwards, its glorious application during eighteen centuries; and in the end, the determination of the future.

Magnificent trilogy, in which should be retraced the origin of Christianity, its doctrine, its establishment; or, if thou choosest, the laborious birth of humanity, the exposition of the law which should govern it, and its first steps in this divine law. Thou understandest that this labour necessitates a knowledge sufficiently profound of the geography, of the natural history of each country, of astronomy, of psychology, of philology, of ethnography.

For an acquaintance with the revolutions of languages and of peoples will serve for foundation and for counterproof to the history of religious revolutions; and besides, as the phenomena of the physical and the social world, as well as the passions of the heart, come by turns to reflect themselves in the beliefs, we must needs know how to disentangle them, and we must needs know them.

Nevertheless, do not be discouraged; there is already behind us much labour accomplished. The *Mithridates* of Adelung, the *Symbolique* of Creuzer, the labours of Champollion, of Abel Remusat, of Eckstein, of Schlegel and of Gœrres, offer us rich mines to dig from; besides, we are two, and we may even join to ourselves other labourers. With regard to that, I have a project which I will communicate to thee by living voice. In a word, *to conquer without peril is to triumph without glory*, and the more difficult the work is, the greater it will be to accomplish it.

Thy ideas about glory are natural enough to a young man: we must not make an end of it, but accept it as a favour. Amorous of his own existence, man desires incessantly to see it prolonged; he lives again in his children, he lives again in his works. He seems to himself to live again in the heart of all those who bless his name. True glory is the gratitude of posterity. As the good man does not scatter his benefits to obtain gratitude, and nevertheless accepts these tributes with a sweet satisfaction, so the true philosopher, the Christian, does not act for glory, and nevertheless cannot hinder himself from being sensible of it. But, as often ingratitude and forgetfulness follow the greatest benefits, the righteous man carries his hopes higher; his reward and glory he awaits from an incorruptible Judge; he appeals from ungrateful man to a God who will recompense.

I have received from M. de Lamartine a very flattering letter, and from *L'Avenir* a very honourable report of my work. I tell thee this because I know that thou art interested in all which interests me, and because in this little pamphlet I have thrown the germ of the idea which must occupy our life.

I have seen Fortoul and H—— again. They are both so romantic that I no longer comprehend them, so romantic that they even become classic to excess. Thou laughest! Thou art wrong. I reply to thee that they are so bewitched by Victor Hugo, that they only swear by him, and maintain that the entire age ought to walk after him. Now, to walk in the leading-strings of a man, I maintain is to be classic *par excellence*. They know no longer neither Lamartine nor Chateaubriand; they din into your ears without ceasing, *Notre Dame de Paris, Plick et Plock, Atar-Gull, Marion Delorme*, etc.; and if you have not read what they have read, Malediction! is the compliment which they address to you. They are so tolerant, these gentlemen! It is almost like *Nemesis*, a Liberal journal, which said lately—

> "And let Liberty, goddess with the agile wing,
> Arms in her hand, her gospel bring."

Then these folks go about declaiming against the Inquisition and against the armed conversions of Charlemagne! *Risum teneatis, amici!*

Here is a very long letter! What would you? One does not weary of conversing with a good friend.

The letter of Lamartine referred to follows. The reference is to a small work which Frederic had actually published now—a kind of beginning of the defence of Christianity to which he had vowed his life, "Reflections on the Doctrines of Saint-Simon." It was about a hundred pages, and was published in April. It was written on account of the coming of this singular sect to Lyons about this time:

M. LAMARTINE TO FREDERIC OZANAM.
Mâcon, August 18th, 1831.

I have just received with gratitude, and read with astonishment for your age, and admiration for your sentiments and your talent, the work which you have done me the honour to address to me. Receive all my thanks. I am proud that a thought from me, hardly expressed, has inspired you with so good a commentary. Believe that the thought was in you; mine has only been the spark which has lighted your soul.

This beginning promises us one combatant more in the sacred conflict of religious and moral philosophy which this age wages against a materialist reaction. As you, I augur well of the success. We possess it not; but the voice of conscience, that infallible prophecy of the heart of the honest man, assures us of it for our children. Let us trust to this instinct and live in the future.

Receive, sir, the assurances of my highest consideration.

LAMARTINE.

Meanwhile, the young clerk had superadded to his clerkship various studies, Sanscrit and Hebrew among them, that he might be able to comprehend the better the primitive religions. He "read enormously," and wrote both poetry and prose for a Lyons publication called *The Bee*. He conversed at large with his elder brother during long and interesting excursions which they made together in the holidays, and he consulted other friends concerning his plans. His brother says that he sometimes engaged him to narrow his plan, which seemed too vast "not to pass the strength and duration of one man's life." The priest-brother, too, seems to have been somewhat afraid lest, in his ardour, Frederic should unintentionally be making some attack on some sacred dogma by the width and breadth and generality of his intended inquiries, and he recommended a prudence "from which," he adds, however, "he (Frederic) never departed."

At the same time, Frederic was not without opportunities for evil. In his daily calling he had met with young men who would willingly have made him their companion, and who related to him their various orgies, while they uttered against religion those sacrilegious railleries which they had gathered from their books. Frederic, however, soon put an effectual stop to these conversations, and let them know that he was neither weak nor wicked, though much younger than they. They had so much restraining power still at work in them, that they neither despised nor hated him for his prowess. On the contrary, they treated him henceforth with respect. His endless law-copying went on, and possibly in the manner of doing it there might be some room for the remorse that crept into his mind, the more that, not content with the necessary studies for his future book, not content with his contributions to *The Bee*, the indefatigable student had laid out the plan of an epic poem in Latin verse on the taking of Jerusalem by Titus. This chapter may finish with a little ode which he wrote for his father on New Year's Day, 1831 :

> As on the borders of the flowing stream,
> The traveller pauses as in lingering dream,
> Lays down his staff some stony seat beside,
> And with bent brow regards the hastening tide ;
>
> So, while our unresisting lives along,
> The wave bears swiftly with monotonous song,
> To mark the waters as they onward race
> I sit me down and dream a little space.
>
> Adieu to you who with a constant flight
> Still flee away, my earliest years so bright ;
> As friends of old who pass for ever on,
> Take my regrets ere yet ye all are gone.
>
> With you, too, flee your joys, each festal day,
> Each blooming wreath, your own hand takes away :
> All you bear off ; even hours of grief depart ;
> All save the yearning memories of the heart.
>
> A son's fond memories time may not control ;
> Safe in the very holiest depth of soul,
> In vain years pass away ; this braves their course,
> And holds its own with an unyielding force.
>
> And thou, New Year, with blessing will we greet,
> New hopes and joys round thy advancing feet ;
> Are they not in our road, and will not rays
> From brighter sun light up more peaceful days ?
>
> Hear thou my word ! Oh, give from out thy hand
> Peace and goodwill to my own beauteous land ;
> Draw spirits each to each, and in thine arms
> Stifle the demon with his war's alarms.
>
> To those from whom all came to me—whose Truth
> And Love wrapped round my childhood and my youth,

Give them to bring to port a favouring wind,
And in full cup pure honey may they find.

Give to their child—to me—with force I ask,
And light, even to the end to work my task;
And of the seed which their own hands have sown,
Grant me to render them the fruits—their own.

CHAPTER III.

EARLY RESIDENCE IN PARIS—MM. AMPÈRE AND CHATEAUBRIAND—LETTERS.

FREDERIC was eighteen on April 23rd, 1831. Late in October, or early in November of the same year, he left his home to study law in Paris. His parents carefully provided, as they thought, for his comfort and well-being in the capital; but his first letter shows that in some way they had made a great mistake.

FREDERIC OZANAM TO HIS MOTHER.

Paris, November 7th, 1831.

You will willingly permit me, my good mother, to make you pay a sum of fourteen sous in order to make you acquainted with news of this poor Frederic that you and I know so well, and who believes himself not forgotten at Lyons, although a distance of a hundred leagues separates him from it.

My passing gaiety has totally made shipwreck. Now that I am alone, without distraction, without outward consolation, I begin to feel all the sadness, all the emptiness of my position. I, so accustomed to the familiar talks, who found so much pleasure and sweetness in seeing again each day gathered around me all those who are dear to me, who had so much need of counsels and encouragements—here am I, thrown without support, without rallying-point, in this capital of egotism, in this whirlwind of passions and of human errors. Who trouble themselves about me? The young people of my acquaintance are too far from my domicile for me to see them often. I have to open my heart to, only you, my mother, you and the good God. But these two are worth many others!

I have a thousand things to say to you; but where shall I begin? Shall I tell you what I have seen? No; you desire to know, in the very first place, where and how I find myself. Here it is: I have been established since Saturday evening in my boarding-house, in a little room to the south, over the gardens very near to the Jardin des Plantes. "Thou findest thyself comfortable, then?" you say. Not at all; I am very uneasy, and my griefs are numerous. I am distant from the school of law, from the lecture-rooms, from the centre of studies, and from my Lyons comrades. Then my hostess has the air of a crafty gossip; her words and her manners have made me presume that she has a strong affection for the purse of the young people. Lastly, and this is my great reason, the company here is not good. There are ladies and young ladies, boarders as well, who eat at table with us, who take the lead in the conversation, and whose discourse and appearance are extremely common. From my room I hear them putting forth great bursts of laughter; for you must know that it is the custom here to join every evening, to play at cards, and they press me to take part in these games. You may easily think that I refused. These people are neither Christians nor Turks. I am the only one who practises abstinence, and by that alone am exposed to a thousand *quo libets*. It is very disagreeable to find one's self in such society. You will tell me what you think of it and what my father thinks, and you will judge if I should make other arrangements.

I begin to know Paris a little, notwithstanding the rain, which is continual. I have seen the Pantheon, singular monument—a pagan temple in the midst of a town whose inhabitants are Christians or Atheists—a magnificent cupola, lacking the cross which crowned it so well—a superb façade whose sombre colour indicates an origin greatly anterior to its extravagant destination. What signifies, in effect, a tomb without a cross, a place of sepulchre without the religious thought which presides there? If death is only a material phenomenon which leaves no hope after it, what mean these honours rendered to dry bones and to a flesh which falls into rottenness? The worship of the Pantheon is a veritable comedy, like that of Reason and of Liberty. But the people have need of a religion, and when they have taken from them that of the Gospel, necessity is great to fabricate for them another, were it at the price of folly and stupidity.

I have been amply made up to for these sad reflections by the beauty of the church St. Etienne du Mont—my parish—the pomp of the ceremonies, and the magnificence of the singing and the organ. A general vibration agitated all my nerves in hearing this instrument of a thousand voices resounding under the Gothic vault, all uniting to glorify the Lord and to chant His praises, as David said, on the harp and the cither, on the flute and trumpets!

*   *   *   *   *

Fortunately Ozanam had a visit of civility to pay, which introduced him both to better and pleasanter company. It was to M. Ampère the elder, and the following letter to his father gives the account and the results of it :

TO HIS FATHER.

Paris, November 12th, 1831.

Do not disturb yourself, I beg you, my good father, if I so often take the liberty of writing to you; but it must needs be that I keep you well informed respecting my affairs, and I have something very important to communicate to you.

On Thursday I went to pay a visit of civility to M. Ampère, Member of the Institute, whom I had seen at Lyons with M. Perisse. After having given me a very cordial welcome, he addressed to me some questions about my situation at Paris, on the charge at my boarding-house; then, rising all at once, he led me into a very agreeable apartment, occupied till the present time by his son, and then—"I offer you," he said to me, "table and lodging with me at the same charge as in your boarding-house. Your tastes and your sentiments are similar to mine; I shall be very glad to have the opportunity of talking with you. You shall make the acquaintance of my son, who occupies himself greatly with German literature; his library shall be at your disposal. You practise abstinence, so do we. My sister, my daughter, and my son dine with me. This will be agreeable society for you; what think you of it?" I have replied that such an arrangement would please me much, and that I should write for your opinion.

Paris, 7th December, 1831.

To-day I am much better, since I have been settled for two days at M. Ampère's. I am installed in a beautiful and pleasant room, planked and wainscoted, having two doors upon the garden, a library full of German, Italian, indeed even Swedish and Spanish books, which I use but little, and some good works of French literature in small numbers. It is the library of M. Ampère *fils*. I have a good stove of Dutch tiles, where I only make a little fire for economy's sake; a marble chimney-piece, ornamented with an antique amphora, but empty for many ages of this good foamy Falerna of which my friend Horace speaks. I send you the geometrical plan of my room. It is warm, light, and lively.

You may, perhaps, laugh at me. However, I wager that this scrawl will amuse mamma. She will imagine she sees me sitting before my table, lying down in my bed, going from my table to my woodpile, and from the woodpile to the stove.

We breakfast at ten o'clock, we dine at half-past five altogether—M. Ampère, his daughter, and his sister. M. Ampère is talker; his conversation is amusing and very instructive; I have already learned many things since I have been with him. His daughter talks very well, and takes part in what is said. M. Ampère has appeared to me very caressing for her, but he converses with her continually of science. Endowed with a prodigious memory for all which is scientific, in whatever order of knowledge it may be, he is forgetful of all household affairs. He has learned Latin by himself; he has only made Latin verses for two years, and he makes them well; he has a wonderful knowledge of history, and reads with as much pleasure a dissertation on the hieroglyphics as a collection of experiences on physics and natural history. All this with him is instructive. The discoveries which have carried him to the position which he occupies to-day, have come to him, he says, all at once, without knowing why. He is finishing at this time a great encyclopedic project.

Well, this is the excellent man with whom I find myself installed. Are you not very glad of it, my good father? I forgot to tell you that a tone of perfect politeness prevails in the house. I forgot, also, to give you my address—" Rue des Fossés St. Victor, No. 19."

I have not yet called again on M. de Chateaubriand. I am waiting for M. de Bonnevie's* letter, which will furnish me with a new reason for presenting myself there. I saw M. de la Mennais the eve of his departure for Rome. I conversed some time with him. All these learned men of Paris are full of affability. I have heard the course of M. Lherminier, one of the most celebrated Professors of the College de France, a learned man and

* M. l'Abbé de Bonnevie was a Canon of Lyons, well acquainted with Chateaubriand. He was a fine benevolent man with a priestly air, whose manner showed "the distinctions of nature and the elevation of grace." "He loved young people, and received them well." The memory of his eccentric taste for long phrases survived him; and a story is told that one day a dog having entered the cathedral where he was preaching, he requested the Swiss attendant to remove him in these terms : " Son of Helvetia, drive out of the temple this importunate symbol of fidelity."

very eloquent, but very unfortunate in gesture and elocution. He teaches a course of comparative law.

I saw yesterday M. Serullas. He is an excellent man, but gifted in the highest degree with scientific distraction. I found him occupied with chemical manipulations, which he took good care not to interrupt; while at the same time receiving me very well, and regaling me from time to time, as he said himself, with the inflammation of some fragments of potassium. But he was not in the vein, and his experiment did not succeed. He carried me into his cabinet, talked to me much about you, my father, to whom he seemed much attached, and he has offered me his services. This man is very lively. He resembles you in this point; but he is altogether employed in his business, and only knows his chemistry.

* * * * *

You see that to-day I am optimist; in my last letter, care had rendered me pessimist, and all appeared evil to me. Now that the affairs of Lyons are calm, that I have society and a room to my fancy, and before me the hope of having books, fire, and money, what is wanting to me? You, my good father—you and all my family. Oh! that is what I want, and what I am longing to see again. How good it will be to embrace each other eight months hence! While I write, midnight approaches; soon I shall no longer know whether it is good-morning or good-evening that I should say to you. What would you! when the heart and the hand are in spirits together, how can we stop them?

Adieu, my father.

Frederic had become now the inmate of a happy,

apparently well-regulated family. Here he remained for two years; and it was the beginning of a lifelong friendship, not only with the father, who died in a few years, but with the son, M. Ampère *fils*. M. Ampère the elder was an earnest and good Christian. He would converse with his young guest of the marvels of nature, and " passing from Nature up to Nature's God," he would exclaim, almost as in a transport, "How great God is, Ozanam! How great God is!"

One day, in one of his frequent downhearted moods, the young man wandered into one of the churches—St. Etienne du Mont—to pray, as is the habit of his co-religionists. One cannot help wishing that this custom obtained a little more amongst us. Our churches, and chapels too, might, as it seems, be put to very great service in this way. Without saying anything of those who have places of retirement in their own homes, among whom there may yet be some who, in the bustle of everyday labour, would be glad for a few moments to turn into a quiet building, there are multitudes among the poor who have no such quiet places, and to whom five minutes or half an hour in a quiet church or chapel would be an immense boon. Meanwhile, the churches and chapels for the most part "stand here all the day idle," their pleasant space, their quiet solitude, of no use to anyone in this crowded world—like capital lying unused. Possibly young Ozanam, trained in the observance of a different faith, had his ideas intermixed with many that neither do nor need to occur to us; nevertheless, we cannot doubt that he really sought help of God, and found it too. " He came," says his brother, "to draw at the feet of the holy altars the courage which failed him, and which He never refuses, Who has said, 'Come unto Me, all you who labour and who bend under the burden of life, and I will comfort you.'" But as Frederic was about to bow his knees, he perceived in a retired corner, among some women, a kneeling man praying in profound abstraction. He soon saw that it was his own host. He began to blush for his weakness, and the faith before which the lofty genius of his friend bowed down, came "like oil poured from vessel to vessel," to strengthen his own courage and to comfort his sadness. He went out like a new man.

TO M. ERNEST FALCONNET.

Paris, November 20th, 1831.

MY DEAR FALCONNET,

* * * * *

Do not say, then, that I forget thee. I, that I should forget this good Ernest, this cousin, this friend of my heart, with whom I have passed hours so sweet, days so full! Oh! believe it not. Very often thou art present to my spirit; very often, in talking with Henri Pessonneaux, with our Lyonnese friends, thy name mingles in our discourses, and we call thee to memory.

Since thou askest me my advice on thy ideas, I avow that I believe that there is confusion on thy part on one point. I see a great difference between the patriarchal school and the theosophic epoch. With the patriarch there is *faith*: inheritor of belief, pure and without mixture, he adores the God-spirit; he is *monotheist*: his worship is as little complicated as his religion. Human sacrifices are unknown to him. The patriarch represents the society all entire over which he presides. But there comes an age when men more numerous have also more wants, when peoples form themselves, when conditions are sketched out, limited, when each takes a condition. Then, preoccupied by the exercise of their special functions, shut up within the limits of their labours, men leave the care of praying and teaching to those whom their genius calls more specially to this function. The priesthood arises. From domestic it becomes public—it becomes in its turn a condition, a profession, sometimes a caste.

At this time, religion ceases to penetrate into the families and to be seated at the fireside. It shuts itself up in the temples; it explains itself no longer as a familiar instruction by the mouth of the father—it is taught by initiation, it speaks by the mouth of the pontiffs. The patriarch, occupied with the care of his house, and the nourishment of his children, prayed in the simplicity of the heart, without having leisure to meditate doctrine. But the priest, alone with his thoughts, attached by duty to theological teaching, without other care, without other uneasiness, will he be able to abstain from meditating, from contemplating that which is become the object of his entire life? Then, imagination and reason carrying away by turns the dogmas to comment on and to embellish, to deepen, or even to disguise from vulgar eyes, will they not finish by raising at the common charge the immense edifice of mythology? This applies to all the castes, to all the colleges of priests: Druids, Shamaneans, Brahmins, Scalds, initiators of all the countries, of Samothracia, of Egypt, and of Greece. In Israel, it is the tribe of Levi, depositary of the traditions after Moses. Moses and Aaron, priests and legislators, succeed to the patriarchal epoch of Abraham and of Jacob, at the time when the Hebrews became a people.

Thus the patriarch is the primitive man—is the man who *believes*. There is synthesis in his thought. The theosoph, *wisdom, knowledge,* is the man of the second epoch—he who *reflects*. It is the man of analysis who isolates the different aspects of the reality, assimilates them to his imagination, oftenest wrongly, sometimes with reason.

There is a dissertation sufficiently long. Thou canst make of it what thou pleasest, and thou canst tell me what thou thinkest of it. I wait impatiently for the manuscript, and I will criticize it with severity. MM. de Chateaubriand and Ballanche have received me well. M. Ballanche said to me in conversation : " All religion necessarily includes a theology, a psychology, and a cosmology." Is not this that which we one day said to each other? Is not this that mysterious triad into which all science resolves itself? Is not this the transcendental metaphysic in which all human knowledge is gathered up? And is not this one manner of understanding the Apostle St. Paul, when he declares that all knowledge is included in the knowledge of Christ crucified?

I engage thee to submit all these ideas pell-mell with thine to M. Noirot, and to tell me what he thinks. See him often ; offer him my respects, and assure him that I shall soon come to plague him with my letters.

I shall see M. de Montalembert, and perhaps M. de la Mennais, to-morrow or the day after, before their departure for Rome.

Until now, Paris has not enchanted me. I have, however, seen a great deal. I have not great facilities for working, considering my inexperience, my ignorance of resources and the provisional condition in which I find myself. *I hope to succeed in founding the reunion of which I have spoken to thee. I have already foundations for that.* Pessonneaux shares our projects, and willingly keeps me company. Adieu, my good friend. May God bless our efforts!

F. OZANAM TO M. ERNEST FALCONNET.

Paris, December 18th, 1831.

The pleasure which thou findest in writing to me, in telling me thy feelings, thy thoughts, thy dreams, thou mayest well think that I share; and thou wouldest often be assailed with my letters, if so many occupations did not come to tie my hands. To-day that I have a little leisure, I am going to converse long with thee, and to reply to thee.

But where shall I begin? I will first reply to thy questions, then I will talk in my turn. Thy two letters —the last especially—have caused me a real pleasure. Wouldst thou really believe that at the reading of this one tears of tenderness moistened my eyes? For I was full of a sweet joy at the sight of thy catholic nerve, and thy young indignation. Courage! thou art now in the way of good. . . . . Guard thyself, above all, against discouragement: it is the death of the soul. Thus acquire the habit of seeing the evil around thee without being shaken by it. In the days of our childhood—in those days which passed peacefully in the midst of virtuous relations and well-beloved friends—we believed, simple as we were, that our family was the universe, and that all the world must practise what we were taught. Thus the moment is very painful when our eyes are opened, when the world appears under its true colours, with the ugliness of its vices, the noise of its passions, the blasphemies of its impiety. We were full of confidence and of candour; our soul was open to every word of man, and every discourse seemed to us to bear the imprint of truth. And behold to-day we must learn the painful art of mistrust and suspicion.

December 29th, 1831.

Fifteen days have passed! My numerous occupations have hindered me from writing to thee, but not from thinking of thee. Now that I have a little leisure, let us take up our chit-chat, and renew our conversation. Thou hast asked me for news, for numerous news about myself, about science, about politics, about religion.

I! Could I be better? A pretty room, a good table, an agreeable society; conversations almost always instructive, often amusing, with my estimable host; a lesson in law and one or two courses in literature daily; lastly, the almost constant company of Henri—surely there is more than needs to make a student's life sufficiently pleasant, sufficiently happy. Well, dost thou think me happy? Oh no, I am not so! For there is with me an immense solitude, a great dissatisfaction. Separated from those whom I love, I feel within me—I know not what of *childish* which needs to live beside the domestic hearth, under the shadow of the father and the mother—something of an unexplainable tenderness which dries up in the air of the capital. And Paris displeases me, because there is no life, no faith, no love; it is like a vast corpse, to which I am tied—all young and living—of which the coldness freezes me, and of which the corruption kills me. It is truly in the midst of this moral desert that we well understand, and that we repeat with love these cries of the Prophet:

" Habitavi cum habitantibus Cedar, multum incola fuit anima mea! Si oblitus fuero tui, Jerusalem, adhæreat lingua mea faucibus meis!"

These accents of eternal poetry often sound in my soul, and for me this city without bounds, where I find myself lost, is Cedar—is Babylon—is the place of exile and of pilgrimage; and Sion is my native city, with those whom I have left, with its provincial kindliness, with the charity of its inhabitants, with its altars standing, and its belief respected.

Knowledge and Catholicism—these are my only consolation, and certainly this side is beautiful; but there also are hopes deceived, obstacles to surmount, difficulties to vanquish. *Thou art not ignorant of how much I have desired to surround myself with young men feeling, thinking as myself; now I know that there are such—that there are many such—but they are scattered abroad as the gold on the dunghill, and difficult is the task of him who would unite the defenders around one flag.* However, I hope in my next letter to give thee more positive hopes.

What seems to be to-day the situation of the scientific ideas; what are the schools, the belligerent powers in the field of philosophy?

We must first consider that after all the discussions

and all the struggles, after all the one-sided problems, a moment must come when reason will resume all her doubts in one alone, and will put forth the general problem. To-day this problem is conceived in these terms : For what is man made? What is the end, the law of humanity? Relatively to the past age, there is progress, since the terms even of the problem suppose a providence, an end, a creative, preserving thought. Now the question in this condition rises from the philosophy of history; to the philosophy of history it belongs to resolve it. Thou understandest, consequently, the importance given in our days to historical studies. So far everyone is agreed. But the scission begins at the very starting-point ; it has for object the very elements of the question. The one side take psychology as the foundation of their researches ; they make a sort of abstract man after the manner of the statue of Condillac : in this man they see all that they wish to see, and they deduct thence a philosophic formula upon which they sketch history as upon the bed of Procrustes, cutting and slaying all which cannot well come into their inflexible framework. These people, who only revive again Rousseau, Dupuis, and Volney—these people, I say, have made this admirable discovery, that the religions have begun by Fetichism ; and they go on repeating it to whoever is willing to hear, discoursing on the law of progress, on the extinction of Christianity, and on the near approach of a new religion. There is what has been lately preached to us by M. Jouffroy, Professor of Philosophy at the Sorbonne, that ancient Sorbonne which Christianity has founded, and whose dome is still crowned with the sign of the cross.

But in face of this school, which confers upon itself the name of *rationalist*, another rises up which takes the name of *traditional;* not that it has broken with reason, but because history is the base, and tradition the point of departure of its system. In its ranks appear MM. de Chateaubriand, de la Mennais, d'Ekstein, Ballanche, de Bonald; and for Germany, Schlegel, Baader, Stolberg, Gœrres. They distinguish two objects of human knowledge: the finite and the infinite, philosophic truth and religious truth; two ways of knowing: reason and belief, analysis and synthesis, or perhaps, as speaks the Church, the order of nature and the order of grace. Now, the finite is pressed upon by the infinite at all parts. The infinite is God, it is the Alpha and the Omega, the beginning and the end. Whence it follows that synthesis is at the same time the base and the crown of humanity, and that religious truth is the source and the end of philosophic truth. On these foundations rise a vast theory of the relations of science and of faith, a large explication of history. And as synthesis is the primitive fact which precedes all knowledge, as its time is the time of childhood, when reason sleeps, it follows from thence that psychology is incapable of examining deeply the nature of it, of seizing the extent of it. Then it is in history that one must search out, must study it; it is for history to tell us again the history of the human kind. They declare further, that Fetichism, far from being the first step of humanity, is the lowest degree of corruption; that the memories of the golden age, and of the primitive fault, and of the expiation by blood are sown among the people. That is what they say, and meanwhile our work ripens with us in our young thoughts, it will come in its time. Never was a history of religions more called for by social wants.—*Tempus erit.*

I have finished translating from Mona that which concerns the mythology of the Lapps; nothing better confirms our ideas. It is a pleasure to see the good German twist himself about to explain philosophically the most moral myths, and searching the worship of the stars in the adoration of God in three persons.

To his Mother.

Paris, December 23rd, 1831.

My good Mother,

I must first thank you for the good counsels of all kinds that you have been anxious to give me. But, unfortunately, all your advice on politeness is paralyzed by this good M. Ampère, who will always be served the last, and who is vexed when one attempts to show him some civility. It is of little use for me to debate. I must absolutely be served the first, or he is annoyed. They have for me all sorts of kindnesses. The other day M. Ampère took me to the Institute, and recommended the doorkeeper to let me enter as often as I pleased. Monday next he is to take me there again, to obtain for me the permission to come to the library of the Institute, which is very rich, and which is less distant than that of the King.

You are very good to concern yourself about my Sunday evenings. Habitually the papa Ampère, as you say, works much and plays little; and as it is he who is the life and soul of the house, it results from this that diversion is rare in it. The Sunday evening passes often as other days; that is to say, that after having chatted an hour or two, I go to shut myself up in my room, and pass my time as I can. Oh! I assure you that I want you much, above all in these moments; the leagues which are between you and me seem very long to me. I think of my good town of Lyons, of those I have left there, and that I love so much. I think of these Sunday evenings of winter which I passed in the midst of you, under the wing of the family, devising a thousand things with my dear Falconnet, or playing with him the fine game of piquet, which was sometimes agreeably interrupted by white wine and chestnuts. To-day, no more of all that. Certainly the family among whom I am loads me with attentions, but I am a stranger to its joys and its griefs. I am there in a sphere which is not mine; no more chit-chats or openings of the heart—no more fêtes. I have allowed to pass unnoticed the pleasant solemnity of childhood, this 6th of December, the day of good St. Nicholas, which we lately kept with such glad hearts. I only remembered it the next day; and I remembered also that there was a term to all these childish joys, and that these artless domestic pleasures are no longer for him who lives in the isolation of the capital.

Thus I shall see New Year's Day pass—this day so much loved. I shall see it celebrated around me by a happy family; a good father loaded with caresses, beside a hearth where I only sit by a title of hospitality. I shall see all this; and I shall think that I—I also—have an excellent father, that I have a cherished mother and well-beloved brothers, and that I shall not embrace them. Oh! if you knew all that these reflections have of bitterness for my soul! God is generous, without doubt, to have softened my exile by the society in which

I find myself placed; but God does everything well. He has seen, indeed, that home-sickness would make me suffer—greatly suffer; and that, weak as I am, I should want many consolations to keep me up to the end.

Now, Christmas is coming. I will pray for you; you will pray for me, my good mother. God will hear us both; He will give us strength and courage; His kingdom will come to us, and whatever may be the future, we will walk with a firm step towards the destinies which wait for us.

Frederic had a very great desire to obtain an audience of M. de Chateaubriand, then in his old age, whose works had greatly excited his admiration; his natural timidity held him back, but at last he succeeded in obtaining an interview. This interview, however, was accompanied by an unexpected test, which, at the same time, only timidity and a feeling of awe in the presence of one upon whom he looked with so much reverence, need have occasioned. M. de Chateaubriand received him very kindly, but after having asked him about his various occupations, he inquired if he intended to go to the theatre. Frederic was brought to a stand by this simple question. His mother had earnestly desired him never to do so; but he was terribly afraid of appearing 'childish' in so august a presence, and he hesitated to say so. His host continued to look calmly at him as if awaiting his reply, and he was compelled to answer. He told the simple truth, and must have been greatly relieved when the venerable old man, whose writings had so attracted his youthful ardour, leaned towards him and affectionately said, 'I conjure you to follow your mother's counsel: you will gain nothing at the theatre, and may lose a great deal.' We will finish this chapter by two letters, or parts of letters, to his cousin, M. Ernest Falconnet, in which M. de Chateaubriand's timid visitor returns to his own self once more, and, one would imagine, in the eagerness of his Catholicity would be afraid of no one. It must be remembered that, although not always—yet often when Ozanam uses the word Catholicism we may translate it by Christianity. It is true that the reverse is sometimes the case; and that when he speaks of Christianity, we are compelled to make a reserve in our own minds.

To M. Ernest Falconnet.

Paris, February 10th, 1832.

My good Friend,

* * * * *

But that which is the pleasantest and the most consoling for the Christian youth, are the conferences established at our demand by M. l'Abbé Gerbet. It is now that one is able to say that the light shineth in darkness: *Lux in tenebris lucet.* Every fortnight he gives a lesson on the philosophy of history: there never sounded in our ears a word more penetrating, a doctrine more profound.

He has yet given only three sittings, and the hall is full, full of celebrated men and of eager young people, I have seen there MM. de Potter, de Saint-Beuve· Ampère *fils*, receiving with delight the teachings of the young priest.

The system of La Mennais laid open by him is no

longer that of his provincial partisans; it is the immortal alliance of faith and of knowledge, of charity and of industry, of power and of liberty. Applied to history, it places it in the light; it discovers there the destinies of the future. For the rest, no charlatanism; a feeble voice, an embarrassed gesture, a gentle and peaceful improvisation; but at the end of his discourses his heart warms up, his countenance lightens, a ray illumines his forehead, prophecy is on his lips.

It is time that I gave thee some details on the German books of which thou hast spoken to me. Novalis is in translation; it is our friend M—— who occupies himself with it. They have recommended to me two works of Mossuer, a "Life of Gregory VII." and a "Life of St. Athanasius," both full of curious details, both written in a Catholic spirit by a Protestant author. I have, then, asked for the first for myself; the second for thee. I know that thou workest much in German. As for me, I translate, whilst waiting, a little work of Benjamin Bergmann. Thou seest that everything is in the plan of our common labours.

To M. Ernest Falconnet.

Paris, March 25th, 1832.

My dear Falconnet,

I have seen with pleasure, I will say almost with gratitude, the interest which thou takest in my efforts to keep up the cause of the Gospel. I will continue to converse with thee on the subject, and I will let thee know all which is accomplished round about us for the triumph of this divine cause. I have related to thee our first skirmishes; I rejoice to tell thee that we have engaged some weeks ago in a more serious combat. It is the chair of philosophy, it is the course of Jouffroy, that has been our field of battle. Jouffroy, one of the greatest rationalists of our days, allowed himself to attack revelation, the possibility of revelation even; a Catholic, a young man, addressed to him some observations by writing. The philosopher promised to reply to them; he waited a fortnight, to prepare his arms without doubt, and at the end of this time, without reading the letter, he analysed it in his manner, and endeavoured to refute it. The Catholic, seeing that he was not well understood, presented a second letter to the professor; he took no account of it, did not mention it, and continued his attacks, declaring that Catholicism repudiated science and liberty. Then we united, we drew up a protestation, in which were declared our true sentiments; it was hastily followed by fifteen signatures, and addressed to M. Jouffroy. This time he could not avoid reading it. The numerous auditory, composed of more than two hundred persons, heard with respect our profession of faith. The philosopher endeavoured in vain to reply; he excused himself confusedly, assuring us that he had not intended to attack Christianity in particular, that he had for it a high veneration, that he would endeavour in the future to wound the beliefs no more. But above all he has established a fact very remarkable, very encouraging for the present time. "Gentlemen," he said to us, "for five years I have only received objections dictated by materialism; the spiritualist doctrines experienced the liveliest resistance. To-day minds have greatly changed; the opposition is all Catholic."

It was sad to see him endeavouring to resolve, by the

forces alone of reason, the problem of human destinies; each day contradictions, absurdities, involuntary avowals, escaped him. Lastly, he ventured to sustain that it was false that there were righteous people unhappy, and wicked people prosperous in this world. Yesterday, he confessed that the intellectual wants were immense; that science, far from supplying them, only served to show all their extent, and conducted man to despair in showing him the impossibility of arriving at perfection. He confessed that material knowledge was not sufficient for our spirit, and that after having exhausted it, we experienced a great void, and found ourselves invincibly pushed to seek supernatural lights. He acknowledged, at length, that there must need for reason a high degree of development in order that she might become the foundation of our moral conduct. Thou seest that from these three facts results evidently the necessity of a revelation.

* * * * *

For thyself, prepare thyself for the struggle by the practice of that Gospel which thou art called on to defend. Pray, pray for us, who begin to take our course, and who stretch the hand to thee with a great and brotherly friendship. Yes, thou hast already here friends who know thee not, who wait for thee, and who will open their arms to thee when thou comest to mingle among them.

Sometimes visit M. Noirot, use his counsels, abuse his patience. I have received from him an excellent letter.

I have finished translating from the German a curious little work of Bergmann on the religion of Thibet. I have begun the version of a Thibetian book, which he has translated into German. It is a genesis, a cosmogonic system in which are strongly imprinted the traces of revelation.

M. de Coux has begun his course of political economy, full of depth and interest. I engage thee to subscribe. There are a crowd at his lessons, because in his lessons there is truth and life—a great knowledge of the wound which festers in society, and a remedy which alone can heal it.

I read the works of M. Ballanche with pleasure, and, I hope, with fruit. They include great ideas mingled with a certain number of errors on the philosophy of history. I read also the celebrated Vico. Lastly, I pursue the study of Hebrew. I beg of thee, occupy thyself seriously with historical and traditional researches, for all is there.

Remember thy friend always.

CHAPTER IV.

CHOLERA—SOCIAL PRESENTIMENTS—VARIED OCCUPATIONS AND ACQUAINTANCES.

IT was in this year the cholera appeared in Paris. Frederic's father sent to recall him, but he remonstrated, not wishing to interrupt his studies. He suffered nothing himself, and perhaps had no fear of the plague, which alone might serve to protect him from it. He stayed on, visiting even those who were ill, and writing to his anxious mother a letter on the subject, which she read to her friends with tears of tenderness, and in which he quoted the words of the Psalmist: "A thousand shall fall at thy left, and ten thousand at thy right; but *death* shall not come near thee, because *thou hast said*, Lord, Thou art my hope, and thou hast chosen the Most High for thy refuge."

One circumstance which he told her for her comfort was the singular one, that though the plague had entered with some violence the street which he inhabited, it had, nevertheless, left untouched the houses on that side on which M. Ampère lived. Ozanam slept immediately above his host, and it is said the latter directed him each evening what to do in case the cholera seized him. "If the cholera seizes me this night, I will strike with my stick on the floor. Don't come to my help, but go as quickly as possible to seek my confessor, the Abbé X——, rue de Sèvres; then you may go after to call my physician." How far this attention was to be reciprocated is not said, but one can hardly fancy so kind a host would not be equally attentive to his guest. Among those who were ill was the Abbé Duchesne, the curé of Notre Dame des Champs, who recovered. Frederic Ozanam visited him more than once, and brought him several volumes to take up his thoughts. It was characteristic of Frederic's diligent inquiry into all things, that some would have thought they were too suitable to the occasion. They were the history of "the three pests most spoken of in literature—*Thucydides and the plague under Pericles;* then that of *Lucrece* and that of Milan, in *Les Fiancés*." Besides the cholera there were political disturbances at Lyons, and Ozanam's following letter savours of dark presentiments which, however, were not all fulfilled. Concerning the disturbances at Lyons in the year 1831, there is a pleasant story somewhere relating to the founder of the "beautiful factory of La Sauvagère in the vicinity of that city." "He had combined the friend with the master in the management of his establishment, and was quite astonished on going out of his house on the morning of the second day of the riots to find a man posted as sentinel at his gate, whom he recognised as a workman dismissed for improper conduct." He inquired what he was doing. "Keeping guard over you" was the answer. All the workmen had entered into an association for his defence, and would relieve each other as guard, when guard was needed, till the disturbance was over. On the gentleman further observing that he was not one of his workmen, he had turned him off, the man replied, " True, sir, but I deserved it. I was in the wrong."

To M. Edward Le Jouteux, Advocate.

Paris, July 23rd, 1832.

My dear Friend,

How happy you are to rest yourself in the bosom of your excellent family, surrounded by relations who cherish you, and whose happiness you make! You hear no longer the rumbling of the political tempest. You are deaf to the confused clamours of these people without number who rise against each other; you see no longer the cholera gathering its great harvest, and the long files of hearses in the streets. The beautiful sky of Touraine, the fertile borders of the Loire, the gentle and peaceable populations—there is the *coup d'œil* which you enjoy. There you live in the country, and there all one's ideas become more smiling, the mind more calm, the health more vigorous, knowledge less austere, religion even more amiable and more consoling. The abstruse compilations of the illustrious Tribonian are no more than a play when one reads them in the shadow of green trees, by the border of a brook, on the flowering grass. Poetic dreams come to mingle with your meditations, and often, perhaps, pretty verses, as those which you showed to me, are the fruit of them.

But if you taste this happiness, it is because you have made yourself worthy of it; it is because during your long sojourn in the capital you have never been shaken, and you have struggled against the fatigues of labour and the seductions of pleasure.

"Vivite felices quibus est fortuna peracta."

'For me, who am only putting my hand to the work, I shall yet have many difficulties to vanquish. I blush almost to confess to you my pusillanimity; but the examination of the first year, which I must soon undergo, is a phantom which frightens me. Little accustomed to the study of law, I have not known how to occupy myself with it as I ought during the course of the year; and at the moment when I have but just made out for myself a method, there is exacted from me the knowledge of the matters themselves. What shall I do? I cannot be irresolute, and I commit myself hardily to the keeping of God, with little confidence in myself. But when this critical moment shall have passed away, I too shall go to find again those who are dear to me. I shall see again my good town of Lyons. I shall make there, if I can, provision of health and of courage for the next year.

Of courage—certainly we need it for the epoch in which we live, and yet more for that in which we are going to live. All elevated minds say that we are arrived at a period of catastrophes and of universal commotions. Such is at least the opinion of MM. de Chateaubriand, de la Mennais, and de Lamartine. The Governments and the peoples are posing in mutual hostility. The protocol of the Germanic Diet, the Reform Bill, the Irish insurrection, the movements of Germany and Italy, the war even of the Grand Turk and of the Pasha of Egypt—all these are the preparatives of the great things which are going to happen;

and this terrible drama opens by the tragedy of hostile brothers, by the desperate struggle between Don Miguel and Don Pedro. Here the Republican party has taken considerable strength from the kind of persecution to which it has been subjected; it no longer hides its designs, it speaks already of guillotine and of fusillades. On another side, the friends of order draw their ranks closer, very resolute to resist even to the end: there is the hatred of extermination between the parties. I believe, then, in a civil war imminent; and the entire of Europe, entwined in the threads of Freemasonry, will be the theatre of it. But this redoubtable crisis will probably be decisive; and on the ruins of the old broken-up nations, a new Europe will arise. Then Catholicism will be understood; then it will be given to carry civilization into the old Orient. This will be a magnificent era; we shall not see it.

For the rest, M. de la Mennais seems tolerably content at Rome. The Pope has caused very obliging things to be said to him—*L'Avenir* even may appear again—but these gentlemen have preferred to wait the return of the illustrious pilgrim. He does not expect to return till the month of September. Before that, many things may have happened.

I hope that at the end of the vacation we shall all be re-united. You will find, I assure you, people who love you well, beginning with him who says that he is, and always will be, your friend.

By this time Frederic had made the acquaintance of several young men like-minded with himself, enthusiastic Christians, and likewise energetic Catholics. They attended the lectures of rationalistic professors, and the accounts of their skirmishes are detailed in Ozanam's letters, some of which have been given. "From this day," says Ozanam's brother, with perhaps a brother's partiality, "the professors of the Sorbonne became more measured in their language, and brought more impartiality into their judgments. Ozanam sent them back by the arms of that science of which they believed themselves alone to have the monopoly. It was thus that he taught them to know him who later was to sit among them and to be their colleague."

To M. ERNEST FALCONNET.

Paris, January 5th, 1833.

MY DEAR FALCONNET,

I write to thee Saturday evening. It is midnight. Soon a new day, great and solemn, will begin— the anniversary of the first homage rendered by the Pagan world to the new-born Christianity. There is something marvellously beautiful in this legend of the three magi—representatives of three human races at the cradle of the Saviour. There is something venerable in this family feast which consecrates joy, which throws a cake by lot, and which creates in its bosom a domestic royalty of some hours, as if to imitate these Oriental royalties sent to the infant Christ. For the rest, whatever may be the origin of this custom, whether it even comes from the kings of the banquet among the Greeks and Romans, it is always one good occasion the more to reunite relations and friends, to cause hearts to flow out. I should have loved this day to seat myself at a table with all those who are dear to me—with thee consequently, my good comrade; and laying aside my philosophic gravity, I would have cried out in all the simplicity of my soul and with all the strength of my lungs: "*The king drinks! the king drinks!*" For I am pleased with all which is old and popular, and I have a deep feeling of sympathy for this primitive freshness, for this good fellowship which is disappearing every day, in proportion as false politeness develops and grows.

And thou, my friend, hast thou taken thy part in these joyous feasts? Hast thou been open to gaiety and pleasure, or rather does melancholy weigh even as a load of iron upon thy soul? Thou hast made me enter into the secret of thy thoughts; thou hast told me thy inequalities, thy enjoyments, thy sadnesses. Art thou always the same? Or, rather, art thou becoming a man, and preparing thyself to preserve this equality of soul which makes the happiness and the safety of life?

Oh, not yet!—I understand thee well—not yet the calm and the impassibility of ripe age; it is youth with its passion, with its tempests; it is the time of great joys and of great troubles; it is as the vessel which is launched for the first time into the sea, unaccustomed to the waves which toss it about—sometimes it sails rapidly and lightly on the top of the waves, sometimes it falls and disappears in the abysses, until a more experienced hand comes to hold its helm and to guide it to the port. That is how life is to us who are commencing. Are we, then, irrevocably condemned to these inquietudes which consume us, to these torments which besiege us; and is there no way of giving to our heart a little peace and consolation?

See, my good friend, we have need, all of us, of

something which may possess and uplift us, which may dominate our thoughts and raise them; we have need of poetry in the midst of this prosaic and cold world, and at the same time of a philosophy which gives some reality to our ideal conceptions—of a union of doctrines which shall be the base and the rule of our studies and of our actions. This double benefit we find in Catholicism, with which we are connected for our happiness. There, then, is the point of departure of all the labours of our intelligence, of all the dreams of our imagination; it is the central point to which they must tend. Thus disappears this vague uncertainty which hurts us, and which leaves us abandoned to our own weakness. Now the feeling of our weakness being one of the principal sources of melancholy, the presence of the Catholic thought in our souls is the first remedy to oppose to it.

Is that all? No, certainly, in my opinion; let us not leave our beliefs in a domain of speculation and theory, let us take them seriously, and let our lives be the continual impression of them. Let us never be unoccupied; let us form, if it must be, castles in the air and gigantic enterprises; but let us not leave our spirit without pasture. Let us begin laborious studies, based on those subjects most suited to our inclinations; but let us not be too much drawn away to reverie and literature. These are excellent things; but they cease to have any value when there is not at the foundation of them precise ideas and facts.

There are plenty of reflections. Now, I am going to tell thee something of what passes around me, to make thee know a little of the world in which I live, and in which thou wilt have to live.

As lawyer, as man, I should have in the world three missions to fulfil; and I ought to be, to arrive at my end, jurisconsult, man of letters, man of society. Here, then, begins my apprenticeship; and jurisprudence, the moral sciences, and some knowledge of the world as seen under the Christian point of view, ought to be the object of our studies.

Several means are given us at this moment by Providence to try us in this triple career: these are the Conferences of Law, those of History, and the reunions at M. de Montalembert's.

The Conferences of Law are held twice a week; they argue there controverted questions. There is in each affair two advocates, and a third who performs the functions of the public prosecutor. The others judge both the cause itself and the merit of the pleadings. It is not permitted to read, most frequently they improvise . . . I have already spoken twice . . . they only gave me an hour to prepare my business; however, they appeared fairly satisfied. For myself, I found myself feeble and hesitating, because I did not feel at all master of my subject.

But the Conference of History is altogether another thing. Composed of forty members, it assembles every Saturday. There all the subjects are free: history, philosophy, literature, all are admitted. All opinions find the doors open, and from that results a very strong emulation; for if one aims to do well, it is not in order to seek applause and praise, it is to give more solid support to the cause which we have embraced. There every attempt, after it has been read, is submitted to a commission, which criticizes it, discusses it, and names a reporter who is its organ before the conference. Nothing escapes the severity of this censure. . . . There is a proposition that corresponding members should be named in the provinces. If thou wilt be one, write to me. Thou wilt have nothing special to do; only, when it seems good to thee, thou wilt send some little work in thy fashion, which I will read in thy name to the conference.

So much for studies. There are, besides, every Sunday, evenings for the young people at M. de Montalembert's. They converse much and in a varied manner; they take punch and little cakes, and return joyously in bands of four or five. I expect to go from time to time. Last Sunday I saw there MM. de Coux, d'Ault-Dumesnil, Mickiewicz, celebrated Lithuanian poet, Felix de Mérode, whom the Belgian nation wished to give itself as king; Saint-Beuve was there also; Victor Hugo was to come. There breathes in these reunions a perfume of Catholicism and of paternity. M. de Montalembert has an angelic countenance and a very instructive conversation.

The points of doctrine on which Rome has desired silence are not brought on to the carpet; the wisest discretion reigns in this respect. But they converse about literature, about history, about the interests of the poor classes, about the progress of civilization; the heart is animated and warmed, and one carries away a sweet satisfaction, a pure pleasure, a soul mistress of itself, resolutions and courage for the future.

The future is for us, young people that we are; let us reserve ourselves, then, and steady ourselves against enemies and molestations. Let us think that the condition of progress is suffering, and that friendship may soften the afflictions which we shall not be able to avoid.

To M. ERNEST FALCONNET.

Paris, March 19th, 1833.

MY DEAR ERNEST,

Shall I tell thee that thy two letters have given me much pleasure? No ; it would be an expression too feeble to express the sentiment which a man feels when his friend opens his heart and lets him read within. Our friendship has never been troubled. . . . I avow that I was wrong to think what I thought, and to write what I wrote ; but listen, my friend: friendship is also a timid and jealous virgin—the least breath of coldness makes her tremble ; and I, at a hundred leagues distance from my dear Ernest, while he is thrown into the whirlpool of fêtes and pleasures, while the world charms so loudly at his ears, might I not fear that my memory might lose some place in his spirit, and that—too far off to make myself heard—my brotherly words might be lost on the road?

No; I have not accused thee. I understand in some sort the possibility of thy forgetfulness. I am thy relation, thy friend ; but beyond that, I am too little a thing to claim a privileged part in thy affections. The time is no more when the Sunday found us sitting at the same hearth, dreaming the same dreams, desiring the same desires, the one completing the thought of the other, and both forming together one single intelligence of which thou wast thyself the cheerful, lively, buoyant part; I, the centre of gravity—solid but heavy. Thy ideas, capricious, but full of grace and delicacy ; thy opinions, often bold, but always original and sometimes true, joined themselves marvellously to my reflections, more serious, more stiff, more borrowed. But in this division the better part fell not to my lot. Age, in condensing, so to speak, the fluidity of thy spirit, would give to it, day by day, the equilibrium which it needed ; and I, in tending towards the maturity of reason, I would acquire always more heaviness and keep always less mobility.

*   *   *   *   *

Since the year and a half that we have been separated, thou hast walked quickly in the way. Not alone hast thou reached me, but thou hast passed me in many ways; thou hast been much occupied with the great social problem of the amelioration of the working classes, of which I have hardly thought. Much better than I thou knowest the German literature and philosophy; thou hast acquired in the usage of good society a facility of speech from which I am very far; in a word, what is much more meritorious, thou hast carried into thy new studies of law a goodwill which will be recompensed later on. For me, on the contrary, except some knowledge of Orientalisms, some very vague ideas of law and of legislation, a certain number of new notions on the philosophy of history, some rapid glances at political economy, drawn above all from the discussions of the conference, these fourteen months passed in the capital have left me very little fruit. And I acknowledge that it is my fault, because I have allowed myself to succumb to a sort of indolence and cowardice almost insurmountable. Thus thou seest how little I can offer thee, and what a feeble contribution I am able to bring to that association of two souls for good which is called friendship. Do not represent to thyself that I say all this by jealousy; no, I speak to thee with open heart.

* * * * *

However, if I have nothing in myself to offer, I rejoice in thinking that a day is coming in which I shall not be useless to thee; and when thou shalt come to Paris I shall be able to introduce thee to a new sphere, where thou wilt not find, certainly, either brilliant fêtes or joyous tumult, but where thou wilt meet, in exchange, joys purer and more fruitful.

Thou knowest what was, before my departure from Lyons, the object of all my desires. *Thou knowest that I aspired to form a reunion of friends, working together at the edifice of science, under the standard of the Catholic idea.* This thought remained for long barren; but a friend had opened to me the door of a literary reunion, not at all numerous—last remains of the old *Société des bonnes Etudes*—but whose customs, little scientific, left hardly any place for philosophy or serious investigations. . . . . Hardly fifteen members were faithful to this studious rendezvous; hardly dared they produce there the great questions of the future and of the past. To-day, thanks to the zeal of some of the old members, this society has grown in a marvellous manner. It reckons sixty persons, of whom several bear names not wanting in celebrity. Numerous auditors assist at the sittings. . . . . . The greater number give themselves up to the study of history, some to philosophy.

* * * * *

The tumultuous domain of politics is outside our excursions. But everywhere else there is full and entire liberty. Thus grave questions arise: young philosophers come to ask from Catholicism an account of her doctrines and of her works; and then, seizing the inspiration of the moment, one of us makes head against the attack, develops the Christian idea not well comprehended, unrolls history to show its glorious applications, and, finding sometimes a source of eloquence in the grandeur of the subject, establishes on solid bases the immortal union of true philosophy with faith. . . . The lists are open; and all opinions, even Saint-Simonian, are admitted to the tribune. Nevertheless, as the Catholics are equal in number to those who are not so, and as, furthermore, they bring more ardour, zeal and assiduity, it is always in their favour that intellectual victory decides: thus, between them, frank and intimate cordiality—a sort of fraternity altogether special; with the others, always benevolence and politeness.

* * * * *

Another source of life are the assemblies of the young and excellent Count de Montalembert. Then the most illustrious champions of the Catholic school open to us the treasures of their conversation; others come there who have defended with the sword and watered with their blood the domain of their convictions—young officers, Belgian or Polish, distinguished diplomatists; then men of another school, who come, as the pilgrims of another empire, to contemplate for some moments the spirit of union and of harmony which reigns among their adversaries. There come by turns MM. Ballanche and Saint-Beuve, Savigny junior and de Beauffort, Ampère *fils* and Alfred de Vigny, de Mérode and d'Eckstein. Last Sunday Lherminier was there. I even spoke a little with him; then a very interesting conversation sprang up between him and M. de Montalembert. We remained till midnight to hear them. Victor Considerant was there also; they spoke much of the actual misery of the people, and drew from it dark presages as to the future. For the rest, they talk very little of politics and much of science. The young people are numerous. M. de Montalembert does the honours with a marvellous grace.

* * * * *

And now, my dear Ernest, let our hands clasp each other more firmly than ever. The future is before us, immense as the ocean. Hardy sailors, let us navigate in the same bark and row together; above us religion, a brilliant star which it is given us to follow; before us the glorious track of the great men of our country and of our doctrine; behind us our young brothers, our companions—more timid—who wait for an example.

* * * * *

To HIS MOTHER.

Paris, June 19th, 1833.

MY DEAR MAMMA,

I have promised you the recital of one of my days, and this promise is not the thing in the world the easiest to keep. For, first, as the Wise Man saith, "The just sinneth seven times a day;" and I, who am only half just, I must sin fourteen times at least. This, then, would be fourteen follies to narrate one after the other, from the idleness which keeps me in bed in the morning, to the carelessness which makes me lose much time in chatting with some one in the evening. Then, what sort of a day should I detail to you? Should it be some obscure day of the week—a working-day, a day of misery and of civil law proceedings? Or, rather, should it be some joyful Sunday with its pious offices and its tranquil pleasures; or, lastly, some one of those rare days of fêtes and enjoyments, such as we spend only two or three times in the year, with pleasant companions, under a clear sky, in the midst of the smiling country?

If I told you that the day of the Fête Dieu, three hare-brained youths went out of Paris by the Champs Elysées, at eight o'clock in the morning, I should perhaps pique your curiosity. If I told you that at ten o'clock thirty students assisted at the Nanterre procession, I should edify your piety without doubt. If I added that at six in the evening twenty-two of the aforesaid individuals refreshed themselves around a table at St. Germain-en-Laye, I should puzzle you still more. Lastly, if I should reveal to you that at a quarter after midnight, or thereabouts, three youths knocked at the door, Rue des Grès, No. 7; that their spirits were good, their legs a little used up, and their shoes covered with dust, and that one amongst them, with chestnut hair, large nose and grey eyes, is very well known to you —what would you say, my good little mother? You would say, "Oh! oh! this seems to me like a silly adventure. This greatly resembles a giddy-goose freak. And were it not for the moral of the procession, I should perhaps make my *grands yeux blancs.*" Well, then, I see that I have touched the chord, and that I have met amongst the two hundred and thirty days of my pilgrimage in the capital, precisely that which will awaken your interest.

You know that at Paris, as at Lyons—but for motives much more plausible—processions are forbidden; but because it pleases some disturbers to pen Catholicism up in its temples in the bosom of the great towns, this is not a reason for young Christians, to whom God has given souls with a little manliness, to deprive themselves of the most touching ceremonies of their religion. So it happened that a few were found who had thought of taking part in the procession of Nanterre—Nanterre, a peaceful village, the country of the good Saint Geneviève.

The rendezvous was appointed a little late it is true, and only in a small circle of friends. The Sunday rose serene and without a cloud, as if the heaven desired to honour it by its splendour. I left early in the morning with two friends; we stopped to breakfast at the Barrier de l'Etoile; we arrived the first at our humble rendezvous. Little by little the small troop increased, and soon we found ourselves thirty. First, all the intellectual aristocracy of the conference: Lallier; Lamache, of whom I will show you excellent historic labours; Cherruel, a converted Saint-Simonian; De la Noue, son of the former President of the Court Royal of Tours, and who makes such beautiful verses; then M. le Jouteux, Languedocians, Franche-Comteans, Normans and Lyonnese above all—and your very humble servant; the greater part carrying moustaches, five or six reckoning five feet eight inches. We mingled among the countrymen who followed the daïs: it was a pleasure to us to elbow these honest people—to chant with them.

  * * * * *

One of us — Henri, I believe — proposed to go and dine at St. Germain-en-Laye. Six or eight poltroons objected to the distance; we let them object, and retrace their steps, and there we were — twenty-two of us, by groups of three or four only, not to make trouble — our soles beating the road to St. Germain. The pleasure doubled the quickness of our limbs; and, gathering as we went the strawberries in the woods, we arrived at the end of our expedition. We went for a quarter of an hour into the church where they were chanting vespers. Afterwards we visited the magnificent château, so rich in souvenirs, so proud of its antiquity.

* * * * *

The night drew on; we lost each other from sight. Some of us mounted into a carriage at Neuilly; and for me, I arrived with two others at my domicile. Monday had just begun.

My heart knows how many times I thought of you all during this day — one of the most charming of my life!

CHAPTER V.

CHRISTIAN ACTIVITY — PRACTICAL WORK — INWARD QUESTIONINGS.

IT is time now to introduce the notice of one of the two special works which Frederic Ozanam had great share, at least, in initiating. The first of these two was the Society of St. Vincent de Paul, which grew out of the Conferences of History which have been mentioned. It was a time of returning Christian activity. Protestants, as well as Roman Catholics, lent their aid in instituting, either alone or in conjunction, many Christian works. Mde. Mallet, a Protestant lady, worked heart and hand with Rosalie Rendu, the well-known Sister of Charity; and in very many directions Christian thought and Christian work were appearing. The conferences of the Abbé Gerbet, which Frederic Ozanam and his young friends bethought themselves to obtain as a further antidote to the University teaching, are mentioned in the letters. The young Christian students felt themselves refreshed like giants with new wine. Those of their fellow-students who did not share their faith were considerably excited by the struggle in which they had engaged, and several of them threw down a challenge to them. They took it up, and upon this ensued an interesting series of colloquies or discussions, in which umpires were to decide whose the victory was in argument. Frederic would often talk to his brother of these religious tournaments, in which both parties appear to have displayed a considerable amount of talent, and also a fair share of temper. No doubt they both enjoyed to a considerable extent this new exercise of their talents. The discussions, however, at length became so lively that they attracted the attention and excited the fears of a good old Catholic gentleman, founder of a journal called *Ami de la Religion*. He feared that very young and ardent hands might injure the cause they were endeavouring to defend, and he intervened by inserting in his journal a warning against them. This sudden pulling up was very grievous to Frederic, and he replied with considerable warmth. M. Picot did not refuse to insert his reply in his paper. Out of these conferences, however, there grew a very interesting work, of which no one like M. Picot could complain. It struck several of the fellow-students to give a practical answer to the various arguments of their sceptical friends. Says Frederic Ozanam twenty years later: 'Some of our young companions in study were materialists; some were Saint-Simonians; others Fourieristes; others, again, Deists. When we attempted to recall to these wandering brothers the marvels of Christianity, they all said to us: "You are right if you speak of the past. Christianity has formerly worked wonders; but to-day Christianity is dead. And you—you who boast yourselves of being Catholics, what do you do? Where are the works which show your faith, and which would make it respected and admitted by us?" They were right; this reproach was only too well merited. It was then that we said to each other: "Very well; let us begin to work. Let our acts agree with our faith. But what shall we do? What shall we do to be truly Catholic, unless that which is most pleasing to God? Let us help our neighbours then, as Jesus Christ has done, and put our faith under the protection of charity." The reproach addressed to the young students had fallen into good and honest hearts, and it brought forth good fruit. They took heed of their adversaries' rejoinder, and considered—not merely with the ardour of zeal, but with business-like consideration—how they should meet it, and the answer was made plain to all. They should work the works of Christianity—do good to their neighbours. They began immediately, says one account, in a very simple way. Frederic and the one friend who had first spoken together carried to a poor man, whom they knew, the small quantity of wood which they still had in possession. Later on, they talked with others; they went and talked with their kind friend M. Bailly. M. Bailly was a very great friend to the young in Paris. Among other things he had instituted a sort of reading-room, to which he gave the name of *Société des bonnes Etudes*. This was very near the School of Law, and here was arranged a large and varied library, seven or eight journals and various reviews. There was a large room for study, open from six o'clock in the morning till ten at night, lighted and warmed in the winter. Here, or in connection with this, also seats could be arranged for literary *séances*, which would hold about three hundred, or they could have

Conferences of Law and Medicine. This specific society had ceased to exist three years before the birth of the Society of St. Vincent de Paul; but it was here that the Conferences of History, of which Frederic Ozanam speaks, were held. M. Bailly had watched over the members of this society with a fatherly care and goodness, and to the Society of St. Vincent he was one of the best of friends. He was its president for seventeen years. When Frederic, with his friends, applied to him in the beginning for counsel, the result was that in a room to which he gave them access, early in 1833, eight young students installed themselves with M. Bailly to preside; and this was the bud of the Society of St. Vincent de Paul. So jealous were they at first of their privacy that when a ninth presented himself, who was unknown to most of them, they found some difficulty in admitting him. With regard to the arrangements for visiting the poor, some of the young men went to the Sister of Charity before-mentioned, Rosalie Rendu, and she instructed and helped them. The thought of their struggles in the Conferences of History, and how better they should sustain themselves in argument, had faded away, dissolved, and been succeeded by the practical thought of this endeavour to work the works of God among their fellows. One more quotation shows the kind of conversation which these young men and their sceptical friends held together. "One of my good friends," says Ozanam, twenty years later, "led astray at that time by the Saint-Simonian theories, said to me with a tone of compassion, ' But what do you hope to do? You are eight poor young men, and you pretend to come in aid of the miseries which multiply in a city like Paris! And when you shall even have increased your number, you will never do any great things. We, on the contrary, we are elaborating ideas and a system which will reform the world and rescue it for ever from its misery. We will do in a moment for humanity that which you will not know how to accomplish in several ages.' You know, gentlemen," adds Ozanam, "what these theories have come to, which caused this illusion to my poor friend!"

At the time when Frederic Ozanam spoke, the little company of eight who were unwilling to be nine, had swelled into two thousand. They had five hundred conferences in France, and they had spread into England, Spain, Belgium, and even Jerusalem. It may be interesting here to give a very brief abstract of this little society. They soon doubled their numbers. They began and ended their meetings with prayer. They generally read a short piece either from the 'Imitation of Jesus Christ,' or from the 'Life of St. Vincent de Paul;' then each gave an account of his visit to the poor; they distributed what they had, and ended by a modest collection. M. Bailly opened to them the columns of a journal, and Ozanam and some others increased their finances by literary work. M. Bailly also interested some of the ecclesiastics in their favour; and although it continued an entirely lay association, this was a great thing done. In less than two years they were a hundred. Some of the members were frightened by their rapid increase, and even questioned whether they ought to admit more into their numbers. But one of its main objects being to form a rallying-point and a place of shelter for all young men who were disposed to be Christians, in their first coming to the metropolis, it was rather necessary to make admission easy than difficult, and the only condition had been that they should live a Christian life. They could not, therefore, refuse any who, on this condition, wished to come; and they moved to a place which was able to hold three hundred persons. They were soon compelled to divide the conference, which was not done without considerable opposition. "As soon as Ozanam saw," says his brother, "the finger of God in the rapid growth of the work, he comprehended that the small charitable association, of which he had at first thought, might perhaps begin to realize the design which he had long meditated: *the reconciliation of those who have not enough with those who have too much, by means of charitable works.*" The society spread first into those towns where numbers of young people gathered together for study; later, into the great centres of population; afterwards, "it extended to localities of less importance, and penetrated even into the villages." "In 1837 it counted in the capital two hundred and thirty-seven young people; it had created conferences at Nimes, Lyons, Nantes, Rennes, Dijon, Toulouse, and even at Rome." They endeavoured to make no noise in the world; this was necessary, sometimes politically—sometimes, perhaps, to defend themselves from other attacks. Their motto was, not to conceal themselves or their work, not to put themselves unnecessarily forward.

One principal work was to visit the poor in their own houses. Each member visited two or three families a week. Receiving-places were established for old clothes, old furniture, etc., also medical services were given. Another principal labour was, procuring work for those who had none. The members interested themselves in all classes of the poor and miserable, from the infants in the *crêches* to the condemned to death in the prisons; and they followed the funerals of those who died. At the time of the Irish famine in 1848-9, this little-known society sent to its relief nearly £6,000. The children of the poor were sedulously looked after. It is said that in 1859, 1,100 apprentices were superintended or looked after by the Conferences of Paris; also the soldiers in the garrisons were attended to. In fact, the whole extent of the needs of the poor seem to have been in a measure considered by this association, either from its first beginning or later.

To return to the history of Frederic individually, who, amid all his multifarious occupations, endeavoured not to neglect his perfunctory studies. He scrupulously gave the specified hours to the study of law; but after this, the attractions of letters and philosophy carried him away in spite of himself, and somewhat to the anxiety of his father, who perhaps thought that his son "had too many irons in the fire." When he did not succeed in passing with all the desired success, this discontent found more expression. As Frederic's brother truly observes, it was very difficult, notwithstanding all his aptitude and his assiduity in labours, for him to achieve with an equal success the bringing to the front the necessary studies to pass an examination in law, and those severe studies which were exacted for a degree in letters, for which he had long been preparing, the more that he joined to all these occupations as accessory a good number of articles for the *Revue Européenne* and for different journals, and was besides a member of several conferences, where often he had to speak. One can hardly help smiling at this review of his brother's. It was zeal without sufficient discretion, doubtless, which allowed him to append so many " accessories" to what was in itself sufficient to engross all his time. Yet, it is difficult to blame him for his literary pursuits, for there is little doubt that the study of the law, so pertinaciously insisted on by his father, was not the one to which his vocation led him, however useful it may have been as an "accessory." His charitable and religious enterprises were eminently called for. Nevertheless, he might have gone "more softly," to quote from a letter written by Lacordaire to him years later, and have taken with advantage a longer time to do all he did. However, just now a time of rest was coming. Dr. Ozanam was too reasonable a man, as well as too affectionate a father, to be seriously displeased for any length of time with a son whose delinquencies were of the nature of Frederic's; and in the vacation, he returned happily to his "dear town of Lyons," where he found father, mother, brothers, a large number of old friends—all which was, in a word, the subject of his "tenderest affections." An interesting excursion into Italy occupied this vacation.

CHAPTER VI.

MORE QUESTIONINGS—CONFERENCE OF NOTRE DAME—HOME RECOLLECTIONS—ABBÉ MARDUET—POLITICAL OPINIONS.

FREDERIC after this returned to Paris to his various studies and good works. He was not free from many questionings of heart, as the following letter to his cousin, Ernest Falconnet, shows.

To M. ERNEST FALCONNET.

Paris, January 7th, 1834.

MY DEAR ERNEST,

Thou sayest that thy future is dark, and thou believest that the purest sun enlightens mine. Oh, how thou deceivest thyself! I feel at this moment one of, perhaps, the greatest troubles in life—the uncertainty of vocation. This may be a secret between us; but such is, at the same time, the flexibility and the softness of my nature, that there is not a study, not any kind of labour which has not charms for me, and in which I could not well enough succeed; and yet there is not one capable of absorbing all my faculties, and concentrating all my strength. I cannot occupy myself with one thing without thinking of a thousand others; and nevertheless, thou knowest no labour can be great if it is not one. Ignorant as I was, I formerly believed that I could be at the same time a learned man and an advocate, and lead two lives at once. Now that I approach the end of my law studies, I must choose between these two ways. I must put my hand into the urn. Shall I draw from it black or white? I am surrounded, in some respects, with seductions. On every hand they solicit me; they put me forward—they push me into a career foreign to my studies. Because God and education have endowed me with some extent of ideas, some largeness of tolerance, they would make of me a sort of chief of the Catholic youth of these parts. A number of young people, full of merit, give me an esteem, of which I feel very unworthy; and men of ripe age make advances to me. I must be at the head of every movement, and, when there is anything difficult to do, I must bear the burden of it. Impossible that there should be a reunion, a conference of law or of literature, unless I preside at it. Five or six magazines or journals ask me for articles. In a word, a crowd of circumstances, independent of my will, besiege me, pursue me, and draw me out of the line that I traced for myself.

I do not tell thee this by self-love. For, on the contrary, I feel my weakness so much, I, who am not twenty-one years old, that compliments and praises rather humiliate me, and I almost feel the desire to laugh at my own importance; but it is no laughing matter, and, on the contrary, I suffer incredible annoyance when I feel that all these fumes rise to my head, intoxicate me, and may make me wanting in that which, until now, has seemed to me to be my career—that to which the desire of my parents called me—that to which I felt myself sufficiently well disposed. Nevertheless, this concourse of exterior circumstances may it not be a sign of the will of God? I know not; and in my uncertainty I do not go before, I do not run after; but I let things come—I resist—and if the attraction is too strong, I allow myself to follow.

While waiting, I do what I can for my law; and although, perhaps, I consecrate too much time to science and literature, I only consider them as secondary occupations until some new order. Thus, once passed my examination for license, I know nothing of my future —all is for me darkness, uncertainty; but what matters it? Provided that I know what I ought to do to-morrow, to what end serves it that I should know what will be my duties six months hence? Is it necessary that the traveller see the end opened, and does it not suffice him to avoid obstacles, to see always ten paces before him? O my friend, I have written all this for thee, for thyself who hast yet three long years of studies to pass through before taking a position.

Have a little circle of chosen friends; connect thyself rather with a few good comrades than with societies of the world. Some hours passed together around the fire, conversing with open heart, will do more good and give more repose than an entire week of soirées, where there must be of two things one; we must hold ourselves restrained and dressed out in the forms of a foolish and cold politeness, or else abandon ourselves to giddy pleasures which are not without peril. Thou knowest it, the world is an iron file, which uses up many young lives: do not give it thine. If thou believest in nothing suffer thyself to say: Short and sweet, and *coronemus nos rosis antequam marcescant.* But Christian, and believing in God, in humanity, in the fatherland, in the family, remind thyself that to them and not to thyself belongs thy existence, and that it is a thousand times better to languish during a half century, giving to others the example of resignation and doing a little good, than to be intoxicated for a few months in a brilliant enjoyment, and to die in the delirium.

But no, thou wilt never languish; the fountain is too gushing to dry up; thy intelligence is too nervous to remain powerless. Thou wilt succeed, thou wilt do good greatly, whatever be the career traced out for thee. Thou wilt not slip on the blood of the bull, as Euryalus; if the one whom thou callest Nisus appears to thee in advance, it is because he set out before thee; perhaps also he will reach the end sooner. But thou also, thou wilt reach it one day. Perhaps also, like these two friends, some common sacrifice awaits us: but sacrifice for him who believes, is it not the shortest way to arrive at the true term, immortality?

My dear friend, here are plenty of counsels; I do not wish, nevertheless, to appear to be giving thee a lesson; we are fellow-disciples, we are brothers. Neither do I take advantage of my right of eldership; and if I have spoken to thee in this manner, it is simply to tell thee what I have in my heart. It is because between us I think that vague sentimental digressions are sufficiently useless, and that it is better to make some positive applications. I beg thee then to do the like for me, and to tell me in this renewing of the year what reforms thou wouldst wish in my character as a whole, in my labours, in my moral direction; thy advice will not be without weight in the balance, because, united from the earliest age, thou oughtest to know me.

I have spoken of thee to these gentlemen of the *Revue Européenne*, who have told me to engage thee to send them something; thou wouldst there find the advantage of connecting thyself with honourable men. My article on China has appeared. I have just written two on India; one is printed in the December number, the other will be in the number following.

Lallier and Chaurand are here, who are chattering in such a fashion that I must finish, under pain of writing by fits and starts. They send thee a thousand regards; the one because he knows thee, the other because he would like to know thee.

I embrace thee with all my heart.

Here comes in suitably the interesting account of the first beginnings of the Conferences of Notre Dame, the earliest seed of which had been sown the preceding January by Frederic himself, in conjunction with his young companions—he being the leader. In the early part of 1833 a petition, with a hundred names appended, had been presented to the Archbishop of Paris by Frederic and two of his companions. The Archbishop received them with great kindness, did not reproach them for their bold attempt, promised to consider what they asked for, talked with them long, and gave them his blessing in departing, saying, "I embrace in your person all the Catholic youth." The purport of this petition was, in view of the sceptical state of society, in view of the needs of the young of the day, to ask earnestly for a more popular style of preaching—a series of conferences in fact—a preaching that should animate the souls of those who possessed faith, and which should attract the wavering and sceptical. They wished for a teaching which should leave the ordinary tone of sermons, in which the questions which then pre-occupied youth should be treated, in which religion should be presented in its relations with society, and which should reply, at least indirectly, to the antagonistic publications of France and Germany, and to the rationalistic Professors at the University whom the courageous young men had already confronted on their own account. The Archbishop, although he was doubtless a gentleman, a man of benevolence, and a Christian, was nevertheless a man of the past generation in thought and feeling—in short, a fine representative of the old *noblesse*, one who, it is said, had never visited at the Court of Louis Philippe—and he and his young visitors found some difficulty in coming to a conclusion. They presented a second petition at the beginning of this year to urge the demand, this time followed by two hundred signatures.

PETITION ADDRESSED TO MONSEIGNEUR DE QUELEN IN THE NAME OF THE CATHOLIC STUDENTS.

MONSEIGNEUR,

When, last year, some young Catholics manifested to your Eminence the desire to hear from the pulpit of truth a special preaching, destined to encourage the faith of those who still believe, and to re-animate it in those who believe no longer, you deigned to receive them with a paternal goodness. Your heart comprehended them, and they brought back to those from whom they were sent words of consolation and hope.

Until now this hope has not been able to realize its fulfilment, and nevertheless the same needs exist to-day, rendered more sensible by a long waiting.

In pursuing for a year longer the studies through which Providence wills that we pass, more than ever we have felt how dry they are for the heart, and barren for the intelligence when the religious spirit comes not to animate them. More than ever we have felt the necessity of a Christian teaching which sanctifies Science for us, and shows it to us as the sister of Faith. The eagerness, general to-day, of young minds for serious studies, has not found the nourishment which it seeks in the vain systems which every day sees changing, and which Reason, left to herself, raises up and pulls down. Religion alone, with her unchangeable wisdom, can fill this void. Already we have experienced a very sweet satisfaction in seeing several of our fellow-students returning to this light, from which they were only alienated because they knew it not. Oh! if we could see this example followed by all this youth of the schools, to whom it is only necessary in order to love Christianity that they should know its beauty; this youth, Monseigneur, that you desired to bless altogether on that day when you blessed some among us who came to speak to you on its behalf!

In this view we come to renew to your Eminence the request which we submitted to you.

It is an age when man, returned from his earliest enchantments and some of his earliest errors, feels the need of a sure doctrine, which on one side strengthens his intelligence, arranges and gives life to his earlier studies in connecting them with a superior order of ideas, and on another side prepares his virtue by tracing out to him the rules of that social life in which he is to take a definitive position. Religion alone can give him the manliness of soul necessary to accomplish his mission. This is why we desired conferences in which one would not be confined to entering into the detail of the proofs of fact of Christianity, to demonstrating the authenticity of its titles, to refuting vulgar objections already fallen into contempt, but in which it should have been developed in all its grandeur, in its harmony with the aptitudes and the needs of the individual and of society. There would have found a place, a philosophy of the sciences and of the arts which should discover to us in Catholicism the source of all which is true and of all which is beautiful, in order that at this source each of us may come to draw according to his necessity and his vocation; in a word, a philosophy of life, which, sounding the problems of human existence, should explain to man his origin, should direct his progress, and should cause him to contemplate his end. We desired that this teaching should fall from the priestly chair, because on the lips of the priest is found a grace which strengthens and converts. To all the door should be open, and those who are in error, and those who believe, drawn together in the same place, simple hearers, should gather in silence the sacred Word, a germ which would grow in their hearts, fertilized by meditation. Perhaps, in the midst of these young people gathered round the same altars, would be born a fraternal love which should draw them together at first, and which, overflowing afterwards, would go to seek for the indigent without, and carry them succour. Then from all these souls, reassured by faith, or consoled by charity, would arise a concert of praises to God, of filial gratitude to the Church, and of blessing for him who would have been the author of so much good—for you, Monseigneur.

Then follow the conclusion and signatures.

Ozanam and two of his friends were deputed to carry this petition, as Ozanam and two others had done the first.

In response to this petition the Archbishop instituted a series of conferences, which were very far from answering the young applicants' desires. Yet it was a step in the right direction. But, notwithstanding "the incontestable talent of the seven preachers"—the Archbishop himself opening the conferences—the people's hearts were going out to another preacher, who was delivering a series of discourses in the College Stanislas. This preacher was Henri Lacordaire, then thirty-three years of age, who was speaking as a young man to young men; as one of this age who was familiar with its allurements, to those of this age who were in the midst of those allurements. The next year the Archbishop yielded to the influence which was setting so strongly, and Lacordaire "took possession of the chair of Notre Dame for the greater glory of God." "The work of the Conferences of Notre Dame was definitely founded." It was carried on and extended in following years. The crowds that gathered and filled the metropolitan cathedral are matters of history, and the waves of powerful impression which passed over the people's hearts and minds cannot but have left a lasting work behind. Frederic Ozanam was yet a young man of twenty-two. The three great works of his life were already begun, the one which was most distinctively his own yet growing in secret. He loved literature with a devoted love for its own sake, but he subordinated alike his loves and his dislikes to one aim.

To M. Ernest Falconnet.

Paris, April 11th, 1834.

My dear Friend,

Thou art uneasy about thy future; in truth, this is the malady of the greater part of young men. Ambition of good, proselytism, charity, personal interest, self-love—all this mingles in the mind, and brings there the impatience of doing some great thing. Impatience wishes to go before the time, and to divine that which is not yet come: one would fain be able to be admired beforehand for the great works which one projects. I know that, dear friend, because there is much of that in a heart which thou knowest, but which I know still better—in mine.

How many times have I not desired to build in advance the edifice of my existence, gathering up that which to me seemed the most proper to make it great and beautiful since my childhood as scholar, when I dreamed of poems in Latin verse, up to the present time, when I dream of so many other things. Dost thou recall those conversations when we were walking, where we spoke of what we would do one day? We loved to open out the road by which we should pass together; we found two phantoms which we called our two lives, and which we embellished at pleasure; we made them as much alike as possible, like two brothers who love to dress alike. We proposed to ourselves common studies, labours animated by the same spirit, tending to the same end. Well, of all these dreams, has one been realized? Do we not find ourselves now divided by place, by taste, by kind of study, and, I fear much, even upon ideas the most important? Would we desire even that our castles in the air of that time were now standing? For myself, I protest that I would not.

Poor creatures that we are! we know not if to-morrow we shall be in life, and we would fain know what we shall do in *twenty years hence!* We are ignorant what are our faculties, what perhaps is for our happiness, and we would trace for ourselves an inflexible route for the development of faculties of which we are not sure, to attain a happiness which is for us a mystery! Besides, consider this. Of what use is it to know what one would do, if not to do good? Of what use to know our destination, if not to accomplish it? Of what good to see the road, if not to walk in it? Now, provided that the traveller sees ten paces before him, will he not reach the end as well as if he had all the rest in perspective? Provided that the workman knows each hour of the day the task which is imposed upon him for the following hour, will he not as surely reach the end of the work as if he had under his eyes the plan of the architect? And does it not suffice to us to know our duty and our destiny for the nearest moment of the future, without wishing to extend our regards to the Infinite? If we know what God wishes to do with us to-morrow, is it not enough?—and what need have we to concern ourselves about what He will command us in ten years, since between now and then

He may call us to repose? I do not say for this that we should be heedless and careless in following a vocation indicated; but I say that we must be content to know a part and follow it with energy and calm, without disquieting ourselves about that which is still hidden.

The thought of the uncertainty of human things should not destroy our courage and extinguish our activity: it ought, on the contrary, to attach us more strongly to present duty, in convincing us of ignorance of the future. Thou wouldst find sufficient peace and contentment if thou canst penetrate thyself with these ideas: That we are here below only to accomplish the will of Providence; that this will is accomplished day by day, and that he who dies leaving his task unfinished is as much advanced in the eyes of the Supreme Justice as he who has the leisure to finish it entirely; that man is no more able to create his moral being than his physical being; that he never makes himself orator, philosopher, artist, man of genius, but that he is made so little by little, and insensibly, by the conduct of God. The greatest men are those who have never made beforehand the plan of their destiny, but who have let themselves be led by the hand. A little confidence in the heavenly Father, without whose will a hair falls not from a human head!

Alas! I hesitate to write thee this. Perhaps already thou no longer understandest me, as I, on one side, begin no more to understand thee. But I am excusable for my unintelligence, for these ideas of thine are new to me; while the language that I use is a language that thou art accustomed to hear, and which, perhaps, because of that, appears to thee antiquated, ascetic—what know I? But, be convinced of it, my dear friend, notwithstanding the coldnesses and the negligences of which thou hast had the right to accuse me, I love thee always. Among my friends thou art always the one on whom my affections rest with the most complaisance, and I know not how to bear the idea that, so near the point of departure, our two roads may diverge for ever. I love thee; and as, with my world of ideas and habits, I am happy, and as thou, on the contrary, thou findest thyself unhappy, I would impart to thy soul a little of that tranquillity which generally reigns in mine.

For some time past, above all since I have seen some young people die, life has taken for me another aspect. I have felt that until now, although I had never abandoned religious practices, I had not kept sufficiently foremost in my heart the thought of the invisible world, of the real world. I have thought that I had not paid sufficient attention to two companions who always walk with us, even without our perceiving them—*God and Death*. I have found that Christianity had been for me, until now, a sphere of ideas, a sphere of worship, but not sufficiently a sphere of morality, of intentions, of actions. The reading of the works of Pellico, above all, has penetrated me with this idea; and the more I attach myself to it, the more I feel in myself of disinterestedness, of kindliness, and of calm. It seems to me also that I understand the things of life better, and that I shall have more courage to support them; it seems to me that I have a little less pride. However, do not believe that I am become a saint or a hermit. I have the misfortune to be far distant from the one, and I have no vocation for the other. While thinking as I have just told thee, I am a sufficiently good fellow, not asking for better than joy;

occupying myself, perhaps, too much with literature, history, and philosophy, doing a little law, and losing always, according to my custom, a considerable time.

Although thou mayest reproach me for this tone of sermon which reigns in my letters, I have yet on my mind something which I must say to thee. For a long time, my dear friend, I have perceived that thou hast wanted a little frankness with me on one point, because thou hast feared, without doubt, to open to me thy soul. I want to speak of faith! I am very sure that in this matter there have passed in thy mind revolutions of which thou hast never spoken to me, and in which nevertheless I should have been anxious to intervene; not, certainly, to teach thee—I am not able—but to share a little thy disquietudes and to give thee some consolations. I do not think that thou hast renounced entirely the beliefs of thy youth, but thou art become indifferent with regard to them; or rather thou hast relegated them to the domain of philosophic opinions, and thou hast accepted Christianity as a noble and holy doctrine, but in modifying it according to thy own ideas. Nevertheless, religious ideas can have no value if they have not a practical and positive value. Religion serves less to think than to act; and if it teaches to live, it is in order to teach to die.

Thou wouldst know that which thou shalt do in ten years hence, that which thou shalt do during the short space of life; but what shalt thou be in eighty years hence and during all the ages after? This is what depends on thee to determine. The value of Christianity is in this, and not in the attraction which its dogmas may present to men of imagination or of mind. I conjure thee, then, to open thyself to me on thy moral condition, for I am convinced that there all melancholies have their source.

Another time, my dear friend, I will write thee a letter a little more cheerful and more varied, for fear that thou shouldst imagine that I pass my day with death's-heads, and that I am preparing to enter the seminary, which certainly is very far from my thoughts and my desires. But, besides my need to give vent to a little of the uneasiness which weighs on my mind with regard to thee, I had my ears filled with sad tidings which they give me of the events at Lyons, which are quite sufficient to make me speak a little more harshly and reflectively than I am accustomed.

My affectionate respects to thy father, and do not doubt that I shall always love thee with all the power of an old and fraternal friendship.

To M. Hommay.

Paris, May 7th, 1834.

My dear Hommay,

You are very kind to have thought of me, and to have written to me in replying to Lallier. Here is a correspondence too well begun not to last. . . . .

I must, my dear Hommay, draw from you twenty sous and your signature for the business which I mention. You know without doubt that the bishops of Belgium have founded a Catholic university. This university is kept up by shareholders. Each share is a franc, payable during five years, or five francs once paid. As such an institution ought to find a great success in a country as religious as Belgium, impiety is moved, and some bands of students from the ordinary university of Louvain have vociferated insults under the windows of the two bishops, and have joined to that invectives in a journal. We have believed we ought to reply in the name of the Catholic youth of the University of France, and we have drawn up a protestation which has been inserted in the *Gazette de France*, the *Univers Religieux*, and three Belgian journals. In a word, all our common friends have signed and subscribed, and there are yet lists open for future adhesions and subscriptions. There is the object for which I ask your permission to dispose of your signature and your purse. Be sure that this will compromise neither the honour of the one nor the stoutness of the other.

All the talk about us is of the new work of the Abbé de la Mennais. M. Lacordaire judges it very severely; he sees in it almost the manifesto of a war against the Church, and he expects a rebellion declared in the next work that M. de la Mennais publishes. For the rest, the journals have judged it very superficially. *La Quotidienne* has made a pompous eulogy on it, without knowing what it said. But the intimate disciples of the great writer, MM. Gerbet, de Coux, Montalembert, who know where this tends, break with him from this day, so that he is all alone. May God have pity on him, and may He pardon those who, by disheartening affronts, have pushed, little by little, this superb genius into a path of wrath and error!

Adieu, my good friend! Let us all love each other. There are great feasts approaching: let us find ourselves again at least before God, since we cannot find ourselves united before men. Since we cannot talk together, let us pray for each other; that will be worth still more.

To his Mother.

Friday, May 16th, 1834.

... You complain, poor mamma, that your son abandons you; that he has no more with you those cordial conversations, those openings of the heart of former times; that he speaks to you no longer of what he does nor of what he feels; you are reduced to *figure* to yourself that you have a son, and you have no other proof of his existence than the money which must be paid for him every month.

I assure you, nevertheless, that if it had only depended on him to give you better proofs of his existence a month ago, at the time of the affairs of Lyons, he would certainly have done it well, and that he would have caressed you so much, embraced you so much, that you would have been well convinced that you have a son *Frederic*. But this has not been permitted me. On another side, if nearly all my last letters have been addressed to papa, it is because they were on business. I had commissions to fulfil, money to ask for, and I know that, on these occasions, it is to the father's side that one must turn. It is true, at the same time, that it is very long since I relieved my heart to you. It is that really this year I do not comprehend at all my manner of being: on one part, examinations, wearinesses, disquietudes, have dried up my soul; and, on another part, all my habits of last year, my conferences, my studies, my researches, have been so turned upside down, that I cannot find myself again. No more of these warm discussions that we had last year at our literary society; no more of these works of time which occupied our minds; no more of these improvisations which warmed our ideas. All our little reunions are disorganized; I am become idle, and except a few miserable articles in the periodical collections and some good lectures, I have done nothing besides my law. I believe, in sum, that if I have gained some white balls on one part, I have lost much on another—or, at least, I have not advanced; so that I am not greatly content with my mental condition.

I am little more satisfied with my moral state. In the first place, weariness and uneasiness have somewhat deranged it; and, again, the sadness of passing things beats down courage; the obscurity of the future disconcerts the best resolutions; in proportion as one becomes older, and sees the world nearer, one finds it hostile to all the ideas, to all the sentiments to which one is attached; the more one comes into contact with men, the more one meets of immorality and egoism, pride among learned men, conceitedness among men of the world, intemperance among the people. At the sight of all this, when one has been brought up in the midst of a generous and pure family, one's heart is seized with disgust and indignation, and one would fain murmur and curse. Nevertheless, the Gospel forbids it; it makes it a duty to you to devote yourself entirely to the service of that society which repulses and despises you.

All this is felt profoundly at my age, and these sad truths, which disenchant all my illusions, leave me sombre and grave as a man of forty years. I feel that my duty is to fill a place, and this place, I see it not. Ambitions are so numerous, capacities so multiplied, that it is singularly difficult to pierce through. How would you that a poor ear of wheat should be able to put forth at its ease, when enormous tufts of darnel cross at its left and right? And then, even when I see my place clearly marked, energy fails me to fill it. You know that this is the perpetual object of my complaint—irresolution and weakness! Impossible to me to say in the evening, "I will do this," and to do it the next day. Perhaps, also, I am too young, and I am wrong to disturb myself with all this, and to wish to be a grown man when I hold yet to childhood by more than one point; but I cannot forget that this year my education finishes, and that in the month of August I may, if I will, be an advocate. Me! advocate!—can you figure that to yourself? After all, an advocate is no great thing.

One circumstance which contributes not a little to leave my inner self in this condition of perplexity is that the only intimate counsellor that I have here—the only one whose wisdom and goodness can at the same time take the place to me of father and mother, M. Marduel—has taken a long journey to Lyons. He was to return this evening, and I expect to see him to-morrow; but he has been away since Easter, so that, as I am a little jealous of making new acquaintances, I have been all this time abandoned to my humour and to the caprices of my imagination. In truth, if there are among the Protestants some young people of good faith, enlightened and religious, I pity them much to want a succour of which my youth has so much need, and without which I should either be completely ruined or consumed with melancholy. The other friends are a slender resource—the ones, those of my age, are as inexperienced, as irresolute, as myself; the others are confined to M. D——, who, since he is married, is no longer a young man, and no longer comprehends anything about the young men of to-day.

All that I have just written has nothing very lively, and it is for this reason that I have not conversed with you on it sooner.

We lead here a life so singular and so monotonous; we have so few distractions and communications without, that we are obliged to fall back upon ourselves. We are placed between dry studies imposed on us by duty—and which we must accept—and seductive studies whose charm attracts us, and of which we must be diffident. We are surrounded by political parties, who, because we begin to wear a beard, would fain draw us into their tracks. Even in religion we hear only controversies, we see disputes in which charity is wanting and scandal abounds. No literary reunion which would not be observed by the spies of the Government, or by certain journals self-styled religious. Taxed as bigots by our irreligious comrades, as Liberals and as rash individuals by older people; questioned at each moment on what we think and on what we do; submitted to the arbitrary power of our university professors, having to fear sometimes for ourselves at the time of outbreaks, and above all, for our relations at a distance from us : it is an existence very strange and very tedious, to which, if it were only a question of my own welfare, I should prefer a hundred times never to have left my hole; but of which I do not complain when I think that I learn here to know the world such as it is, and that, perhaps,

Providence proves me here in order that I may be more useful afterwards.

Now I am vexed at having talked to you so long of this, because you will torment yourself for me. Do nothing of the sort, my good mother, I entreat you. For first, is it not right that I should be put to proof? I am of age to fast; and to-morrow I fast with the Church. Am I not of age also to suffer a little, and to combat as she does? And also these thoughts are not so anchored in my soul that they do not leave place to many others —consoling and joyous. Sometimes there are memories : I love much to recall to myself all that I know of my life since my childhood. Often we speak of these times with Chaurand. The college makes an amusing episode in it, and the first communion—a touching scene, all whose most minute traits are profoundly imprinted in my memory. Then there are the first joys of study— the uncertainties, the researches, the healthy and strengthening philosophy of the Abbé Noirot; and in the midst of all this many friendships commenced on the benches of classes, and which yet continue— Ballofet, Falconnet, Henri; all our plays, from Noah's Ark and the soldiers to our sentimental promenades and serious parties at chess. Afterwards, the study of the clerk, the tediousness of the *copy*, the eternal conversations with the first clerk, the pamphlet against the Saint-Simonians and the pleasure of being printed. And afterwards, as background of all the picture, the family life, your caresses and your spoilings, your gentle words when I worked at the table beside you; consulting you on my themes when I was in the sixth, and reading you my French discourses when I was in rhetoric; the counsels, and sometimes the benevolent fault-findings of papa; the long excursions made with him; his histories, to which I listened with so much pleasure; this eldest brother, whom we only saw from time to time, and about whom we were so uneasy; this little brother, whom I had seen born and grow; the good relations of Florence, who came one after the other to show us how amiable and excellent they were. Finally, a nearer memory, our delicious journey, the stay in Rome—so calculated to overawe the soul—the stay in Florence, so dear to the heart. So much for the past. The future has also its part, and hope makes it for me. I imagine to myself that, with the help of God, a day will come when I shall pay you in filial piety and in satisfaction a little of what you have expended on me in solicitude, strength, and health. These enjoyments are not the only ones. I read beautiful and good books, and sufficiently varied. Dante, Manzoni, Walter Scott, Lamartine, Titus Livius, Pascal—to this company of illustrious dead I join the society of good and pleasant living friends. I have very dear friends—Henri, Lallier, Chaurand and others, with whom I am on intimate terms. I have estimable persons who receive me well, as M. Ampère. I hear good speakers in the public courses, and eloquent preachers in the Christian pulpits. I satisfy my curiosity in the museums, and exercise my limbs in the fields. I do not dine badly—my room is pretty; money, thanks to you, is not wanting; I have a library very well chosen; and, whatever may be my weakness, whatever may be my defects, I preserve the hope of not being too unworthy of my parents—of being one day a zealous Christian, a steady citizen, and a virtuous man. In sum, I assure you that I do not find myself unhappy, and that, all reckoning made, I find up to the present time, in the greater part of my days, more of well-being than of evil. Thus, I repeat to you, my good mother, do not be uneasy for me.

Meanwhile, here is my letter filled, and in an hour and a half of conversation I have covered four pages. Adieu, my good mother. This time I have conversed with you a very long time. Oh, have no fear that I will desert you.

The Abbé Marduel referred to in this letter to his mother was Lyonnese, and at first settled in Lyons. Having been later fixed in Paris, Frederic's elder brother had found him so useful and kind a friend that he believed he could not do better than recommend Frederic to him likewise. He was certainly worthy of the respect and love which were showed him, and during the whole time of Frederic's first stay in the metropolis he was his "guide, philosopher and friend." And when he returned and brought a wife there, he not only recurred to the good old man himself, but took his wife with him, and the relation was not dissolved till the Abbé's death. It is not straying from Frederic's life to say a few words of a man to whom he must have owed much, setting entirely aside the exercise of any priestly function. "Hardly," says the Abbé Ozanam, "had we exchanged a few words with him than we found ourselves at ease with him as with the best of fathers. Although much occupied, he never had the air of being pressed. He listened to you, and spoke to you as if he had nothing else to do." Affable and kindly to an extreme, he yet waged continual war—making known his sentiments especially in blessing marriages—with the familiar habit which had lately taken root, the *tutoiement* of parents by their children. His house was furnished with chance articles, but he had a large and rich library in which were some curious and rare books. Unfortunately, his charity was not tempered with prudence; he got himself into trouble by having endorsed a cheque for another, who not being able to pay, it returned to him; and he was not only obliged to sell some of his goods to have means to honour his signature, but also to withdraw at an advanced age into comparative retirement, on account of the noise the affair made. After a time, however, he returned to Paris, and there, it would appear, died.

To M. Ernest Falconnet.

Paris, July 21st, 1834.

My dear Ernest,

I have received lately two visits, which have given me great pleasure. The first, that of thy excellent father; the second is thine. It is thy packet of good letters, friendly and sincere talks as I desired them. It is the opening of thy heart, the history of thyself—a history for which I was so anxious, an opening for which I longed. For see, my friend, when one has put between him and his friends two hundred leagues, one fears always to lose sight of them; one dreads, on returning, to find them no longer the same; one fears, on seeing them again, no longer to comprehend them. And that is why I have, in some sort, submitted thee to question. That is why I have knocked at the door of thy most intimate feelings. I have desired to make the most sacred cord of thy heart vibrate, to see if it still uttered the same sound as mine.

And now I rejoice myself in this experience, because I see that we are still as near the one to the other, still brothers by thought as we are by blood. I am happy to see that after having suffered what I have suffered, sought as I have sought, thou believest as I believe. Thus, without seeing each other—youthful pilgrims—we are arrived by the same route at the threshold of the same temple.

Only—but this is not the place to explain my idea—I consider Catholicism in a more absolute manner. I see in it the necessary formula of Christianity, as Christianity seems to me the necessary formula of humanity. I believe in worship as profession of faith, as symbol of hope, as terrestrial realization of the love of God. Because of this, I practise my religion according to my strength and according to the habits which have been given me from childhood ; and I find in prayer, in the sacraments, the indispensable support of my moral life in the midst of the temptations of a devouring imagination and of a deceitful world.

As for political opinions, there also we agree—that is to say that, like thyself, I desire the destruction of the political spirit for the profit of the social spirit. I have, without contradiction, for old royalism all the respect one owes to a glorious invalid ; but I would not lean myself on him, because with his wooden leg he knows not how to walk at the pace of the new generations. I deny not, I repulse not any governmental combination. But I only accept them as instruments to make men happier and better. If thou desirest formulas, here they are:

I believe in authority as means, in liberty as means, in charity as end.

There are two principal kinds of governments, and these two kinds of governments can be animated by two opposing principles.

Either there is the use of all for the benefit of one alone; and this is the monarchy of Nero—a monarchy that I abhor.

Or there is the sacrifice of one for the benefit of all; and this is the monarchy of St. Louis, which I revere with love.

Or it is the use of all for the benefit of each; and this is the Republic of the Terror—and this Republic I anathematize.

Or it is the sacrifice of each for the benefit of all, and this is the Christian republic of the primitive Church of Jerusalem; it is, perhaps, also that of the end of time, the highest condition to which humanity can rise.

Every government, it seems to me, is to be respected in this, that it represents the divine principle of authority: in this sense I understand the *omnis potestas a Deo* of St. Paul. But I think that in face of the power, there must also be the place of the sacred principle of liberty. I think that one must energetically claim this place. I think that one must warn with a voice courageous and severe the power which uses others for its own benefit, instead of sacrificing itself. The word is made to be the barrier which one opposes to force; it is the grain of sand where the sea comes to break itself.

Opposition is a thing useful and praiseworthy, but

not insurrection. Active obedience, passive resistance, *les Prisons* of Silvio Pellico, and not *les Paroles d'un Croyant*.

Now, we others, we are too young to intervene in the social strife. Shall we then remain inert in the suffering and sighing world? No; there is a preparatory way open to us; before doing public good, we can endeavour to do good to some individuals; before regenerating France, we can solace some individuals amongst her poor. *Thus I desire that all young people of mind and heart would unite for some charitable work, and that they would form through all the country a vast generous association for the comfort of the popular classes.*

I have done very little this year, except my law, at which I have laboured more than usual. At this moment I am struggling with the subjects of the fourth examination, which are very extensive, and leave me no leisure. I write thee in haste; it is one o'clock in the morning. I must end this letter, too short as conversation, too long and too desultory as letter of ceremony; thou wilt excuse the one and the other, wilt thou not? And also, in less than a month, we shall speak at our ease of all those things which the pen renders so badly.

Adieu.

CHAPTER VII.

VACATIONS — LAMARTINE — SELF-DISGUST — ANXIETY ABOUT HIS MOTHER—THE GRANDE CHARTREUSE—ASSOCIATION OF CHRISTIAN ARTISTS.

THEN came some quieter holidays — holidays which nevertheless left a delightful impression on his memory:

To M. LALLIER.
Lyons, October 15th, 1834.

A month and a half has passed away since you conducted me in friendly fashion to the carriage which brought me joyous to Lyons. A month and a half has passed away since my father, come before me, clasped me in his arms; and it seems to me that I have just arrived. I have not yet had the time to take up again my old domestic habits; hardly have I had time to know myself again. Having passed my last vacation in Italy, I am here, after two years absence, almost a stranger. There are old acquaintances wanting; there are little cousins come into the world during my exile, and of whose existence I was ignorant; others, whom I left almost children, have learned their philosophy and are preparing to leave for Paris; these are married, those have lost their wife. My old confessor is dead; they have renewed almost all the priests in the parish. The material even of the town has changed. The cannon of the days of April have overturned houses, but in revenge our hills are crowned with new forts. . . . Commerce does little, and the workmen emigrate for Switzerland; but we have a superb garrison, reviews . . . the uniform carpets the quays, the great sabres trail agreeably on the pavements of the public places; if some manufactures are deserted, the houses of debauch and the prisons are filled. . . . Numbers of people have broken up their houses, and nothing vexes me more than not to find in their places the tradespeople whom I was accustomed to use, or the friends on whom I called in passing. So that, in this poor Lyons, I know no longer whereabouts I am. Yet I have found new enjoyments there; our family of Florence has come to fix itself amongst us; my uncle, my aunt, and my cousins show me the kindest affection. With this, the tenderness of my father, my mother, and my two brothers, is there not sufficient to render me happy?

Well, my dear friend, I believe I may say it without offending Providence, no, it is not sufficient. God has put into our soul two wants which resemble each other, but which must not be confounded. We need relations who cherish us, but we need also friends who are attached to us. The tenderness which comes from blood, and the affection which proceeds from sympathy, are two enjoyments which we know not how to do without, and of which the one cannot replace the other. The tenderness of relationship has the more sacredness in this, that it is established immediately by the Creator Himself; friendship is the more flattering that it is rather our own work. Relations weigh heaviest in the balance without doubt; yet the other scale must not remain empty. Often at Paris you have heard me regretting the paternal roof, the embraces of my mother, the counsels of my eldest brother, the caresses of my little brother; now that I have all this, I regret our comrades of Paris, the charitable kind-heartedness of M. Bailly, the long evenings passed together, and you above all, who gave me so often good advice and good examples, who showed me an attachment so sincere and so Christian.

You know it well, of all the young people whom I knew in the exile of the capital, it was you whom I preferred; it was you whom I went to seek when you were hidden in your little room, and when you were in your sombre days; it was you, in your turn, who so many times inspired me with holy and salutary thoughts, who consoled my sadnesses, who gave me courage. But these are things which we must feel and not express; in a word, I want you much—we all want you as long as we are here at Lyons—we of your old fellow-disciples. Twice we have dined together —de la Perrière, Chaurand, Biétrix, and many others —and twice we have drunk to your health, amidst the great acclamations of everybody. The last time it was at our house, and my father and my mother, desirous of knowing you, have joined with ready hearts in the toast which we proposed to you.

Of all my pleasures, one of the greatest is the pilgrimage that I have made to Saint-Point, to see M. de Lamartine. Dufieux, who knew him, had obtained of him the permission to bring me. We left together one Sunday morning for Mâcon, where we arrived in the evening after having passed through a charming country. There we learned that M. de Lamartine was at his château of Saint-Point, five leagues from Mâcon, in the mountains. The Monday, then, after breakfast, we set out on a light pleasure-car, which a little ragged Phaeton conducted, and we followed the road of the ancient and celebrated Abbey of Cluny. Then, when we had from far perceived the ruins of this old house of God, we turned to the left, in the grand and beautiful valley in which is situated the residence of this great man. On a knoll, at the foot of the mountains, is a hamlet overlooked by a church, *quasi* Gothic, and an ancient château. It is Saint-Point. This château belonged formerly to the redoubted Count de Saint-Point, rival in cruelties of the Baron des Adrets. This hamlet was, twenty years ago, an assemblage of rude country-folk, ignorant and bad. M. de Lamartine has brought civilization into these places. He has repaired, embellished, enlarged the château; he has raised the steeple again; he has purchased a house to establish there a hospital and schools; he has opened roads to establish communications between the village and the high-road; he is now building a magnificent bridge over a ravine. These benefits have attracted new and numerous inhabitants into the valley. White houses rise up on all sides; all breathes ease and contentment; the manners have become gentle and pure, and the stranger, going to visit the poet, meets honest men who offer to serve him as officious guides. Behold us, then, at the gate of the château. An elegant porch, form Gothic, decorates the entrance; three seigniorial towers lend it a sufficiently majestic aspect. We cross the threshold of the parlour. Madame de Lamartine receives us with the greatest goodness. She is a highly respectable lady, very good and very pious. She is English, and converted to the Catholic religion. This day there was, as it happened, at Saint-Point a number of people, and among others a family of English, and we saw, to our disappointment, that we should not be able to enjoy without sharing the society of him whom we came to seek. However, M. de Lamartine arrived. He showed to Dufieux a very particular friendship, and received me myself in a very affable manner. He took us both into a summer-house, where we three talked alone nearly two hours. He expounded to us his great and generous political ideas, his beautiful literary theories; he asked much concerning the youth of the schools, and the mind which animated them, and appeared to me full of hope for the future. His ideas are connected together by a very solid logic; his language is brilliant, figurative; he seems philosopher still more than poet by the thought, and more poet than philosopher by the word. I have rarely seen a man unite more noble qualities. Aged forty-three years, he carries on his countenance the impress of trouble supported with dignity, of glory accepted with modesty. His forehead is very broad, his eyes large and bright, the curve of his mouth gracious and severe at once, his features thin, his stature high.

At table and in the parlour he seemed to me full of amiability. He pressed us very much to pass a week with him; and as we could not do it, he made me promise to go and see him at Paris this winter. We dined and passed the night, and the next day he took us to see his two houses of Milly and of Monceaux. Along the high-road the country people saluted him with an affectionate air. He accosted them and chatted with them, asking them news of their vintage, their interests, their families. They, too, seemed to love him much, and the little children ran after him crying, "*Good-morning, Monsieur Alphonse!*" At Monceaux I found de Pierreclau. We dined together, and in the evening we took leave of our illustrious host, and returned into our obscurity.

That is quite enough, is it not? Here I am always with my honeyed words which cannot cover less than a hundred pages; with my immoderate admirations and my grand laudative phrases. What would you? The life of this man has very much struck me; notwithstanding that, before visiting M. de Lamartine, I had read and re-read a certain chapter of the "Imitation" against human respect, I was veritably fascinated in considering to what height genius and virtue can raise a creature like ourselves.

Oh! more than ever have returned to me all my uncertainties, my literary ambitions, the desire of doing good confounded with the desire of acquiring glory, and nevertheless the consciousness of my nothingness, the feeling of my social position, and of the necessity in which I am placed of gaining my bread and working for money. These uncertainties are not at all ended. I have submitted them to my brother; he thinks it is not yet time to cut the Gordian knot; he urges me to pursue at the same time the studies of law and those of history. I have obtained of my father to return two years to Paris. I shall there quietly earn my doctorate, and at the same time I shall learn the Oriental languages. For the rest, no more articles for the journals; only some rare labours for the conference, if there is one, or for the *Revue Européenne*, if it is not dead, and in any case to exercise myself. I leave the rest of my future to Providence. Willingly I will accept the place which it pleases it to assign to me; however low it may be, it will be sufficiently good if it is well filled.

I am without any news from Paris; no letters, none of our journals. If you know anything write it to me; I begin to feel the ennui of provincial life. We shall bring you to Paris a band of good Lyonnese who will increase all our reunions; although, to speak the truth, I do not care any longer for the historic conference than as means of recruiting the conference of charity.

* * * * *

To M. X.——

Lyons, November 4th, 1834.

MY DEAR FRIEND,

Your letter filled me with joy. This joy I have not kept for myself alone; I have communicated it to some of my friends who make a part of our little society, and who are here for the vacation. I have written immediately to the members now at Paris, to tell them this good news,* and to have the report you ask me for. But permit me to congratulate you, from this time, for the good you have begun, and for that which you prepare to do. You have found colleagues worthy of you; you have found a wise guide. The field is before you; misery has there traced large furrows; you will sow

* Of the foundation of the first Provincial Conference of St. V. de Paul, at Nismes.

benefits there with open hands; you will see them grow and fructify. God and the poor will bless you; and we, whom you will have surpassed, we will be proud and joyful to reckon such brothers. The wish that we formed is then accomplished; you are the first echo which has responded to our feeble voice; others will rise soon perhaps; then the great merits of our little Parisian society will be to have given the idea of forming similar ones. A thread suffices to begin a cloth; often a stone thrown into the waters becomes the foundation of a large island.

I believe, then, that you have taken all that there was of good amongst us in taking from us a charitable idea, which was already without doubt in your heart, but which had not yet expression. In such a work one must abandon one's self much more to the inspiration of the heart than to the calculations of the mind. Providence itself will give you counsels by the circumstances with which it surrounds you, by the thoughts which it sends to you. I believe that you will do well to follow them freely, and not to charge yourself much with rules and formulas.

Besides, the end which we propose to ourselves in Paris is not absolutely the same as that which you propose to yourselves, I think, in the province. At Paris we are birds of passage, distant for a time from the paternal nest, and over whom Incredulity, this vulture of the thought, hovers to make his prey. We are poor young intelligences, nourished in the bosom of Catholicism, and scattered in the midst of a foolish and sensual crowd. We are the sons of Christian mothers, arriving one by one within strange walls, where Irreligion seeks to recruit herself for her losses. Well, it is a question, before all, of assembling these feeble birds of passage under a shelter which shall protect them ; of providing these young intelligences with a rallying-point for the time of their exile ; that these Christian mothers may have a few tears less to shed, and that their sons may return to them as they sent them away. It needed then to form an association of *mutual encouragement* for the young Catholics, where they might find friendship, support, examples ; where they might meet, so to speak, a shadow of the religious family in which they had been nourished ; where the older ones might receive the new pilgrims from the province, and give them a kind of moral hospitality. Now, the strongest bond, the principle of a veritable friendship, is charity ; and charity cannot exist in the hearts of several without gushing over ; it is a fire which is extinguished without nourishment, and the nourishment of charity is good works.

For you—you seem to me called to a mission yet more generous. . . . . You act directly for the poor ; you form, besides, a permanent reunion, and not unceasingly renewed like ours ; you spread your benefits in your own town and not in a stranger city. Your work will then be at once more durable, more apparent, more powerful ; you may remain less numerous, and, though you should not be more than a dozen, if you are united with a true friendship, you may do great good in a town of thirty thousand souls. We, on the contrary—we are obliged to extend ourselves, even at the risk of relaxing, in order to embrace in our circle the greatest possible number of young people.

I do not know if I have expressed myself in an intelligible manner; but I wished to draw your attention to the difference in the end, because it seems to call for the difference in the means. I do not enter into longer details respecting our little society of Paris. I believe I have told you all in our conversations; and the report of M. de la Noue will teach you more than I can do. Since we have existed, we have distributed nearly two thousand four hundred francs, some books, and a tolerably large quantity of old clothes. Our resources consist in the collection which we make among ourselves every Tuesday; in the alms of some charitable persons who are anxious thus to aid our goodwill; in the cast-off clothes of our wardrobe. As it is probable that at the renewal of the scholar-year our number will increase and rise to a hundred, we shall be obliged to divide ourselves and to form several sections, which will periodically have a common assembly. When these new arrangements shall be ready, I will inform you of them. For, notwithstanding what I have said to you, of the difference which it appears to me should exist between our two societies, it ought not to diminish the union and harmony; on the contrary, in the same manner that the divergent rays all come from the same centre, thus our efforts, varied and tending towards divers points, resolve themselves into one same charitable thought, and proceed from the same principle. It needs, then, that there should be accord between us to double our force; it needs that there should be frequent communications, which give us a laudable emulation for good, and which make us one community, each proud of the success of each.

* * * * *

Ozanam returned to Paris at the close of the vacation

to study law, as before, "by obedience," and to endeavour to improve upon the dryness of the study by an intelligent attempt to find out from history and philosophy the reason why the laws had been put together. Meanwhile he studied for the diploma of licentiate of letters, in hopes of after obtaining that of doctor. He succeeded in obtaining the licentiate. A review, called the *Revue Européenne*, at this time applied to him for help in its resuscitation, begging him to compose an introduction to float it again.

TO M. VELAY.

Paris, February 5th, 1835.

MY DEAR VELAY,

I reply very late to thy letter, but I observe to thee that I am yet in the week of visits for New Year's Day, and that thus I come in good time to present thee my affectionate wishes. I wish thee, then, happy days at Metz—days which shall not be too much encumbered with tedious studies, which will not seem to thee too long, which will leave thee some leisure to think on thy friends the Parisians. For them, I assure thee that they do not forget thee at all; and if thy military step no more makes itself heard ascending the staircase of the Hôtel des Ecoles; if thy glorious sword sounds no more on the floor of our rooms; if we have no more on the Sunday thy accustomed visit—thou livest in our memories, thou comest into our conversations. Thou art cited—regretted. We ask when thou wilt return; and when one of thy letters arrives for some one amongst us, he is courted that we may each have our share.

Thou regrettest, thou sayest, the Conferences of M. Lacordaire. Well, my friend, console thyself; we hear him no longer. It is a great trouble to us, who have need of the bread of the Word, who had accustomed ourselves to this excellent and strong nourishment, to be deprived of it all at once, without anything replacing it.

It is to us a grief still greater to see those of our erring brethren who at this powerful voice had returned to the way of truth, returning from it to their errors—shaking the head and lifting the shoulders. Perhaps heaven desires this silence, this humiliation of the Catholics, as one sacrifice more; perhaps we had too soon lifted up our heads. We put our pride in the word of a man, and God put His hand on the mouth of this man in order that we might learn to be Christians without him, in order that we might learn to do without everything, excepting faith and virtue.*

A slight compensation for these treasures of religious eloquence which M. Lacordaire lavishes upon us, has been offered me these last days. I have heard M. de Lamartine at the Chamber. How great and beautiful he was that day! How full his discourse was of gravity, brilliance and harmony! How far he was from this vagueness and those vaporous theories with which they have reproached him! He was simple, he was a logician, he was generous; he was more—he was charitable. He alone represented the Christian thought in this discussion.

Mayst thou have companions who will render agree-

* This trouble passed away, for the next spring Lacordaire was in the pulpit of Notre Dame.

able to thee thy two years at Metz! Thou wilt know well, thou, to render them useful to thee. Thou wilt have, I hope, more leisure than at l'Ecole Polytechnique. Thou wilt be able to see again from time to time thy good and ancient friends—the books of history and of literature. Then, when thou shalt have shaken off the last dust of the bench, when thou shalt have no other servitude than the brilliant servitude of the uniform, then thou shalt be very happy. Master of thy time, delivered from the care of material existence, occupying an honourable rank in society, thou shalt no longer have anything to occupy thee but intellectual and moral labours. I envy much thy lot from this point of view. I, a poor creature, who, whilst waiting till fortune comes, shall be attached to the judicial soil from morning to night, save reading from time to time the chapter of Seneca on the contempt of riches. Now I study in a manner serious enough Hebrew and Sanscrit; but what good will it do to the client, if it please thee, that his advocate should know Sanscrit and Hebrew? Better grow mouldy over the code.

* * * * * *

To M. X——.

Paris, February 23rd, 1835.

MY DEAR FRIEND,

From the first day of my arrival here, I have thought of the report for which you asked me. Our president, M. Bailly, has sought the report in his papers, and a short time ago he told me of the uselessness of his search. So this document is lost. It is not a great misfortune for us; there was in this abridged history of our work a thought which was perhaps of pride. God, who wishes that the left hand should not know what the right hand giveth, has permitted that we should lose a document which only served to give us a little ridiculous vanity. Charity should never look behind her, but always before, because the number of her past benefits is always very small, and the present and future miseries which she should solace are infinite. See the philanthropic associations—there are only assemblies, and reports, accounts, memoirs—they have not a year of existence when they possess already large volumes of official reports. Philanthropy is a proud dame for whom good actions are a kind of adorning, and who loves to look at herself in the mirror. Charity is a tender mother who keeps her eyes fixed on the child she carries at the breast, who thinks no longer of herself, and who forgets her beauty for her love.

Neither do I think that this loss will be grievous to you. It is better that you raise your work by your own proper force, under the inspiration of your heart, under the influence of local circumstances, under the direction of the venerable priest who presides over you; with all this, you will do very easily without a model, which is besides very imperfect. You will not do as we; you will do better than we.

This prediction is not a flattery; it is the expression of what I have felt at the reading of your letter, so burning with charity, so full of this apostolic fire which has set the world aglow, and of which your soul has gathered up such lively sparks. I should have been an egotist and evil-disposed if I had kept for myself alone this enjoyment. I have read to my assembled colleagues, in presence of the curé of the parish, who consented to come and preside over us that day, a great part of your letter. The impression which it left on them can only be conveyed by these words of one of them : " Indeed, it is the faith, it is the charity of the first ages." Oh yes, my friend ; the faith, the charity of the first ages ! It is not too much for our age. Are we not, like the Christians of the earliest times, thrown into the midst of a corrupted civilization and of a crumbling society ? Let us cast our eyes on the world which surrounds us. The rich and the happy, are they much better than those who replied to St. Paul, " We will hear thee another time " ? And the poor and the people, are they much more enlightened, and do they enjoy more prosperity than those to whom the Apostles preached ?

Then for equal evils there needs an equal remedy. The earth is chilled ; it is for us Catholics to re-animate the vital heat which is being extinguished ; it is for us to recommence thus the era of the martyrs. For to be a martyr is a thing possible to all Christians ; to be a martyr is to give our lives for God and for our brothers : it is to give our lives in sacrifice, whether the sacrifice be consumed all at once as the holocaust, or whether it be accomplished slowly, and smoke night and day like the perfumes on the altar ; to be a martyr is to give to heaven all which we have received from it—our blood, our gold, our soul all entire. This offering is in our hands ; this sacrifice, we are able to make it. It is for us to choose to what altars it will please us to carry it, to what divinity we will consecrate our youth and the times which follow it ; to what temple we will gather ourselves to meet—at the foot of the idol of egoism, or at the sanctuary of God and humanity.

The humanity of our days seems to me like the traveller of whom the Gospel speaks. It also, whilst it pursued its way in the roads which the Christ had traced for it—it has been assailed by robbers, by the thieves of thought, by wicked men who have stolen away that which it possessed—the treasure of faith and of love, and they have left it naked and groaning, lying at the border of the path. The priests and the Levites have passed; and this time, as they were true priests and Levites, they approached this suffering being, and wished to heal it. But, in its delirium, it knew them not, and repulsed them.

In our turn, feeble Samaritans, profane and men of little faith as we are, we dare nevertheless to accost this great invalid. Perhaps he will not be affrighted at us; let us try to probe his wounds, and to pour into them oil; let us sound in his ear words of consolation and of peace; and then, when his eyes shall be opened, we will put him back into the hands of those whom God has constituted the guardians and physicians of souls, who are also, in some sort, our hosts in the pilgrimage here below, since they give to our wandering and hungry souls the Holy Word for nourishment and the hope of a better world for shelter. This is what is proposed to us; this is the sublime vocation that Providence has made for us. But how little worthy we are of it, and how we bend beneath the burden! I speak of us here, students of Paris, colony of the people of God in a foreign land. It seems that the spectacle of this misery should render us more enthusiastic and stronger. It seems that having before us great vices, and above us great virtues, we ought to be as a serried battalion in the face of the enemy, ranged under banners which it loves. And, unhappily, it is not at all thus. I do not know what languor seems to overwhelm us. I do not fear to say of the greatest number that which is true of me in particular. Nevertheless, I hope that God will not abandon us; above all, if we have brothers who pray and who merit for us.

In the name of our society, I congratulate yours on its courage; I thank it for the attachment which it desires to show us. . . . . In the earlier times of Christianity, the communities of Asia sent the torch of the faith to the people of Gaul; and when Gaul became Christian, Asia had ceased to be. . . . . Let us act so that it may not be thus with our Parisian work; let us act so that for long yet, and always, if it may be, there shall be in this city a hearth for religion, where the sons of Christian mothers may gather themselves to preserve together warmth and light to increase the one and the other, and to carry them back into their provinces.

I will not give you literary news; there is little important; but you will do me a great pleasure in sending me something of Reboul; a still greater in coming yourself to see us in Paris.

Adieu. Do not forget me; but forget my negligences. I am the first of these idle and discouraged people, of whom I spoke to you lately.

To M. Dufieux.

Paris, March 2nd, 1835.

MY DEAR FRIEND,

*   *   *   *   *   *

But if it is true that I am not ungrateful—if it is true that I have preserved for you a sincere affection—how is it that it should remain dumb; and what is this cold friendship, without word, and without works, a sort of moral petrifaction?

Alas! my dear Dufieux, this question which I ask myself, in the name of friendship, I repeat every day to myself in the name of all my other duties. My conscience does not spare me; and placed between the desire of doing well and much, and an incredible weakness which hinders me from doing anything, I pass my days in bitter reproaches for the non-execution of my past resolutions, and in new resolutions which I shall execute no better, and which prepare for me new reproaches for the future. I may say it, because I say it to my shame and to the glory of God. Perhaps no one has received more than me of generous inspirations—no one has felt holier jealousies, more noble ambitions. There is no virtue, there is no work, moral or scientific, to which I have not been invited by that mysterious voice which sounds at the bottom of one's heart; there are no praiseworthy affections of which I have not felt the attraction—no friendships and precious relationships which have not been prepared for me—no encouragements which have been wanting to me—not a favourable breeze which has not breathed on my stem to bring forth the flowers. There is not perhaps in the vineyard of the eternal Father of the family one stock which He has surrounded with more cares, and of which He might say with more justice: "*Quid potui facere vineæ meæ et non feci.*" And I, an evil plant, I have not opened out to the Divine breath; I have not plunged my roots into the soil which He loosened around me; I am dry and withered; I have known the gift of God; I have felt the living water bathe my lips, and I have not opened them—I have remained a passive being. I was shut up in my supineness. In this moment even, when the call from on high sounds in my ear, when I feel the inspiration withdrawing a little as if to threaten me, but not to abandon me for ever—in this moment even I know not how to will; I know not how to act. And I feel accumulating on my head the responsibility of favours which I neglect every day.

I have told you my trouble, I have said it tumultuously and without order, as I feel it; but that you may not refuse to believe me, that your indulgent charity may not attribute to a moment of excitement the lines which I have just written, I will explain myself more clearly.

Two things above all make our hearts beat with a generous envy, we young Christians: these two things are science and virtue. I was early taught to relish them, and I believed myself made for them. In our conversations of these holidays, I related to you my dreams in this regard. I had resolved for the two years which remained to me to pass in the capital, upon labours more serious, and a moral reform more complete. I had placed my desires under the auspices of our celestial Mother, and I confided in my good intention. Now, since that time, three months have passed away, and I am still empty-handed. Continual uneasiness, tedious application, have begun to extinguish my ardour; and when I have had all the leisure and all the facilities desirable, I have fallen into a sort of fatal languor, which I know not how to shake off. The study which I formerly loved fatigues me; the pen weighs in my fingers, I know no longer how to write. We have still literary conferences, but the poor things are dying, and it is not I, most certainly, who will save them. Force— this gift of the Holy Spirit, so necessary to the men of this age to tread their way without falling, through so many perils—force is not in me. I float at the will of all the caprices of my imagination. Piety seems to me sometimes a yoke, prayer a habit of the lips, the practices of Christianity a duty which I accomplish without spirit, a last branch to which I cling that I may not roll into the abyss, but of which I know not how to gather the nourishing fruits. I see the young men of my age advance with head erect in the paths of a real progress; and I, I halt, and despair of being able to follow them, and I pass in sighing the time which one should avail one's self of for walking.

This is my miserable condition, and this recital serves for explanation of my negligence towards you, if it cannot serve as excuse. If you do not pardon me, you will at least pity me; you will change your friendly adulations into salutary reproaches, into encouragements, into good counsels, and above all into prayers. You comprehend also another motive for my silence. When one writes to a friend like you, one needs to speak of one's self, and one loves not to speak of one's self when one feels ill. I waited instinctively to feel myself better before having a talk with you. In fine, yesterday I had the happiness of receiving Him who is the strength of the weak, and the medicine of the languors of the soul, and to-day I write to you in the sincerity of my regrets for the past, and of my good resolutions for the future. Oh! pray, I implore you, that these at last may not be deceitful!

You, my dear friend, you are the most perfect contrast which can be opposed to me. As much as God has loaded me with favours, so much He has loaded you with sufferings and trials; and while I have succumbed and am bending down notwithstanding His benefits, you come forth stronger and stronger from the crucible of trouble in which His hand has placed you.

* * * * *

TO HIS FATHER.

Paris, March 15th, 1835.

MY DEAR FATHER,

I thought of not writing to you till to-morrow, because I hoped to have the leisure to talk longer with you; but I like better to write to you to-day, although it will compel me to be short. In point of fact, the courier leaves at two o'clock; it is half-past eleven. Lallier has just gone out from breakfasting with me, and at half an hour after noon I must be at Notre Dame to hear M. l'Abbé Lacordaire, who continues, under the presidency of the Archbishop, and in presence of an immense auditory, the Conferences which he began last year in a little chapel.* These Conferences are magnificent; they are attended by all there is of most distinguished in the capital—M. de Lamartine, M. Berryer, etc., a crowd of literary and learned men, and a very great number of

* At the College Stanislas.

young people from the schools. The space reserved to men takes up all the grand nave; it holds from five to six thousand. I am charged with making the analyses of these conferences for the *Univers;* they will pay me twenty-five francs for each; there will be eight. If the purse gains little by it, I assure you that the spirit loses nothing. It is impossible to hear anywhere else things more eloquent. However, M. l'Abbé Cœur, our compatriot, is distinguishing himself also by his preachings at St. Roch; and on another side, Lauzet has made yesterday, in the Chamber of Deputies, a discourse which has been followed by unanimous admiration, and which they compare to the best discourses of Berryer.

Now I will complain to you, my dear papa, of an act of dissimulation which your goodness has suggested to you, but which has not succeeded in deceiving me; on the contrary. Mamma has been ill; she has even been so rather seriously, and you tell me in your letter that she begins to recover her strength. Her strength—she had then lost it—she has then been suffering much, and you have not informed me of it; and there pass in the house things which interest me so much, and I know nothing of them. I am no longer able to rest myself in this correspondence, by which I hoped to participate in all the joys and all the sadnesses of the family. You have done it to spare me uneasiness, but this is not just. This poor mother has had so many cares for me, should I not have at least a little for her? And when she suffers, is it proper that I, her son—I should be as gay as usual? No, this is not right; so much the more, my good father, that it is useless to hide it: the heart guesses.

To M. Velay.

Paris, May 2nd, 1835.

MY DEAR VELAY,

I confess that all the thunderbolts of thy wrath would not be enough to punish my faithlessness. Two months and a half have passed away since I received a letter from thee, and I have not replied to thee. I could, however, allege a plausible excuse. I have been bringing myself into the mind to reduce to its most simple expression, to its most positive expression, that which I had learned of literature during my three years' sojourn at Paris, to cause, if it were possible, my knowledge to pass into parchment, and to take the degree of licentiate in letters.

It has been necessary to review Burnouf from one end to the other, and to convince myself that I had never known my Greek. It has been necessary to go over again a crowd of authors, and afterwards all history, of which several parts are tolerably foreign to me. These labours have occupied a long month, at the end of which I have obtained this most happy diploma of licentiate, which will serve me as footstool, I hope, to enable me to receive doctor the next year; then I shall be, if it please God, doctor in law and doctor in letters, which will not cause the pot to boil more than if I possessed them not. At the same time, we have been occupied in resuscitating the defunct *Revue Européenne*, these gentlemen having desired that I should compose the introduction to it. I have found myself greatly absorbed by this task, and have not had an instant free up to Easter. I tell thee all these things, not to show my own importance—for there is nothing of that, since I have not, so to speak, laboured but by force—but to excuse myself from negligence in thy regard.

The great rendezvous of young people—Catholic and non-Catholic—this year has been at Notre Dame. Thou hast without doubt heard the Conferences of the Abbé Lacordaire mentioned. They have only one defect, that of being too few. He has delivered eight in the midst of an auditory of nearly six thousand men, without counting women. These Conferences on the Church— its necessity, its infallibility, its constitution, its history, etc.—have all been very beautiful; but the last has been eloquent beyond all that I have ever heard. Mgr. de Quelen, who had assisted at all the Conferences, addressed the last time solemn thanks to M. Lacordaire, and has named him Canon of the Cathedral. This brings balm to our feelings. We have had need of it to console us for the last book of M. de Lamartine on the East. This great poet is at the same time so impressionable, that in traversing Asia he is impregnated with a part of its ideas and tendencies. He gives extreme praises to the Alcoran, and by the strength of optimism and tolerance he evidently departs from orthodoxy. Because orders had been given everywhere that he should be well received—because the pachas and the chiefs of the tribes have welcomed him as a great lord, threatened as they were with losing their heads if they failed in respect, his fine soul, which knows not how to suspect evil, allowed itself to be attracted by these outsides, and is smitten with admiration for the Oriental manners.

However, the evil is not without remedy, for it is only

the exaggeration of a good quality. Besides, the book contains no formal apostasy. But it is evident that the sky of Palestine is reflected with all its vividness in the clear spirit of the poet. Time will efface what there is of impure in this image. For the rest, there are also in this same work admirable things; above all, every time that the father shows himself, holding in his hands this poor Julia who was about to die at the feet of the mountains of Jerusalem.

All the Lyonnese here present send thee their kind remembrance. It is impossible to me to name them all.

To M. X——.

Paris, May 16th, 1835.

MY DEAR FRIEND,

I bear you a grudge for having said so little of yourself in your last letter, and for having said so much of me. That which I do is a very small thing. I have great trouble in working; the ideas that I express laboriously are not my own. I try to make myself the echo of the young Christians in the midst of whom I live. But how feeble this echo is; how cold are these words slowly put together, in comparison of this luminous faith, this burning charity, this courageous hope, which palpitates in souls like yours, like those of some whom you resemble! If you knew how feeble I am! how my goodwill is easily broken by the encounter with circumstances! how I pass from ambitious presumption to discouragement and inaction! what vanity in my thoughts, what powerlessness in my works! Yes, I dare say it—Providence has surrounded me with so much care, it has so well provided for me the benefits of education, it has given me prodigally such good relations, such wise teachers, such exemplary friends, that often I allow myself to believe that it intends from me something more than a common virtue; and nevertheless my soul is as a barren sand which the rains of heaven inundate without fructifying.

And yet, in the days in which we are, there need great virtues and strong men. Without doubt the empire of evil begins to be undermined in all parts, and the time approaches when Truth shall be anew saluted Queen of the world. But as long as the earthly life of the human race shall last, evil will not disappear from the midst of it. Evil is always on some part of the earth—sometimes as tyrant, sometimes as slave. It never makes such redoubtable efforts as when it sees its tyranny departing from it. To seize again its falling sceptre it re-unites all its forces; to every religious reaction corresponds necessarily a contrary reaction of impiety. Thus, whilst the idols of the eighteenth century are deserted, whilst the solitude of our temples is peopled anew, whilst indifference is dying out, and whilst M. Lacordaire sounds out the Word of God to an auditory of six thousand men crowded into the grand nave of Notre Dame, rationalism is not idle. It multiplies its periodical reviews; it organizes a seductive propagandism around young people; it surrounds them with its emissaries; it besieges our most illustrious men; it provokes the defection of those who lately were our glories; it dethrones the Abbé de la Mennais from those heights where his genius and his faith had placed him; it makes us tremble for the virginal muse of Lamartine.

These things are sad, but they are true. We are punished, Catholics, for having put more confidence in the genius of our great men than in the power of our God. We are punished for indulging pride in themselves, for having repulsed with some fierceness the affronts of the incredulous, and for having showed them, to justify us in their eyes, our philosophers and our poets, in place of showing them the eternal Cross. We are punished for having rested on these feeble reeds, however melodious they were; they are broken under our hands. Henceforth it is higher that we must seek our help. It is not a weak staff which we need for journeying through the earth: it is wings—those two wings which carry the angels, Faith and Charity. Those places which have become empty must be filled. In the place of genius which fails us, grace must conduct us. We must be courageous, we must be persevering, we must love until death, we must combat until the end. We must not reckon on an easy victory. God has made it difficult to us, in order to make our crowns more glorious.

Alas, my dear, I know not if you feel what I feel, but I feel sometimes so much discouragement and feebleness that I have need to write thus exhortations and strong resolutions to elevate me. I am like children who lift up their voices when they are afraid. I feel myself better when I have opened my heart into the heart of a friend who is better than I. Thus, without knowing it, you do me good; and these lines which you will read in a few days—these lines of which you are the object—before reaching you, will have a little strengthened my heart, and will have given me energy for some time.

* * * * *

The next letter, written from Villefranche, near Lyons, opens with an account of his vain attempt to reach Lyons in time to keep his mother's fête, an occasion which was always very especially celebrated in the family.

To M. Lallier.

Villefranche, near Lyons, Sept. 23rd, 1835.

My dear Friend,

More than a month has passed away since we made our adieus, and promised ourselves to visit each other by letters from time to time in our vacation. In waiting for your visit I come to make you mine, impatient as I am to know something of you, what are your occupations for the present, and what are your ideas for the future. Besides, you are not ignorant that the love of silence is not my favourite virtue, that my happiness is to pour out into the soul of a friend all that I think, all that I feel, all the fantasies of my imagination, all the dreams of my mind; and transported for five weeks under other skies, I have seen, felt, and thought a multitude of things that I need to tell you.

And, first, there were the pleasures of the return—pleasures which were not obtained without pain. You know that I left Paris the 12th. I desired to reach Lyons the 15th, my mother's fête; I desired not less to have mass that day, fête of the holy Virgin. It was necessary for me, therefore, in the morning to stop at

Mâcon, twelve leagues from my home, to assist at the holy sacrifice, hoping to find afterwards a carriage which would take me through in a day. I had reckoned without my host. I found no other carriage than that with which all the sons of Adam are provided from their birth, and I was obliged to pass all this great day of the Assumption in treading on foot the dusty road. At last, some leagues from Lyons, I found a poor tilted cart which brought me at eight o'clock in the evening to the house, at the moment when all the family, assembled to do honour to mamma, were troubling themselves with my delay. Father, mother, brothers, uncle, aunt, cousins —all were there. I leave you to imagine the joy of the first embrace.

Nevertheless, with this first embrace was certainly mingled some sadness. The uneasiness which I had felt about the health of my good mother had been only too well founded. You remember that day of trouble and that charming* letter of which I told you: this trouble and these alarms, my father and my brothers had shared them. Mamma had been subject during more than two months to a weakness and languor of which one could not foresee the end. Accidents sufficiently grave were added to this indisposition, and the fears that they had had at Lyons were not less than those I had experienced at Paris. Happily, at my return there was a great improvement. My good mother was no longer suffering, but she carried the traces of her sufferings past; and in kissing her I was startled by the thinness of her face. Tranquil for the

---

* Alarming(?)—*charmante*, probably, is a misprint for *alarmante*.

present, I am yet very anxious for the future. I see that this health, which is so dear to me, is really enfeebled; that her sensibility has become extreme; that a small thing is sufficient to trouble her—to disturb her; that her virtue and her angelic goodness are always in strife with her delicate and nervous organization. With this she redoubles her good works, and imposes on herself fatigues before which I myself, young and strong, shrink back. I have much anxiety for the next winter. My dear friend, if you have two places to give me in your prayers, give one of them for the health of my mother, and the other for me. If you have only one, let it be for my mother. Praying for her is praying for me. To her preservation in this world is, perhaps, attached my salvation in the other.

Besides domestic cares, I found at Lyons an impression of general terror. The cholera, which struck such dreadful blows in the southern provinces, seemed to be advancing towards our gates. It had ascended the Rhone, to fifteen leagues from our city, chasing before it multitudes of fugitives who came bringing among us frightful recitals, and a terror still greater than the evil. Our lively and impressionable population was greatly moved. Whilst the rude and uninformed spirits began to talk of rumours of poisoning, and prepared themselves to reply to the invasion of the plague by disturbances and violence, a religious crowd besieged Notre Dame de Fourvières, and knelt down in the open air on the space before the church to chant their songs of sorrow. At the same time, a number of devoted persons presented themselves to serve the poor at the time when the epidemic should come. More than fifteen hundred of these people were inscribed beforehand.

* * * * *

At length we breathe. I cannot tell you how happy I am at this momentary repose from all my inquietudes, at having no longer to preoccupy myself either with the approaches of an examination, or with the coming of the cholera, or, above all, with the illness of my mother. I find in my family many consolations and enjoyments. My eldest brother is my guardian angel. For a long time we have projected going together to make a pilgrimage to the Grande Chartreuse. We have accomplished it; we have made on foot a journey of sixty leagues through Dauphiny. There, in the mountains which form the footstool of the Alps, in the midst of a magnificent nature, at the end of a valley cut up by torrents and cascades, bordered with a luxuriant and grand vegetation, in the midst of a hollow in the rocks—some sombre and arid, some covered with moss and flowers—at the foot of elevated and snow-covered peaks, is found the Grande Chartreuse—the chief residence-general of the order founded in this same place by St. Bruno.

* * * * *

For the present I am always the same, the same that you know well, always abundant in words and poor in works, always suffering from my powerlessness and my misery, and not being able to raise myself . . . . with difficulty deciding to take a step towards the good; and after having taken it, always fearing to have done wrong . . . . without ceasing discontented with myself, and not knowing how to destroy the causes of this discontent; finding neither strength nor repose, except in friendship, the lessons and the examples of others. Providence has not willed that this succour should fail me. It has given me excellent friends. You know several of them; and if I suffer from anything in this moment, it is from their absence. However, I have my brother, who keeps me up and helps me much. I have heard him and another ecclesiastic, whose wisdom I esteem, speak of the apostolate of the laity in the world, in a manner altogether reassuring for us.

If you come into my country, at the next vacation, you will find numerous friends, without counting me— me, who am and will be all my life your devoted.

To M. Henri Pessonneaux.

Lyons, September 24th, 1835.

A thousand thanks, my dear Henri, for the services which thou hast rendered me, for thy good letter, and the interesting news which are contained in it. The history of M—— has greatly rejoiced us. I distrust vocations which speak so highly and so long beforehand; that which is violent does not last. Silent and discreet vocations are much more sure. It appears that we are come to that time of life where the road divides into two, and where we make an irrevocable choice. Here are several of our friends who push their way into the straight road of the seminary; here are many who descend into the broad career of marriage. I will give thee the change of thy piece in announcing to thee that C——, at the age of twenty-one years, is learning to light continually the torches of Hymen with some notes of a hundred thousand francs. It is a blessing: the end of the world, announced by the sombre spirits of our time, is adjourned until a new order. The last number of the *Revue* contains a poem of Francheville, which strongly resembles an epithalamium; and there is a talk of things which the known virtue of the young man commands me to regard as a preliminary of marriage. Such are the news which it is permitted me to publish. What would it be if I could reveal all which is told into my ears!

To fortify myself against the contagion of example, to strengthen myself again in the love of solitude and of liberty, I have been with my brother in pilgrimage to the Grande Chartreuse. I need not say that we went on foot, and that we did not die of sadness on the road. The first day we accomplished more than twelve leagues; thus I am henceforth thy equal. I will not tell thee what we have seen, because thou hast already made the same pilgrimage. All that I can say is that I have found there a nature that I should not have the talent to describe, and men whom I should not have the strength to imitate. Yet the impression that this journey has produced upon me differs greatly from the idea I had formed of it beforehand. I had only heard of sublime horrors, of torrents, of precipices, of deserts, of frightful austerities; and I have only seen a delicious solitude, a magnificent vegetation, rich prairies, forests where the greenness of the beech mingles with the blackness of the fir, rocks intermingled with rosebushes, brooks falling in elegant cascades on to a bed of turf and moss, on all sides tufts of blue campanulas, large and graceful ferns like dwarf palm-trees, great flocks on the mountains, birds in the woods; and there, in the valley, the monastery majestic and grand, the monks in their ancient dress, with serene countenance, expressing in all their features happiness and quietude; the chant rising at every hour of the day with strength, with harmony; the hymns of the night rising towards heaven at the hour when crimes are multiplied, and when the judgments of God are prepared; lastly, the charming chapels of Notre Dame *à Casalibus* and of St. Bruno, with their fountains and their memories of seven hundred years. I know not if the idea is not eccentric, but the Chartreuse, thus placed in this hollow of the mountains, seemed to me like a solitary nest where holy souls, gathered together and sheltered under the maternal wings of religion, developed peaceably to fly away one day to heaven.

Religion, mother full of condescension and of goodness, has united around this sacred nest all the harmonies of nature, all the graces of creation. And it is a remarkable thing that the anchorites and monks of all times, in retrenching the artificial enjoyments of society, in exiling themselves from the tumults and pleasures of the towns, in treating their flesh hardly, have always sought out for the place of their solitude picturesque positions, grand aspects, magnificent landscapes, and have never refused themselves the pleasure of the eyes. It is a remark which is verified every moment in Italy: all the summits of the mountains are there crowned with monasteries. It was the same in old France. If there was in some part a boldly elevated mountain, a laughing valley, a forest with melancholy shades, the traveller was sure to see raised there a steeple surmounted with a cross. . . . Nature, in her simplicity, in her virginity, is profoundly Christian. She is filled with solemn sadnesses and ineffable consolations; she only speaks of deaths and of resurrections, of past falls and of future glorifications. The mountains, above all, say much to the soul, of which they are, in some sort, the image. Richness and nakedness, heights without measure, abysses without bottom, innumerable and divers landscapes, immense disorder, traces of ancient upturnings, expansions, efforts to reach heaven, always powerless, always renewed! Is not there the image of our poor existence? The mountains with their variety resemble human nature, as the sea with its immensity resembles the divine nature. It is thus that on the globe which we tread under foot are written in ineffaceable characters the lessons of a sublime philosophy, and this philosophy is no other than that written in characters not less ineffaceable in the pages of the Gospel.

From the Grande Chartreuse we went to visit the Grand-Som, a very elevated mountain whence one can see the whole of Dauphiny, a part of Savoy, and whence is descried all the chain of the Alps. We had snow up to the knees, and the traces of wolves were freshly imprinted all around. Afterwards we descended to Grenoble by le Sapey; and during an entire day we enjoyed still more admirable points of view. In this part of Dauphiny the vines are suspended to the trees, as in Italy. The land there is as fertile as in Piedmont. The population there made a good appearance, seemed rich, and very religious to judge by the number of persons who saluted my brother, the Abbé, along the roads, or that we saw at church on Sunday. Grenoble is a pretty town seated on the border of the Isère, and surrounded with inaccessible fortifications. However, Lyons is worth more; above all when we have there our family and our friends.

In this last relation, thou makest for me a great void here. Where are our long conversations, our Jeremiads made in common, and which terminated always by some words of encouragement and of hope? Where are our evening walks, our castles in the air, our students' follies? Here the present vacation does not at all resemble those which are passed. The fear of the cholera froze the spirits on our arrival. We remained rude and isolated; no friendly dinners, no country parties.

* * * * *

To M. X——.

Lyons, October 29th, 1835.

MY DEAR FRIEND,

Receive my compliments on the poetic fecundity of thy country. Flowers love the sun, and genius opens out more brilliant and stronger under the vivifying climate of the South. But if poesy easily takes root in your natal soil, and puts forth vigorous boughs, it appears that charity germinates there also without trouble. For the grain of mustard-seed which you have planted the last year begins to grow; and soon, I hope, it will become a great tree, and the poor will rejoice under its shadow. You are but twelve; you are only joined together for about six months; and already, by your cares, several marriages are become legitimate. Grace has descended with the nuptial benediction upon seven families,.and the numerous generations which will spring from them will owe to you, with the benefit of being able to name their fathers, the prosperity and virtues which God fails not to shed on alliances contracted according to His law. The work which you have done is very great; it would suffice to honour your life. Your elders in Paris will be jealous of it. Alas! their successes are very far from equalling yours. It is true that on one side we have not the advantages of position that you have, neither have we as you to do with a people ardent, impassioned, of deep feeling, accessible by that even to the moral and religious emotions.

*　　*　　*　　*　　*

Oh, how often we would wish to meet people who would receive us with blows, provided that we might find others who would listen to us, and who would comprehend us! But no; these are languid souls, who receive us always in the same manner, always with the same reserve at the end of a year as at the first day, who carefully abstain from contradicting a single one of our words, but who change nothing in their actions. However, from time to time some good is done.

Good is done, above all, among us, who mutually sustain and encourage each other. We are yet only in our apprenticeship to the art of charity. Let us hope that one day we shall become clever and laborious workmen; then on the different points where Providence shall have placed us, we will rival each other as to who will cause to be born around them the greatest happiness and the greatest virtue; then when you give us a share in your success, we will reply to you by ours. And from all points of France shall arise a harmonious concert of faith and love to the praise of God.

The great action which you are meditating will only serve to redouble your zeal and your strength. "When two or several shall assemble in My name," said the Saviour, "I will be in the midst of them." It is in this divine name that you are going to join yourself to a wise and pious wife: the promise will be accomplished upon you. In giving your love to a person who will be so justly dear to you, you will withdraw none from the poor and the unhappy whom you have loved first. Love partakes in this of the divine nature, that it can give itself without being impoverished; that it can communicate itself without dividing; that it multiplies itself; that it is present in many places at the same time; and that its intensity increases as it gains in breadth. In your wife you will love first God, whose admirable and precious work she is; and afterwards humanity—the race of Adam whose pure and amiable daughter she is. You will draw from her tenderness, consolations for evil days; you will find in her examples of courage in perilous times; you will be her guardian angel, she will be yours. Henceforth, you will no more experience those weaknesses, those discouragements, those terrors, which we are seized with at certain hours of life, for you will no longer be alone. You will never more be alone. Your virtues give you the legitimate hope of it. The alliance you are about to contract will be an immortal alliance; that which God has joined—that which He has forbidden man to separate, He will never separate Himself; and in heaven, He will clothe with the same glory those who here below were companions of the same exile.

But I stammer a language which I know not at all yet; I speak of things which have not yet been revealed to me. With me imagination developed early; sensibility has been more tardy. Although my age is that of passions, I have hardly felt their first approaches. My poor head has already suffered much, but my heart has yet known no other affections than those of blood and friendship. However, it seems to me that I have felt for some time the symptoms telling the coming of a new order of sentiment, and it frightens me. I feel a great void making itself in me which neither friendship nor study fills: I am ignorant what will come to fill it. Will it be God? Will it be a creature? If it is a creature, I pray that it may be late before she presents herself, when I shall have become worthy of her; I pray that she may bring with her what is necessary of exterior charms to prevent place being left for any regret. But I pray above all that she may come with an excellent soul; that she may bring a great virtue; that she may be worth much more than I; that she may draw me on high; that she may not make me descend; that she may be generous, because often I am pusillanimous; that she may be fervent, because I am lukewarm in the things of God; that, lastly, she may be compassionate, that I may not have to blush before her for my inferiority. These are my wishes, my dreams; but, as I have told you, nothing is more impenetrable to me than my own future.

Live happy, you whose path is now all traced out: "*Viviti felices, quibus est fortuna peracta.*" But when in the midst of your enjoyments you shall have a moment free, pray for me, who know not yet whither I go.

To M. Lallier.

Lyons, November 10th, 1835.

My dear Friend,

Your letter long expected has at length arrived. I thank you, not for having written to me, but for having so written in a manner so good and so friendly. I fear, on the contrary, that the letter I wrote to you at Joigny has given you some pain. You have perceived, I am sure, that it had a certain tendency to make me out of some value to you, to make you feel my friendship. If you perceived anything of this you were not deceived. I confess to you, my dear friend, notwithstanding all my efforts, I feel always at the bottom of my heart the prick of egoism. I cling infinitely to the esteem, and yet more to the affection of others. You know how often at Paris, talking with you, I begged, as it were, for commendation; oftener still I have begged, indirectly, some words of kindliness on your part. I harassed you in your silence, because I took it for coldness. Many times, nevertheless, you gave me testimonies which surpassed my expectation. One evening, for example, you told me that you prayed every day for me by name, and these words have never since gone out of my heart. In writing to you then, I wished to provoke some similar testimony of your friendship for me, and you have loaded me with it. I was wrong. I wanted confidence—pardon me for it, I pray you. I will try to be henceforth more disinterested in my affection for you.

How right you are in what you say of interior combats! Alas! I have the misfortune of comprehending perfectly these grievous combats. In the midst of the enjoyments with which I am loaded, a vague and multiform uneasiness never leaves me. My conscience has had terrible storms to suffer. Now that it is tolerably calm, it is the turn of the mind. The desire to do something consumes me. I have a thousand things before my eyes which all solicit my attention, and of which I can seize none.

* * * * *

I think still of leaving from the 25th of this month to the 3rd of the next month, without being able to decide anything yet, because my brother is absent. When I shall be at Paris, I must have my own furniture. You will be in the same necessity. Could we not rent a little apartment together? Wait for me for this, if this is possible to you. Solitude would be fatal to my repose: my imagination eats me up. Alone, it always seems to me that some demon may be at my side. With Christian friends I feel immediately the accomplishment of the promise of Him who has engaged Himself to be found wherever we gather together in His name. We should live as two brothers. I should pray you to mortify my indomitable self-love; we would seek together to become better; we would combine our labours of charity; we would ripen our projects of work; we would give each other courage in our times of dejection; we would console each other in our times of sadness; but I see that I am again becoming egotistical.

Adieu.

To M. LALLIER.

Lyons, November 23rd, 1835.

MY DEAR FRIEND,

Your good letter, that I received about a month since, has been a great consolation: nothing is in truth more consoling than the remembrance of those to whom we are closely tied by the heart. I believe I have already said it to you; the joys of the family are very precious, blood has rights, inborn and imprescriptible; but friendship has rights acquired and sacred, joys which cannot be supplied; relations and friends are two sorts of companions which God has given us for the road of life, the presence of the one class cannot make us forget the absence of the other. Must it be, then, that we cannot have happiness without alloy, nor pleasures without regrets? That we are not able to return to those who are dear to us without separating ourselves from others who are dear to us also? Does God wish by these continual separations to cause us to make an apprenticeship to death? We cannot pass anywhere without leaving some rag of our affections, as the lambs who leave their wool upon the thorns. During the short journey that I made two years ago in Italy, I felt much this fatality of our nature. All these beautiful things which I looked upon caused me less joy at the first sight than sadness at the moment of departure. I entered Rome with weariness, I left it with tears in my eyes. Rome, Florence, Loretto, Milan, Geneva—all these places have kept something of myself; and every time when I think of it, it seems to me that I ought to return there to take this something which has remained.

Now if monuments, memories, landscapes have thus divided and captivated my soul, what must not good and excellent friends have done for me, whose sympathies have so oftentimes consoled me—whose examples have kept me up, who have hindered me from being alone and losing myself? This is why I am sad in thinking that this next year will be the last that I shall pass at Paris. I am happy with my parents; it seems to me that they need me—I feel that I need them. I could not decide to leave them in their old age; and nevertheless, it will be hard, it will be cruel, to me to leave the place of my exile — to bid adieu to those who have made it supportable to me; to bid adieu to our fraternal reunions, but above all to you and to Pessonneaux.

You have given me a proof of your deep and cordial attachment in taking so lively an interest in what I told you of my mother. Perhaps I owe it to the fervour of your prayers, she is now much better, and gives me no more uneasiness. My sinister presentiments have fled away; and I hope to preserve, for long yet, her from whom I have received all there is of good in me. I hope to preserve her for long, and to pay her according to my power the pains, the labours, and the tears that I have cost her. How I pity you for being deprived of such a happiness!

But if my guardian angel is on earth, yours is in heaven; if mine is near to me, yours is nearer to God. What I owe to her counsels, you owe to her intercessions. You know the great mystery of the communion of saints; you know that this mystery does not permit us to believe ourselves alone here below, and that it surrounds us with the most excellent and the dearest souls as so many witnesses and glorious patrons, in order that the heart may not fail us in our trials. And then, life is very short; and soon the hour will come when, according to the language of Holy Scripture, we shall go to rejoin our people—this great people who have preceded us in the paths of faith and love. Oh, let us be good during ten, twenty, thirty, or forty years more, and then will arise for us the day of the eternal rendezvous!

* * * * * *

To M. de la Noue.

Lyons, November 24th, 1835.

My dear Friend,

Your little epistolary visit has been very pleasant to me. Your remembrance is one of the dearest remembrances that accompany me every year at my departure, and which leave me not during my long vacation. It is very kind on your part, elegant Parisian, gracious poet, to come thus to knock at the door of a dull provincial, to risk yourself through the foggy atmosphere and the miry streets of our commercial city.

* * * * * *

You come, then, to tell me that you have been pleased to accept for me a title, and you ask me for my ratification. At the same time you tell me of the foundation of a society whose end is to glorify religion by the arts, and to regenerate the arts by religion. It is nearly six years since such an idea took possession of me, and has not since left me. The power of association is great, for it is a power of love. In the past century a reunion of men swore to crush *l'infame*, and they brought Christianity to the gates of the tomb—to the gates only, for since our Lord left the sepulchre, it could no more enter. At the same time they debased philosophy, eloquence, poetry, and all the arts, for they put mire on their hands to make them cast it on Christianity, and their hands have kept trace of the stain. It seemed to me that at our epoch an alliance of Christian men might work with success at the restoring of all these holy things dishonoured. This end would be accomplished by the foundation of a society which should embrace in a triple framework : artists, and in the number I comprehend all those who love the arts ; men of letters, and under this title I join all those who, by taste or by condition, occupy themselves with religious, philosophic, historic, literary studies; and learned men *(savants)*, and I assemble in this category all those who give themselves up to the investigations of nature. Such a society would have for general end to develop human intelligence under the auspices and for the glory of Christianity; and for special ends : 1st, to gather together all the believers who occupy themselves with arts, letters, sciences, in an encouraging fraternity ; 2nd, to procure by foundations of prizes, or by other means, the composition of a large number of works beautiful and religious ; 3rd, to sustain young artists, *littérateurs*, and *savants* by furnishing them with means of cultivating the talents which God has imparted to them, and hindering them thus from flinging themselves into false paths ; 4th, to assist those who fall into misery or affliction, in order that we may no more see Camoens, Gilberts, dying in the hospital, in order to save from suicide some new Chatterton or some new Leopold Robert; 5th, to exercise an active proselytism on all those who come young and upright to run their career, and to draw thus under the Catholic standard the intellectual *élite;* 6th, lastly, when a broader legislation allows it, to establish Catholic colleges, academies, universities. But, however beautiful these dreams might be, I never had the claim to realize them myself, and I have always hoped that God would charge Himself with doing the work, provided that we helped in it. I believe firmly that the solid institutions are not those that man makes in his way, with deliberate purpose, with the elements of his creation, but those which develop by themselves with elements which exist already. Thus, when I have seen our little societies of history, of law, and our little society of charity formed, I have rejoiced, hoping that from this humble nucleus might develop perhaps one day a great tree. I rejoice equally in the news that you tell me; and the formation of a religious association for the arts is to me the guarantee of a like association for letters and for the sciences.

I should conceive yet greater hopes if I saw at the head of this institution a very capable man. But what matters it? God often uses feeble and fragile instruments to execute great things. One must be called to a providential mission, and then talents and defects disappear, to give place to the inspiration which guides. But, on the other side, if there was presumption, if one went without being called, if by his fault the work failed, it would be a great misfortune. A work which has failed is often discredited for ever; it is easier to build on new ground than on ruins.

I believe, then, that it is needful to reflect maturely, and see if the incipient work has guarantees of duration and success. One should know, above all, if it proposes a practical end. For it is not sufficient to bring together a certain number of names, and to arrange a table divided into six sections. It is not even enough to found a journal : there are so many journals, and they live so short a time. Will there be reunions among the members, conferences, some bond of charity? Will it be an association simply religious, in the most extended sense, or positively Christian, orthodox? Be sure, my dear friend, that orthodoxy is the nerve, the strength of religion, and that without this vital condition all Catholic associations are powerless. It is pleasant to dream, but when we dream we sleep, and when we sleep we are not acting. To act we must see with an undisturbed eye, with an assured conviction, the sacred end towards which we march.

These are generalities. Now let us speak of myself, since it is of myself that the question is in your good letter. I leave in eight days for Paris. This year will be the last of my stay, and my time will be taken up entirely by the trials which I shall have to undergo to take the degrees of Doctor in Law and Doctor in Letters. I have reckoned beforehand that, to fulfil my plans, there must be a determined labour and long vigils. There will remain to me then little leisure to satisfy the obligations of the Society of which you speak to me, yet much less to fill in it the task of vice-president. There is nothing so sad as being a dead member.

Afterwards, in seven or eight months, I shall leave again for my province, which perhaps I shall quit no more. Consequently, what should I be good to you for? Lastly, I love the arts much, but I have very little acquaintance with them. Hardly am I initiated into those difficult studies designated by the name of æsthetic.

Altogether, my dear friend, you have presumed on me too much in accepting in my name the dignity of which you speak to me. I must contradict you. You have acted without commission. Do you know that I, an advocate, could prosecute you for it? When I shall be at Paris, we will talk of this; and, if I am not too much occupied, I will willingly accept the title of simple member, to have in the reunions of this Society one point more of contact with you.

* * * * *

CHAPTER VIII.

LEAVES PARIS FOR LYONS—ABSENCE OF VOCATION—ITALY—DANTE—SOCIETY OF ST. V. DE PAUL—ENDEAVOUR MADE TO OBTAIN A CHAIR OF COMMERCIAL LAW AT LYONS, AND TO HAVE OZANAM NOMINATED TO IT — RECONCILIATION OF THE TWO CLASSES, THE RICH AND THE POOR, BY CHRISTIAN CHARITY —LAW OCCUPATIONS.

FREDERIC OZANAM, in 1836, was still in Paris for his last year of studies. He was employed in working for the degree of Doctor of Law, and at the same time for that of Doctor of Letters. Notwithstanding his passionate attachment to letters, writing for him was a very laborious employment, and never a recreation, though it acted the part of one. His scrupulosity, his fastidiousness, a natural difficulty in arranging his materials so as to please himself, made his writing not only a labour, but a severe one. His conscience, at the same time, was not at ease as to the time and labour which literature had taken from his study of the law, in which he thought if he had given to it exclusively the five years of his stay in Paris, he would have obtained a rank which was now beyond his power, and which, no doubt, would have greatly pleased his father. "But he could not decide' to bid an eternal adieu" to his literary studies, which, notwithstanding their thorns, had for him an incomparable charm.

To M. Dufieux.

Paris, February 8th, 1836.

MY DEAR FRIEND,

I received, a few days ago, your good letter, and I thank you for it with all my heart. These few lines, written by a friendly hand, come so well to renew the chain between two souls that distance of place has separated! When two men walk together, it is often their custom to walk with the same step. They set forth the left foot at the same time, and during a certain time they instinctively keep this equal movement; however, little by little, one slackens, or else the other quickens, and then it is necessary that with a look they put themselves into harmony, and that anew they regulate their march. It is thus with two sister souls who advance together in the road of life : from time to time a word, a look, is necessary to harmonize their movements and re-establish their agreement. Above all, if of these two one is weaker and more easily discouraged, more impatient of the roughness of the way, it has need of a charitable support; and this is what I find, my dear friend, in your correspondence. How I should wish to be able to show myself worthy of it, in writing to you, as you ask, frequently and at length. But I am weighed down under the burden of my duties of this year; I despair almost of being able to accomplish the task I have prescribed to myself; time escapes and betrays me; there does not remain to me enough to satisfy both the duties of study and the duties of friendship.

If I had an energetic will, I might easily attain to marking the hours and the days; by leaving to each occupation its natural place, by making labours and enjoyments succeed each other, I should find a place for study and a place for pleasure. But many times, I have told you, my best resolutions have still remained unaccomplished: I have never been able to realize that economy of time so necessary for a good employment of our passing life. To-day I trace a rule; to-morrow I go and break it. I work by starts, by efforts in bringing all the strength of my mind to bear upon a single point. I do not know how to act with method, with calm—to bring to the front two, or several studies—and it is this above all which distresses me.

Formerly I soothed myself with the consoling idea that my life might be divided into two parts: one for action, the other for study; one for the tumult of business, the other for the peaceful culture of letters—and now I see myself fatally thrust on to the grievous alternative of abandoning the one or the other of these two futures which I had thought I could join. My poor head is not large enough for one thought to lodge there without expelling all rival thoughts. Now for about a month I have worked a little, either at an examination in law, or at my thesis in literature that I am preparing; and yet because I desired to divide myself in this way, I have done very little.

Letters could never be to me a recreation: you have seen by your eyes what it costs me to write. And yet, whether it be self-love, whether it be any other motive,

I cannot bring myself to bid an eternal farewell to those friends so severe, who make me pay so dear for their familiarity. From another side, I consider that if I had consecrated to the exclusive study of law the faculties which God has given me, and the five years' stay at Paris which my parents have given me, I should have been able to acquire at the bar a rank that now I cannot hope to reach. All these reflections agitate and torment me, and the close necessity in which I am about to find myself, of taking a definitive position, weighs me down. I am afraid of causing much pain to my dear parents, and yet you know whether they deserve to be loved. Here, many people who wish me well seem, by their suggestions, to be willing to redouble my agitation and my annoyances. It is certain that I shall leave Paris for ever in five or six months; but what shall I do at Lyons? There is the point on which turn all my uncertainties. They would engage me frequently at the bar, and yet it seems to me that it would be very hard for me to remain confined in the narrow sphere of the forum. Is this pride? Is it vocation? Is it inspiration from above, or temptation from below? All that I have done for five years—is it reason, is it folly? O my dear friend, pray that the good God would answer all these questions which I ask myself every day! It seems to me that I am resigned to do His will, whatever humble part, whatever grievous mission He prepares for me. Only let this will be known to me, and let me be no longer, as I have been, for five years, divided against myself; that is to say, feeble, powerless, useless. Alas! He has granted me such numerous graces that they are to me a subject of alarm. Each year of my life has received from heaven more mercies than trials, and yet, I assure you, if there were not the feelings of my moral unworthiness, I should greatly desire that this life might soon finish, and that the day might succeed to this cloudy twilight in which I am enveloped, walking without knowing on what stone my foot shall rest, nor towards what end my course is directed.

Pardon me if I have entertained you with my troubles. It is because you have known similar troubles, because you have traversed this burning desert in which I take my first steps. For you life is opening plainly, and I see with joy what solution you are about to give to this dangerous problem. Yes, you will be happy with all the happiness which can be known upon earth. Yes, you will be recompensed for so many sacrifices and so much resignation. Your fine faculties will be able to develop in peace and liberty. . . . . You understand admirably the poetry which the men of our days must have; you feel it better still. It is no longer inward songs, solitary conversations of the soul with nature and with God. It is no longer barren sighs and complaints without echo. It is fraternal hymns, intelligible, popular, all impregnated with the colours of history, all vivified by the interior breath of tradition, all filled with these three great things—Faith, Hope, Charity. When man is given up to the seductions of the exterior world, the first movement with which grace inspires him is a return to himself. But this movement is not the last. If man forgot himself in the contemplation of himself, he would be nothing but a philosopher—that is to say, a very little thing. It needs that from himself, he mount again to

God ; and that from God, he come down again to his fellows. From the love of the Creator comes forth the chaste and virtuous love of the creatures. The second commandment is like unto the first. This is why the religious contemplatives themselves, all exiled as they are from our noisy societies, do not believe themselves alone. From the peaceful meditation of their cell they go out to pray ; and when they pray, they pray for all— they repeat the prayers that we repeat here. They do not say to God, My Father ; they say to him, Our Father. Poetry must do the same. In the midst of the Pagan orgies, to which she was abandoned, a ray from on high has struck her. She has blushed ; she has withdrawn herself to sigh in the desert. You have heard, in the *Meditations* and in the *Harmonies*, her melodious griefs. But in this isolation she has pleased herself with herself. She has believed she was able to communicate with God without interpreter and without veil. She has become individual, rationalist ; and we have seen her, with grief, stop herself half-way on the road of truth. Nevertheless, she must put herself again on the march. Some one must take her by the hand, must bring her back into the society of men, into the society of believers.

*   *   *   *   *

I hardly know what I write to you, for my head is tired. For the rest, we will talk of all this together when we shall see you here. Try that it may be in the month of April. Come with the flowers, poet. I went to M. de Lamartine's a short time ago. Surrounded with political men, he scarcely said anything to me ;

but, to make up, Madame de Lamartine showed me great kindness. My visits to Montalembert have not succeeded so well. I have not yet been able to meet him. When I see him, I will not forget you.

* * * * *

TO M. DE LA NOUE.

Paris, June 11th, 1836.

MY DEAR FRIEND,

I am very grateful for the poetic confidence which you are pleased to make me. Your idea seems to me very beautiful, and I believe that you have all which is necessary to develop it in a powerful manner. As for me, I could not give you light on the obscure point you mention to me. Besides my own insufficiency, there is a darkness there which no eye has ever penetrated. Nothing is known, I believe, of the antediluvian world, except that which Genesis reveals. The two races of Cain and of Seth, their early struggles, their fatal unions, a nature more vigorous and more grand, lives of several centuries, the alliance of strength, of knowledge and of sin, all three in a gigantic condition—these are the images which crowd imposingly between the closed doors of Eden and the open cataracts of the deluge. Evoke these images, poet, and they will obey you; they will place themselves in light on the scene which you have prepared for them. The silence of history is the liberty of poetry.*

* * * * *

Frederic Ozanam's religious faith did not desert him in his times of need: " more and more it lighted up his soul

* M. de la Noue died in 1838, at the age of twenty-six.

as his studies became deeper, his prayers more fervent." He often had recourse to what was for him a means of grace, and felt that a divine Saviour and Master met him at "this Sacrament of love." Among those works which he regarded as the necessary aliment of his charity, that which had his preference was visiting the poor. It was open to all; it became the source of nearly all the other works so varied, nevertheless, which, as time went on, the Society of St. Vincent de Paul undertook, such as the work of apprentices, those of clothing, rent, libraries, ovens, etc. "His extreme sensibility caused a truly paternal tenderness for the poor to spring up early in his soul, and those whom he visited became to him as members of his own family. He visited them hat in hand, and on leaving them would say, far more in the spirit of faith than for politeness, "Your very humble servant.'" The Society of St. Vincent was to Frederic a means of filling up the void which the distance from his family created. In their weekly meetings he met dear friends and good Christians, into whose hearts he poured his own joys and sorrows according to the needs of his temperament; and he found at the same time a vast field for the exercise of his zeal. Here he used all the influence which his character gave him, in acting upon those around him who in their turn needed it—the youth of the schools especially.

Dr. Ozanam wished his son to enter the bar at Lyons. He was delighted as the time approached for him to leave Paris, and busied himself in preparing beforehand for him a pleasant room as his peculiar property. Carefully the affectionate father furnished it, and, above all collected a library into it, placing there some of his own books: happy to be able to despoil himself for the sake of the young advocate, who was soon to find in his family's town—such were the father's dreams—his sphere for action, and perhaps for fame. Frederic, however deeply he had felt his separation from his family, and very sensible though he was of the fond affection and hopes of his father, and of his own happiness in returning once more to the bosom of his family, could not now leave Paris without regret—the cradle of his beloved Society, the theatre of the Conferences of Notre Dame, the place of extensive libraries and of learned men, the residence or sojourning-place of many beloved friends. But he had now obtained his doctor's degree in law, and he returned to Lyons as his home at the vacation of 1836.

During the time of rest he and his brother made some little excursions together, taking with them on one of these occasions their young brother Charles, then in his twelfth year, this being his first pedestrian excursion. The elder brothers passed some days with a friend near Mâcon; and "one charming morning, when all three had set off to visit the ruins of the old and celebrated Abbey of Cluny," they met Lamartine. He asked them all to dine with him, and, together with his wife, gave them the kindest welcome. A large party of intellectual men were gathered there.

TO M. LALLIER.

Lyons, November 5th, 1836.

MY DEAR FRIEND,

Tuesday evening I had begun to write to you. It was the solemn day of the Communion of Saints. Perhaps—and the supposition is not injurious—perhaps it is for this, that by a singular exchange, at the moment when I finished the first page of my letter, there came to me one from you. Thus your thoughts came all ready to hold converse with mine, as in those Sunday evenings when we met each other at du Lac or de la Perrière. But never a clock replied to another clock in a tone so different, as your epistle, the just welcomed, to mine unfinished. Still quite preoccupied with the somewhat sad news that la Perrière had received from you, I pitied and I blamed at the same time your melancholy; and I was given up on this subject to long considerations which savoured, I suspect, of the sermon of M. le Curé on the Gospel of the day. And behold, in one of the moments of gaiety, into which you pass often at the conclusion of your times of *ennui*, you write me a thousand joyous things, and talk about the future as a man without care and without business. Necessity was then to put into the fire the page that I had scribbled for the benefit of your melancholy, and to trace other lines more suited to the present colour of your spirit.

I am completely of your advice, and I profess that it is folly to consume one's days in accumulating that which one will never enjoy—folly even to heap up for one's children. For the children who see a heap of gold formed behind them, are furiously tempted to sit down upon it and to fold their arms; and to prepare them a fortune is very often to invite them to the sin of idleness. And then children are sometimes only a respectable pretext; lift the veil, and you will see egotism —the egotism which finds in property a means of extending and prolonging in some sort the personality, which is very glad to have much about it for the present, and to leave much behind it for the future. Happily, this applies to none of those to whom I owe love or respect, although at Lyons this vice be common.

I desire to give thanks to God for having caused me to be born in one of those positions on the limit of embarrassment and ease, which habituates to privation without leaving one absolutely ignorant of enjoyments; where one cannot slumber in the gratifications of all one's desires, but where at the same time one is not distracted by the continual solicitations of want. God knows, with the weakness natural to my character, what dangers there would have been for me in the soft indulgence of riches, or in the abjection of the indigent classes. I feel also that this humble post in which I find myself puts me in a position the better to serve my fellows. For if the question which to-day disturbs the world around us is neither an individual question nor a question of political forms, but a social question; if it is the struggle of those who have nothing with those who have too much; if it is the violent shock of opulence and of poverty which makes the soil tremble under our tread—our duty as Christians is to interpose ourselves between these irreconcilable enemies, and to bring about that the ones may despoil themselves as for the accomplishment of a law, and that the others may receive as a benefit; that the ones may cease to exact and the others to refuse; that equality may operate as much as is possible among men; that voluntary community may replace taxes and forced loans; that charity may do that which justice alone knows not how to do. It is a happy thing, then, to be placed by Providence on a neutral ground between the two belligerent parties, to have among both ways opened and means of communication, without being compelled, in order to act as mediator, either to mount too high or to descend too low.

And yet, in writing this, it seems that I do myself some violence, and that the numerous erasures which are made in these last lines bear testimony that a contrary thought disturbs me. While acknowledging in the past of my life that providential conduct which I cannot weary of admiring, I cannot hinder myself from casting a doubtful and somewhat sombre glance upon the future. The moment of deciding a destiny is a solemn moment, and all which is solemn is sad. I am troubled by this absence of vocation which makes me see the dust and the stones on every path in life, and the flowers in none. In particular, that to which I am now nearest, that of the bar, appears to me little attractive. I have talked with some business men; I have seen the miseries to which one must resign one's self to obtain employment, and the other miseries which accompany employment. One is accustomed to say that advocates are the most independent of men; they are, at least, as much slaves as others, for they have two sorts of tyrants equally insupportable; the attorneys at the beginning, and the clients later on. Enough, my dear friend, enough of my murmurs, enough of these disquietudes of a man of little faith; and if you desire that it shall not be a fault to have told them to you, receive them as a sort of confession which asks counsels, friendly exhortations, and reproaches at need.

Do not believe, nevertheless, that these wearisome preoccupations fill up all my hours : the hours for some time past have passed away for me in a pleasant and varied manner. I have made with my eldest brother two charming little excursions: one to Saint-Etienne, where I have seen miracles of industry; the other into Mâconnais and into Beaujolais, where I found the hospitality of M. de Maubout, and the society of M. de Lamartine: nature beautiful in autumn, populations surprising by their fidelity to the faith and to religious practices. I have worked a little at the organization of our little Conference of St. Vincent de Paul. I have brought back my mother from the country; but in return I have seen my eldest brother leave for his missions, my little brother for his school.

It may be that at Joigny you have yet to learn from me two literary events, which without doubt are already old at Paris, but which have left with me a lasting bitterness: I mean the putting of *Jocelyn* into the Index, and the appearance of the new work of M. de la Mennais.

*   *   *   *   *

I know that God, that the Church, need not poets nor doctors; but those who do need them are the feeble believers whom these defections scandalize. They are those who believe not, and who despise our poverty of spirit ; they are ourselves, who have need sometimes to see before us men greater and better, whose foot might mark out our path, whose example might encourage and elevate our weakness. We cannot, young Christians, think to replace these men ; but could we not make the change of them, and fill up by number and by labour the void which they have left in our ranks?

This question, in which my self-love finds its own account a little, is nevertheless asked above all in your interest. Often I have admired in you a humble opinion of yourself, a contempt for earthly things of which I afterwards deplored the excessive consequences· . . . . Yes, we are unprofitable servants; but we are servants, and the salary is only given on the condition of work which we do in the vineyard of the Lord in the place which shall be assigned to us. Yes, life is contemptible if we consider it in the use which we make of it, but not if we see the use we might make of it, if we consider it as the most perfect work of the Creator, as the sacred vesture with which the Saviour has willed to cover Himself: life, then, is worthy of respect and of love. Let us pray the one for the other, my very dear friend; let us distrust our wearinesses, our sadnesses, our doubts; let us go simply where a merciful Providence conducts us, content to see the stone on which we must place our foot, without wishing to discover all the length and all the windings of the way.

You know if it will be hard to me to be deprived of you this year. Let us often overpass the distance by thought; let us write to each other; let us counsel; let us sustain each other. I believe that you must certainly have need of it, since you are a man; but I have yet more need of it.

Be my interpreter to all our old friends. Please to give to those who ask for them my themes of which you have the depôt. Do not neglect, if you can, to see

N―― occasionally; you will be useful to him. Let me know something of our little apprentices.

All your friends here recommend themselves to your memory. My father and my mother give to you in affection that which you charged me to offer them in respects.

Adieu, my dear Lallier! May I soon see you again!

To M. JANMOT.

Lyons, November 13th, 1836.

MY DEAR FRIEND,

Here are nearly two months since I received thy good letter, and thou wilt address to me perhaps lively reproaches for my delay. I find, however, my excuse in thy far-away pilgrimages, which have left me completely in ignorance where I might find thee. Thy mother herself for a month has had no news. At length, a few days ago, they told me of thy return to Rome, and immediately I set myself to pay thee a visit. Poor visits are they that are thus made in haste and uncertainty; stupid conversations, where one speaks all alone, where one replies to words already forgotten by the other interlocutor, where one moralizes when he should cause to laugh, where one laughs when he should console. Friendship is nevertheless obliged to hold itself content with this last resource which remains to it; it is for her to divine the impressions of the present hour, and to bring hearts into relation and discourses into harmony. I think, then, that at the moment when these lines reach thee thou wilt be still under the lasting influence of the beautiful tour which thou hast just made through Umbria. It is indeed, if I mistake not, one of the most admirable countries of admirable Italy. The majesty of high mountains crowning sweet and laughing valleys; contrary climates disposed as in an amphitheatre to give place to all the riches of vegetation, from the pine and the oak to the orange and the aloe; the cities seated or suspended here and there on proud heights; and each city, each hill, each brook, each stone where the foot can tread, filled with memories. Spoleto, whose humble gates were closed before Hannibal, while those of Capua opened only at the noise of his steps; and the lake Trasimene, where two giant people sustained blows so terrible that during the combat an earthquake overturned towns and was not felt; Orvieto and its Etruscan antiquities, heritage of a civilization dead without having left a history; the desolate lake of Bolsena, and the island where a Queen died of hunger; and later, the Christian traditions which have purified, embalmed all these places. Here, the miracle of Bolsena eternized by Raphael; there, the marvellous legend of St. Marguerite of Cortona: but above all must hover the grand memory of St. Francis.

* * * * *

It is in these roads by which thou hast passed, that he went inviting the little birds of the heaven to sing the glories of the Lord, and redeeming with the price of his mantle the lamb whom the butchers led to the slaughter. But it is Assisi, above all, which must be full of him—Assisi and its cloisters, which contained of old six thousand monks, and its two churches—symbol of the two lives of the saint, the one terrestrial and mysterious, the other immortal and resplendent—its two churches, where the good and pious painting of the middle age has developed from its cradle to its maturity, from Cimabue and Giotto till the time of Perugino and his disciple. For it seems that nature and history had not yet done enough for this blessed country, and that art has there shone willingly to surround it with a third and not less brilliant aureole. The Umbrian school, with that one which painted the Campo Santo, certainly appears to me, as to thee, and reserving the mistakes into which my ignorance may draw me, to have walked in the veritable way which was forsaken afterwards at the time of the Renaissance.

Thou wilt not have crossed the threshold of the sanctuaries of Assisi without reading the magnificent history of St. Francis in the eleventh canto of the *Paradise* of Dante:

> Fertile costa d' alto monte pende . . .
> Di quella costa là dov' ella frange
>   Più sua ratezza, nacque al mondo un sole,
>   Come fà questo tal volta di Gange.
> Però chi d' esso loco fa parole
>   Non dica Ascesi, che direbbe corto,
>   Ma Oriente, se proprio dir vuole.°

Dante should be there, the necessary commentator of Giotto, his contemporary and his friend. What men, what pencils, and what voices to celebrate the name of a poor man, of a mendicant, who was taken for a madman! It is because, according to the word of Lacordaire, he was

> ° The fertile side of a high mountain slopes . . .
> From this side there, where broken yet it lies
> In less abruptness, a new sun doth streak,
> Like to this one from Ganges' wave, the skies.
> Therefore who henceforth of this place shall speak,
> Let him not say Assisi—that were small—
> But Orient, if the right word he shall seek.

that very thing, he was beside himself with love. His immense love embraced God, humanity, nature: and considering that God made Himself poor to inhabit the earth, that the greater number among humanity are poor, and that Nature herself, in the midst of her magnificence, is poor, since she is subject to death, he desired to be poor himself also. The characteristic of love is to assimilate itself as much as is in it to the things beloved.

And we, my dear friend, shall we do nothing to resemble these saints whom we love, and shall we content ourselves with sighing over the barrenness of the present time, whilst each of us carries in the heart a germ of holiness which the simple will would suffice to cause to bud forth? If we know not how to love God as these loved Him, without doubt this ought to be to us a subject of reproach; but yet our weakness may perhaps find for it some shadow of excuse; for it seems that we must see in order to love, and we only see God by the eyes of faith, and our faith is so weak! But men, but the poor, we see them with the eyes of flesh; they are there, and we are able to put our finger and our hand into their wounds, and the traces of the crown of thorns are visible on their forehead: here incredulity has no more place possible, and we should fall at their feet and say to them with the apostle, *Tu es Dominus et Deus meus.* "You are our masters, and we will be your servants; you are for us the sacred images of that God whom we see not, and not knowing how to love Him otherwise, we will love him in your persons."

Alas! if in the middle age the sickness of society could not be cured but by the immense effusion of love—which was made above all by St. Francis of Assisi;

if later, new troubles called for the helping hands of St. Philippe de Neri, of St. John de Dieu, and of St. Vincent de Paul—how much are not needed now of charity, of devotion, of patience to heal the sufferings of those poor people, more indigent now than ever, because they have refused the nourishment of the soul, at the same time that the bread of the body is failing them! The question which divides the men of our days is no longer a question of political forms; it is a social question; it is to know which shall gain the day, the spirit of egoism or the spirit of sacrifice—if society shall only be one great undertaking for the profit of the strongest or a consecration of each for the good of all, and especially for the protection of the weak. There are many men who have too much, and who desire still more; there are many more who have not enough, who have nothing, and who desire to take if it is not given to them. Between these two classes of men a struggle is preparing, and this struggle threatens to be terrible; on one side the power of gold, on the other the power of despair. Between these opposing armies we must cast ourselves, if not to prevent, at least to deaden the shock. And our age as young people, our mediocre condition, renders more easy to us this *rôle* of mediator which our title of Christian renders obligatory.

Here is the possible utility of our Society of St. Vincent de Paul. .... You have already done an excellent work in establishing a conference there (at Rome); and you have been aided by an admirable instinct when you have given as its object the visiting the poor French in the hospitals of Rome. God will give you the blessing which He gave Himself to His first work, " Grow, and multiply." It is little, however, to grow; we must at the same time be united: in proportion as the circumference extends, each of its points must communicate with the centre by uninterrupted lines.

A conference, thou knowest, exists at Nîmes; another is just formed at Lyons—we are fifteen, almost all of thy friends; we have much good to do, and we have done little of it. There are five conferences at Paris. There needs now a correspondence which shall gather us all up. I do not know if you have the Paris rule; if you ask it, I will cause it to be sent to you. . . . .

I am much ashamed, my dear friend, to use language so urgent, when I am myself so cold and so sluggish. Thou askest me what I am become, and I hardly know it myself. I have finished my fifth year of law, and am received doctor; now I am fixed at Lyons, where I am contented. But I find here no other career than that of the bar, and, believing it too painful for me, I am trying to prepare for myself another, to which I feel myself better disposed—I mean teaching. It might easily happen that chairs of law or of letters might be established here. I shall endeavour to hold myself ready; and at this moment I occupy myself with my thesis for the doctorate of letters, which I have not been able to pass this year for want of time, and for which I shall return for some weeks to Paris.

I think I have already told thee that one of my theses is on the philosophy of Dante. This has led me to a long study of this poet, whom I admire more and more. I study also his epoch. . . . . Happy those whose life can be consecrated to the searching out of the true, the good, and the beautiful, and who are never importuned by the vulgar thought of pecuniary utility! And yet, even in this searching out one is sometimes seized with a scepticism which paralyzes intelligence. Thus it happens to me when I consider the instability and the dissimilarity of human judgments in the matter of the *Beautiful.* Fénélon compared Gothic churches to bad sermons: thou makest of St. Peter a grand colossus without common-sense. Profane!—what shall I believe when great priests dispute?

However, till some new order, and without fearing either the epithet of eclectic or the reproach of inclining to tripartite divisions, I admit three legitimate forms of Christian architecture: the form Romanic of the beautiful churches of ancient Rome, and of which in my souvenirs the type is St. Clement. The form Gothic of the cathedrals of Milan, of Lyons, and of Paris. The modern form of cupolas, a symbolic form which realizes in its manner an image of heaven, and which, attempted for the first time in St. Sophia of Constantinople, repeated at Pisa and at Venice, is carried out more boldly at Florence, and which, lastly, is posed majestically as a crown on the front of the Eternal City. For of the whole of St. Peter's, it is really the cupola alone which I have found irreproachable. It is indeed, with that of the Invalides, the only one whose curve has appeared to me perfectly harmonious. As for the seeming mediocrity of the structure of the pile, it is not that which I admire, but the effect which results from it, and in virtue of which the greatness of the church appears always growing in proportion as one visits the details, and we finish by feeling overwhelmed by its immensity.

Enough on this point. Nor do I wish to seek dispute with thee on the subject of the Italians. I could reply to the anecdote which thou hast told me by another more terrible, of which Chaurand, la Perrière, and I, have been witnesses at Paris. But to what serves it thus to give an evil opinion of humanity? Let us not do as Ham; let us cover, on the contrary, its grievous nakedness, and let us leave each other under better auspices, since here I am at the close of this letter.

The friends here embrace thee; repeat it to our friends there. Remember me also a little.

Thy friend.

Shortly after returning to Lyons, before settling down, Frederic received an advice from some of his friends which seemed in some measure to harmonize his own desires and the duties of his calling. Several of the influential inhabitants of Lyons had conceived the idea of obtaining from the Government the establishment of a Chair of Commercial Law in their city, and of procuring Frederic's nomination to it. This project, which, of course, involved teaching and study of a different order from the mere practice at the bar, made it desirable that he should return to Paris for awhile, as also did the desire which he had for some time cherished to obtain a degree as Doctor of Letters.

TO M. AMPÈRE.

SIR, Lyons, February 16th, 1837.

In the humble and peaceful family life which I have led for six months, I often let my thoughts return to the time when, leaving Lyons for the first time, I arrived, a young man of eighteen years, in the midst of the noisy and dangerous solitude of the capital. Then I recall the tutelary house which opened to shelter my inexperience, the family which was willing to admit me into the number of its children, and him who, in the midst of his infinite occupations and his honours, found the time and did not disdain to act to me as father. These memories always leave me in a sort of astonishment; and, my whole heart moved by the bounties of Providence, I ask myself with uneasiness what He has desired from me in placing my youth under such rare auspices.

The affection which you yourself have more than once showed to me, and particularly towards the end of my stay at Paris, has made me believe in the prolongation for the future of this influence which I have so happily experienced in the past. There may be found in the designs of Providence a continuous action of certain men on the destinies of others, and this action may be hereditary. Among so many better things which you have inherited, permit me to reckon the patronage with which your father honoured me.

In a conversation which I had with you last year, I confided to you the hesitations which were common to me with all young men who pass from a studious to an active life, my repugnance for the agitation of business, my quiet tastes, my dreams of study, and the moral necessity under which I nevertheless was to be near to my parents, and to make for myself at Lyons a laborious existence. I confided to you, at the same time, the idea which had been suggested to me, and which seemed to conciliate my mental inclinations and the exigencies of my position. There was a question made of obtaining from Government the establishment of a Chair of Commercial Law at Lyons, and my nomination to this Chair. This thought, which would have been rash if it had been personal to me, had been conceived and adopted by several respectable persons of our town.

To-day things seem to approach their accomplishment. The Chamber of Commerce of Lyons has framed a demand to the Minister of Commerce, which must be communicated to the Minister of Public Instruction.

In asking from you the favourable intervention which I had asked from your father a year earlier, I have not believed I need change anything in the simple expression of my desires, as nothing has been changed in him to whom they are addressed. Representative of his fine intellect, you are also for me of his goodness; and this occasion will not be the first in which I shall owe you gratitude.

I am, sir, in waiting to deserve the title of friend which you have sometimes given me,

Your tenderly devoted servant.

To M. X——.

Lyons, March 9th, 1837.

DEAR FRIEND,

I am not too much contented with myself, and nevertheless I find in myself one thing, one single thing which does not displease me. It is the need of loving, of possessing, of preserving friends who love me. Above all, when friendship is formed, so to speak, of itself, by a concourse of unforeseen circumstances, by the will of God who has used these circumstances to draw two men together, then this friendship seems to me more precious still, and in some sort sacred. Such is that which has been formed between us for six years, and which time and distance have not diminished. Is it not so?

We must agree nevertheless that friendship, being a harmony between souls, could not subsist in a prolonged absence, if they gave not from time to time some signs of good accord; and these signs may be of two sorts, words and actions. Words borne by the trustworthy paper come to teach him who forgets that he is by no means forgotten; they scatter disquietude, put grief and annoyances in common. It is, indeed, an epistolary commerce where one always gains and never loses. Nevertheless, there are bonds yet stronger than words— these are actions. I do not know whether you have observed it: nothing familiarizes two men between themselves so much as eating together, travelling together, working together. Now, if acts purely material have this power, acts moral have it much more; and if two or more agree to do good together, their union will be perfect. Thus at least He assures us who says in the Gospel: " In truth, when you are assembled in My name, I will be in the midst of you."

It is for this reason that, at Paris, we desired to establish our little Society of St. Vincent de Paul, and it is also for this reason, perhaps, that heaven has willed to bless it. You will see in the annexed circular, that under the auspices of our humble and illustrious patron are already united in the capital two hundred and twenty young people, and that the work has sent colonies far away, to Rome, Nantes, Rennes, Lyons. Here, in particular, our intentions prosper, and are realized. We are more than thirty. Money does not fail us; and the benevolence of the ecclesiastical authorities, after some slight clouds, is shown to us in all its plenitude. You will see that in Paris they greatly desire to draw tighter this confederation of men of goodwill, in establishing between them regular relations, in order that they may know each other, may encourage each other, and may sustain each other mutually by the force of example, and by the force of prayer. The society of Nîmes, the first-born of those of the provinces, will not refuse herself to this fraternal invitation: her sisters will be happy and proud to enter into communication with her.

Do not you find that it is marvellously pleasant to feel your heart beat in unison with the hearts of two hundred other young people scattered over the soil of our France? Do not you find that in casting the good work which is just done as a humble mite into the common treasury, one loves to see it lose itself amid a thousand good works which have been placed there at the same time, and all confounded together in order to be one single offering to Him from whom all good proceeds? And, independently of the present enjoyment which results from this community of charity, are there not there great hopes for the temporal future, even, of the society where this new generation will take its place, and for the eternal future of each of us, for whom that which all have done shall be remembered?

Alas! we see every day the schism begun in society

become deeper. It is no longer political opinions which divide men. It is less than opinions: it is interests. Here the camp of the rich, there the camp of the poor. In the one the selfishness which wishes to keep hold of all; in the other the selfishness which wishes to carry away all. Between both an irreconcilable hatred, the menaces of an approaching war, which will be a war of extermination. One only means of safety remains—it is, that in the name of charity the Christians interpose themselves between the two camps; that they go, benevolent fugitives, from one to the other; that they obtain from the rich much alms, from the poor much resignation; that they carry to the poor presents, to the rich words of gratitude; that they accustom them to regard themselves anew as brethren; that they communicate to them a little mutual charity, and this charity paralyzing, stifling the selfishness of the two parties, diminishing each day the antipathies, the two camps will rise, they will destroy their barriers of prejudices; they will throw away their arms of anger; and they will march the one to meet the other, not to fight, but to mingle with each other, to embrace each other, and to make but one fold under one shepherd—*Unum ovile, unus pastor.* Adieu! Tell me at length of your friends, of yourself, of your town, of your Reboul, and of so many other things in which your friendship will know how to guess what interest I shall take.

To M. Paul de la Perrière.

Lyons, March 10th, 1837.

My dear Friend,

I have to return thanks to you, whether for the services that you have already rendered me, or for those which you still offer me. . . .

Should I interest you in telling you two words of the life which I lead here? It is always this strange life between inconstant studies and importunate occupations. I reckon disrespectfully among these last, the rare pleadings which have taken me to the Palais. The famous affair of interdiction, pending at the time of your departure, has been pleaded twice since, and will be judged perhaps to-morrow. On two other occasions I have spoken at the bar of the Civil Tribunal and the Correctional Police for extremely small interests. This week the Assizes have given me much work.

* * * * *

They really complimented me on my discourse; but, you know, my poor words have the happiness of obtaining felicitations sometimes, convictions scarcely ever. Here, my dear friend, is the most memorable scene of this life at the bar, which I have had the advantage of leading for four months.

I thought to write to-day to N———, but, behold, to-day is ended, since midnight has struck. Not having the time to write to him to-morrow, which is no more to-morrow, I beg you to communicate to him what may be able to interest him in this letter, and to make *ensemble avec lui*. In particular, I beg him not to take too much to this habit of writing without thinking, which is common now to many people who are not *clerks*. I do not press him for my article, but I make a conscience of it to him in the interest of his own intellect, which has need of a little exercise, if he wishes not to go to sleep in the vapour of requests and judgments. . . . . Present my respects, I pray you, to M. Bailly. If you see M. de Kerguelen, charge him to say two words of friendship for me to the litttle apprentices Marius and Blondeau. Here all your friends remain tenderly attached to you. Put in the first rank

Your devoted.

CHAPTER IX.

DEATH OF HIS FATHER—HIS MOTHER'S DECLINING HEALTH—PERPLEXITY AND DISTRESS OF ALL KINDS—ENDEAVOURS TO OBTAIN THE CHAIR OF LAW—DISGUST WITH THE BAR—ENERGETIC PLEADINGS—VIEWS ON MARRIAGE—SOCIETY OF ST. VINCENT DE PAUL—STUDIES ON DANTE.

FREDERIC OZANAM was still in Paris when a terrible disaster visited his family. Dr. Ozanam was now in the sixty-fourth year of his age—a yet robust and healthy man, occupying himself, as we have seen, with the delightful expectation of seeing his second son establishing himself under his own roof. The numerous cares and sorrows of his life had not destroyed his natural vivacity of spirit. Walks with his family, or quiet family parties, where he was a most agreeable companion, were his favourite recreations. He was very fond of music, and played himself tolerably well on several instruments.

Of the visits which he and his wife mutually paid to the poor an amusing story is told. Some of these poor lived up several flights of stairs, and husband and wife, each conscious of some infirmity in the other, had "forbidden" each other to mount higher than a certain stage.

On one occasion, however, they each went, unknown to the other, to visit a poor invalid who lived beyond the forbidden height. They met on the staircase, and each taken in a flagrant act of disobedience, had nothing for it but to forgive and go home together. A tendency to giddiness in the head was the husband's infirmity ; and, robust as he was, so that it is said that it seemed as if only an accident could put an end to his life, this one infirmity, perhaps only temporary, may have been the partial cause of the deplorable accident which deprived him in a few hours of life. On the 12th of May, 1837, in the evening twilight, visiting one of his poor patients, he mistook the staircase descending to a cellar for the one to the higher stories, and fell on his head. That same day at dinner, *à propos* of something which is not mentioned, he had remarked, "Death is nothing, but the judgments of God are to be dreaded." Yet it was not to be called a judgment in the case of this good man. "God gave him time to receive the last sacraments," says his son Alphonse, "of which he had himself procured the benefit for several of his sick."

Frederic was yet in Paris. There was no railway then, no electric telegraph. It took three days for him, only half informed, to reach his friends ; and it was only when he met them all again that he became fully aware of the nature of the calamity which had befallen his house. In every point of view it was a crushing misfortune, coming, too, just at a time when, if possible, it might be felt the more. Madame Ozanam, overwhelmed with grief and in uncertain health, could do little to reassure her family in their bereavement. "My poor friend—my poor Oza !" she cried, using a familiar name which she gave her husband. "Oh, my God, how unhappy I am!" she exclaimed; then added pathetically, "and yet how I bless Thee for having given me such good sons!"

When death so rudely broke into this family circle, the youngest son was still a child, the eldest son, the priest, was taken up with his "missions;" and upon Frederic, young, inexperienced, and looking for something so very different, came, in addition to the grief which he shared with the others, the burden of settling his father's affairs, of becoming master of his house, of, in some sort, taking his place. It was a dreary and doleful necessity. "Preoccupation and inquietude of all sorts" came down upon him, of which the greatest was the illhealth and condition of his mother.

The calamity which parted him with such terrible distinctness from the comparatively happy and uncareful time of the past threw all other causes of concern into still deeper shade; and the dark experiences and perplexities of the next two years and a half—till his mother's death—are best told in the letters themselves.

To M. X——.

Lyons, June 1st, 1837.

MY DEAR FRIEND,

Among all the consoling voices which came from far to show sympathy in my misfortune, yours has been the first, and has not been the least grateful. You know, you too, what a solitude is made in a family by the loss of one of its chiefs. If the death of a mother is most heartrending for her sons, that of a father is most overwhelming. It causes, perhaps, less tears to be shed, but it leaves behind it a sort of terror. As a young child, accustomed to live in the shadow of another, if he is left for an hour alone in a house, penetrated with the feeling of his own weakness, is frightened and begins to weep, so, when one has lived so peacefully in the shadow of a paternal authority, of a visible providence in which he trusted for all things, in seeing it all at once disappear, in finding himself alone, charged with an unaccustomed responsibility in the midst of this bad world, he experiences one of the most grievous troubles which have been prepared since the commencement of the world to chastise fallen man. It is true that my mother is still here to encourage me with her presence and bless me with her hands; but cast down, suffering, desolating me by the uneasiness her health gives me. It is true that I have excellent brothers; but however good those are with whom we are surrounded, they cannot supply the absence of those who protected us. Myself, above all, of an irresolute and fearful temperament, I need not only to have better men than myself about me, but to have them also above me. I need intermediaries between my littleness and the immensity of God; and now I am like him who, living in a stormy region, under the shelter of a large roof in which he had put his confidence, should see it rudely blown away, and should be left forlorn under the infinite vault of the heavens.

I do not know if I make you comprehend my principal kind of affliction; add to it the spectacle of the affliction of my family, the rapidity of the blow which has struck us, the affairs of a succession importunately mingled with the sadness of a mourning, and many things too long to say.

For the rest, we feel a great consolation in thinking

that the piety of my father, strengthened during these last years by a more frequent use of the sacraments, the virtues, the labours, the griefs, the perils of his life, have rendered easy to him the access to the celestial dwelling-place; and that soon, if we are good, we shall find him again at the eternal rendezvous, where death shall not be. The more are multiplied in the invisible world the number of the souls who were dear to us and have left us, the more powerful shall we feel the attraction which draws us thither. We hold far less to the earth when the roots by which we were attached to it are broken by time.

What would it serve me, my dear friend, to tell you of my griefs, if I could only sadden you by my recitals? And what a cruel pleasure it would be to make for friendship a community of troubles! But when we pour these troubles into a heart loving and religious at one time, we draw forth from it a prayer, and this prayer rises agreeable towards heaven, which hears it always. It is, then, before God that I desire that you would remember my misfortunes, and the needs of my entire family. You have, besides, other preoccupations sweeter, and which have more claims on your spirit. You are a father; and if this joy is measured by the sadness which one feels at ceasing to be a son, it should be very great. Enjoy the happiness which God grants to you for your deserts, so much more excellent than you seem in the least to comprehend. You believe you owe something to the acquaintance which we made together six years ago; and I, I am sure of finding much there. I do not know if my company in a large town could be any profit to you; I know that yours revealed to me the possibility of certain virtues of which I believed not that youth was capable; I have welcomed with lively gratitude the amiable guest* whom you have sent me, to be, you said, the interpreter of your gratitude. Two things above all astonish me in this man: an energy which is not of his time, and a choice of style, a constant erudition, an abundance of learned allusions which speak of readings multiplied beyond the rare leisures of a manual profession.

I would converse with you more, but time fails me, and the courage even for long conversations fails me also since my misfortune. I would beg you, then, to be patient. Tell du Lac to pray for my father, for my mother, and for me; I will write to him soon.

A Dieu, my dear friend—to Him alone who draws distances near, consoles in absence, and knows how to reunite sooner or later those whom He has made to love each other.

To M. AMPÈRE.

Lyons, June 2nd, 1837.

SIR AND FRIEND,

The last year, at this time, you had lost an excellent father, France one of her glories, and myself a patronage which honoured and encouraged my youth. My mourning was confounded with the general mourning which must needs have been one of the consolations of yours. Nevertheless, you willingly admitted me to share your sorrows in a more intimate manner. I recall to myself a day when you came to visit me in my

* Reboul.

little chamber; both of us had tears in our eyes. I said to you how I felt myself urged to return to my family, to profit by all the hours which heaven would grant to my aged parents. The example of your misfortune made me think with trembling of the possibility of a similar misfortune.

To-day, you know it, these sad presentiments are realized, and the severities of Providence are also heavy on me. I also, during a short absence, I received alarming news. I arrived—it was too late—I arrived to embrace my mother and my brothers alone. My father had left them. He was no longer there; he would never be there again. I had only bade him an adieu for three months, and I found myself separated from him by the whole interval of a life. Those who have not experienced it cannot tell what a void is made by the privation of one single man, when so much respect and love surround him, when one was accustomed to do so many things because of him, and to rest on him in so many things, when he was really among his own—the visible presence of the Divinity. My father had not obtained in science a name illustrious in the first order—his name was not celebrated in far-off countries; but his labours and his virtues had made him loved and esteemed by his colleagues, by his fellow-citizens, and above all, by the poor in whose service he has died. Public regrets have not been wanting to him. He was not known to you; but me you knew—me, his son; and if ever your benevolence has found in me something which did not displease you, it was from him, from his counsels, from his examples, that it came to me. Thus the affection that you have always showed to me assures beforehand that this year also there will have been between us community in afflictions. One finds one's self almost happy not to suffer alone.

Henceforth, family duties fix me at Lyons more imperiously still than in the past. However, I hope in a few months to see Paris in passing, and there at length to finish the tests for which I am preparing myself, and which, for the second time, are interrupted. As for the affair, on the decision of which I am awaiting, the circumstances in which I find myself oblige me to desire in a more lively manner than ever to succeed. Near my mother and my brothers, the Chair of Commercial Law, which has been asked for, would give me a position sure, honourable, peaceable.

The finances of the family were only straitened; the law, to which he was compelled to devote himself, brought in no flow of money, while it continually disturbed his mind by the practices to which it seemed to compel its followers. The extreme depression of some of his letters is sufficiently accounted for by their contents, and they probably acted as a needed safety-valve for what might well be felt at his time of life, and with his temperament, as overwhelming troubles. The presence of the old servant, Marie, must have been a great stay in many ways; but she herself was now advancing in years. His brothers came to him when they could, and he had many friends. Yet all these were, and must have been, humanly speaking, but slight relief for the daily and hourly loneliness and anxiety of his life.

To M. HENRI PESSONNEAUX.

Paris, June 19th, 1837.

MY DEAR FRIEND,

Pardon if I have remained so long without replying to your good letters, and particularly to that of thy father.

You have made it for me, nevertheless, a new duty to love you by the interest which you have taken in my misfortune. The testimonies of sympathy are so much more precious as the grief is greater; and, in proportion as God withdraws from us our nearest relations, we feel the need of drawing yet nearer to our more distant relations. My good mother is always a great sufferer: sadness consumes her heart, and an interior malady never leaves her head. However, her intellect is perfectly sound, and her virtue, piously resigned, causes the admiration of all those who surround her.

Happy the man to whom God gives a holy mother! But why must it be that in proportion as the aureole of sanctity surrounds more brightly this cherished head, the shadow of death seems to approach it? Why, in the tongues of men, is perfection synonym of the end? Why does God give nothing here below? and why does He only lend? My dear friend, pray with me that my mother may be preserved to me, that she may be preserved to my brothers, who also have so much need of her; that this house which thou hast known happy and full of love, may not be desolated, filled with mourning, empty of all enjoyments, given in spectacle as an example of human vicissitudes, become a scandal for the impious, who, seeing Christian families so hardly treated ask insolently where is the God in whom they had hoped : *Ubi est Deus eorum ?*

For me, it is always in Him that I hope ; and, up to the present, I am resolved to follow the indications which He gives me in the unequal circumstances of life.

I continue by letters the proceeding which in Paris I took by myself. In waiting, I do not at all abandon literary labours, which are for me one of the most salutary earthly consolations. I still occupy myself a little with Dante.

Adieu. I embrace thee tenderly.

To M. Letaillandier.

Lyons, August 21st, 1837.

My dear Friend,

You had reason to be astonished at my silence. Believe me, nevertheless, that imperious and continual business has alone hindered me from answering you. However grievous my ordinary preoccupation might be, and however happy may be the event in which you have given me a share, this contrast should never hinder the exchange of our thoughts ; because, for us Christians, the most contrary events of life are seen in the same light, are brought back to the same principle, which is God. Before Him, there are no inconsolable griefs, neither are there joys without mixture ; there are no more suffering hearts or satisfied souls who cannot converse together in this admirable language that religion has made for us. As you have shared my mourning in the midst of your smiling projects, I also, in the midst of my sadnesses, I have smiled at your near-approaching happiness. For your happiness is not for you what vulgar men dream : it will be serious, sought out in an order of enjoyments where many sacrifices are met with ; it will attach itself to new virtues which you are about to practise. The benediction of heaven will be upon your head, but cares unknown to this day will sit heavily on your brow. Fatherhood is also a sort of royalty—a kind of priesthood. Your vocation is difficult, but it is beautiful, but it is grave, but it is certain. You are fortunate thus to reach the term of these agitations which torment so great a number among us: uneasy, ill-assured of the destiny which Providence prepares for them in this world. *Vivitis felices quibus est fortuna peracta.*

Alas! my dear friend, it is only two years ago since we lived together as brethren ; and the memory of this time is sweet to me. Our two lives were joined in one, and in so short an interval, see how already a frightful divergence is made. You are about to have two families, both prosperous, both full of hope ; and I, I see dissolving the only one I had. The void grows around me. My poor mother is ill, my two brothers are wanting to me during the greatest part of the year. You are meeting a future which all promises brilliantly for you ; and I, the loss of the one who supported my steps arrests me at the threshold of my career, and leaves me hesitating, trembling, given up to my own counsels. Nevertheless, I am not jealous. God be blessed for having sowed roses on your path! and if He has put thorns in mine, let Him still be blessed, provided that, on the one part and on the other, His eye watches over us, that His love accompanies us; provided that He makes us remember each other frequently here below; that He cause us one day to find each other elsewhere! You have here many friends who rejoice in your happy alliance, but who murmur at the same time to see the hope which they had nourished of drawing you near to them carried away. I speak especially of Chaurand, of la Perrière, of Artand; for if I would name all those who are attached to you, I should have to say all the Conference of St. Vincent de Paul, for the Conference of Lyons is very closely joined with the Society of Paris. This union makes our strength, and this strength augments each time a new conference is formed in some part, as in these last times at Dijon and at Toulouse. Shall you do nothing at Mans? Will you not give us brothers, you who were one of our fathers, you who were, I remember me of it, the first author of our society? See, do not as others whom family ties cause to forget everything else. You have in your heart sufficient love to shed it abroad outside even of your domestic hearth. You will have need of many more graces than in the past; this is not the case in which to do fewer good works. May each one of us, as we grow in age, grow also in friendship, in piety, in zeal for good!

* * * * *

He recurred now with some satisfaction to the idea already set afloat of the establishment of the Chair of Law at Lyons; but a long time and a great many *démarches* were necessary before this was accomplished. Indeed, not until the poor mother who had greatly longed for it, and had helped it by her prayers, had passed away from those who loved and needed her, although she had the satisfaction of knowing that it was close upon a satisfactory arrangement. "Six different powers had to agree to arrive at the conclusion." These powers were, the Lyons Chamber of Commerce, the Ministry of the Royal Council of Public Instruction, the Municipal Council of Lyons, the Ministry of Commerce, and that of the Interior. With all these complications, it was not wonderful that the affair dragged a wearisome length along—the more wearisome because the pecuniary aid which its settlement would bring was so really needed. During the debates, the Minister of Public Instruction, M. Cousin, intervened with a proposal to Frederic to take a Chair of Philosophy at Orleans. He would greatly have preferred this, but for one thing, the condition of his mother. He could not leave her.

To M. LALLIER.

Pierre-Benite, near to Lyons,
October 5th, 1837.

MY DEAR FRIEND,

Since you wish it, I am going to keep you informed of the current of my existence since the time when I quitted you.

You are not ignorant of what there is lasting in certain griefs. When the wings beneath which we have lived so long a time fold themselves; when the shadow which covered our head suddenly fails us; and when alone we carry the burden of the heat is it surprising that henceforth sorrow should be a thing of every day? This immense void which the absence of God makes in the soul of every man, is increased for us by the absence of a father or a mother; and I doubt not, my dear friend that here is one of the causes of that inward melancholy which we both feel.

The health of my mother, who is threatened with slowly losing her sight, is also for me a great affliction. I have had other family tribulations, which it would be too long to enumerate to you. All the administration of our little fortune weighs henceforth on me, and my inexperience makes the burden yet more heavy. Excepting quarrels among brethren, we have had all the annoyances of a succession where there is a minor. Independently of these cares, common to all the family, I have those of my profession. I have pleaded this year about twelve times; three times only in the civil, where I have always gained. . . . . The emotions of the pleading at bar are not without charm to me, but the emoluments come in only with difficulty; and the relations with the people of business are so painful, so humiliating, so unjust, that I cannot bend myself to them. Justice is the last moral asylum, the last sanctuary of present society; to see it surrounded with impurities is for me a cause of indignation every instant renewed. This kind of life irritates me too much. I come back almost always from the tribunal deeply wounded: I can no more resign myself to see the evil than to suffer it.

However, I am far from wishing to abandon a profession which actual circumstances make more than ever a necessity to me. After the vacation I shall give a lesson in law to three young people whose money I hope to see.

* * * * *

The horizon of my future is not bounded there; but if it is larger, it is tolerably stormy. The Royal Council of Public Instruction having sent back the demand* to the Minister of Commerce, this last is disposed to encourage the institution of the chair in a pecuniary sense, if the Chamber of Commerce and the Municipal Council will provide the principal expenses; and now they discuss the shares which the Chamber, the Council, and the Ministry should contribute. The institution, and the dotation once decided, then there will be the question of the nomination. Then I shall present myself, surrounded by those who wish me well; and it must be a singularly unhappy chance which would cause me to fail. Although these negotiations should have no other effects, they would always have that of having proved to me the affection of all my friends; for the wishes of the ones have no more failed than the exertions of the others.

For the rest, in all this I keep myself passive. I feel a sort of religious, perhaps superstitious, respect for the present uncertainty of my destiny. I have put myself under the protection of Providence, I fear to lay my own hand upon the matter. It seems to me that the happy or unhappy success of this affair will decide whether I shall remain in the world or whether I shall leave it when events have rendered me free. You perceive there what is the rashness of my dreams, and on to what sacred ground they venture to bear me. But, in truth, I envy the lot of those who devote themselves entirely to God and to humanity. And from another side, the question of marriage suggests itself often to

---

* Demand made by the city of Lyons for the foundation of a *Chair of Commercial Law*.

my mind: it never leaves it without leaving there an incredible repugnance. . . . .

It may be that there is in this some unjust contempt for women. Nevertheless, the Holy Virgin and my mother, and some others, would make me pardon many things to these daughters of Eve. But I declare that in general I do not understand them. Their sensibility is sometimes admirable, but their understanding is desperately light and inconsequent. Have you ever seen conversation more capriciously interrupted, less followed out, than theirs? And then to engage one's self to a society without reserve, without end, with a human creature, mortal, infirm, miserable, however perfect she may be! It is, above all, this perpetuity of engagement which is for me a thing full of terror; and this is why I cannot hinder myself from shedding tears when I assist at a marriage, as when I find myself at an ordination, or a taking of the habit. I do not understand the gaiety one is accustomed to meet at weddings.*

You see that life does not appear to me sown with roses, and, if your heaven is sombre, mine is not less so. I will tell you, to hide nothing from you, that images yet more dark show themselves sometimes. It is a little more than a week ago that the prolonged thinking on my miseries, interior and exterior, so thoroughly upset my spirit that I had come to an absolute impossibility of thinking or acting. My head was on fire, whirled in all directions by distressing thoughts; and the most distressing of all, perhaps, was the very idea of

* One of the last earnest prayers towards the end of Frederic Ozanam's life contrasts sadly enough with this, that " he might live to grow old beside his wife."

my actual condition. The excess of the evil made me have recourse to the doctor—to the doctor, I mean, who has the secret of moral infirmities and the depôt of the balm of divine grace. And when I had opened, with an energy which on these occasions is little common to me, my sadnesses and the subjects of my sadnesses to the charitable man whom I call my father, what do you think he replied to me ? He replied to me by these words of the Apostle: *Gaudete in Domino semper.* And was not that a strange utterance? Here is a poor man who has just had the greatest of evils in the order of spiritual things, that of offending God; the greatest of evils in the order of natural things, that of becoming an orphan. He has a mother aged and sick, whose every movement he notices—all her looks, all her features every day, that he may know how long yet he may keep her. He sees himself cut off by absence or by death from several friends to whom he was tenderly attached, and other separations yet more grievous threaten him. He is, moreover, in all the distresses of an undecided career, loaded with cares and businesses, of which the most fortunate disturb his mind still. If he falls back upon himself to escape the troubles without, he finds himself filled with weakness, imperfection and defect; and the secret humiliations and sufferings which he causes to himself are not the least painful of all. And he is told not merely to resign himself, not to console himself, but to rejoice—*Gaudete semper!* It needs truly all the boldness, all the pious insolence of Christianity, to speak in this manner. And yet Christianity is right.

Melancholy has its dangers. It confounds itself often

with idleness, and it even occupies the place of this last in the old enumerations of capital sins.

* * * * *

In this condition, we often reproach ourselves with the imperfections which least depend on our will. We love better to despair of ourselves than to condemn ourselves. We would willingly lay the blame on the Creator for not having gifted us more advantageously. We are almost jealous of the faculties and virtues of others. Thus love is weakened, and egotism conceals itself under the deceitful austerity of our regrets. We are so much displeased with ourselves, because we love ourselves too well. And indeed, see how we take delight in melancholy; first, because it is one way of occupying ourselves with ourselves; second, because in default of merits which we would find in ourselves to admire, we are happy, at least, to manifest grief for not having them. It is a feeling in appearance honourable. It is a sort of justice; it is almost a virtue. And also it is more convenient to dream than to act. Tears cost us less than sweat, and it is our sweat that the inexorable sentence demands from us.

It may then be the beginning of wisdom to make a man retire into himself, and indeed ancient and pagan wisdom knew this precept; but, if we desire not that the man thus retired into himself should die there of shame and discouragement, a ray from on high must descend into the prison. There must be something which is not human, which will come nevertheless to visit the man in the solitude of his heart, and which will cause him to go out again to enter into action. This something is love; it is it alone which changes remorse into penitence, which fructifies grief, and makes it germinate in generous resolutions. It is it which gives confidence, and by confidence courage, for it makes that view of ourselves to disappear which confounds us in the sight of God, with whom it clothes us, in whom it makes us feel, be, and move—*In ipso movemus et sumus*—who lightens us with His light and strengthens us with His strength. In these high regions, all changes its appearance, and, contemplated in the economy of the Divine Will, the most fatal events are explained, are justified, and we may see in them a consoling sign. Thus these evils from within and from without, from which we lately suffered, henceforth only affect our sensibility—the lower stage of our soul. Its higher part is raised above them. Better preoccupations dwell in it. A joy serious, but real, surrounds it; and the prodigy is accomplished, and the precept of the Apostle is realized—*Gaudete semper*, because it is God Himself who is the cause of this joy unknown to nature—*Gaudete in Domino*.

Perhaps, my dear friend, this savours greatly of the sermon. And, nevertheless, what employment more worthy of friendship than that of seeking together the remedy for those evils which we think we have in common? I believe there are three sorts of manners of life between which we must choose—the external life, which loses itself in material joys, and which is that of the pagans, and of the lowest class of humanity; the internal and reflective life, which concentrates itself in the meditation of the infirmities and the needs of the soul, but which is sterile and dead if one stops there, like the ancient philosophers and some weak minds of our days; the superior and Christian life, which draws us out of ourselves to lead us to God, where henceforth we find the central point of all our thoughts —the central support of all our works.

Now, if I must believe you, you must be ranged with me in the second category, from which it is easy to fall back into the first, if we do not rise to the third. Let us help each other then, my dear friend, with counsels and examples: let us seek that confidence in grace may equal our distrust in nature, and that not only in the order of religious virtues, but even in our temporal occupations. Let us be strong, for the disease of this age is weakness. Let us consider that we have already lived more than a third of our probable existence, that we have lived by the benefits of others, and that we should live the rest for the good of others. Let us do this good in the way it is offered, without ever holding back by a false humility.

And you particularly, my dear friend, do not deceive our hopes. .... Without abandoning your profession you may make good writings and good works. .... Prepare yourself for one or other of these missions.

Our little Society of St. Vincent de Paul has become sufficiently considerable to be regarded as a providential fact, and it is not without some reason that you occupy an important place in it. Do not deceive yourself; as general secretary, you are, after M. Bailly, the soul of the society. It is on you that the union of the different conferences depends, and by the union the vigour and endurance. See then what duties are imposed on you, and activity is the first of all. Be often present at the particular assemblies; see from time to time the president; keep the place at the meetings of the council for direction; stimulate sometimes the too great calm of the president-general; do not neglect the correspondence with the Provincial Conferences. If you will credit me, when a conference has failed to write at the fixed time, you will write to it yourself a little before the following time, to engage it to be more faithful to the rendezvous. Neither allow the circulars to be too long waited for. That which you addressed to me two months ago was very good, and answered to an urgent want: the visiting of families is not so easy as one imagines; the instructions on this subject are of an extreme utility, it would be good to come back to them. You will have read in the *Université Catholique* some lines of this poor M. de la Morvonnais, which seem to me to oppose, with great advantage, the system of domiciliary help to that of bureaux for mendicity. Perhaps we shall agree on this one day, and a better organization of the charitable boards will resolve the question, so much agitated, of the forms which public charity ought to take. Meditate on these points, but do not ask light from me; for, for my part, I perceive inconveniences well, but resources very little. Between prudence in religious matters and pusillanimity, between extreme reserve and extreme familiarity, there is a medium difficult to keep.

* * * * *

I will speak to you in a letter which I will address to M. Bailly for the council of directors, of a work which we have undertaken without prejudice to the visiting of families, and which it would be desirable to see established everywhere where conferences exist. It is the propagation of Christian instruction among the soldiers of the garrisons. We have got up here a library and a school for reading, writing, and arithmetic, for the soldiers, and already the results are consoling.

* * * * *

To M. LALLIER.

Lyons, February 7th, 1838.

MY DEAR FRIEND,

* * * * *

The business of which I spoke to you comes to a conclusion. The Municipal Council only waits for the approbation of the budget of the town by the Minister of the Interior to proceed to the nomination of candidates. I have made more than sixty visits, I have seen thirty-four municipal councillors, and, thanks to the goodness of many people, I have gained the almost entire certainty of being presented. I know not why, I feel pressed to draw you into this affair; or rather you know already with what hope I flatter myself. If I obtain this post, where everyone tells me of the formation of a connexion which I would not desire to exhaust, it only needs for you to come and share with me the advantages of this position. In a town where reputations are quickly made, where you have already acquired so much affection and so much esteem, you will perhaps find yourself better than at Paris.

This proposition is serious and conscientious on my part, however interested it may appear. In presence of the ruins which are made in the family which nature had given me, I need that the one which friendship has created should not abandon me. I am a witness every day of the most grievous of spectacles, the decay of the forces of my poor mother; at the same time that her sight is going, her moral energy is enfeebled; her sensibility seems to augment in proportion, with all the disquietudes, all the sadnesses which one can conceive in a soul like hers. Instead, then, of finding in her the support necessary to my age, and to my first step in the world, I must sustain her by word as well as by my arm. The continual missions of my elder brother take from me the resource of his good counsels, and perhaps the designs of God upon him may draw him yet further from me. But it is, above all, the communication of sentiment and of idea; it is sympathy, intellectual encouragement, moral assistance—it is these intimate offices of friendship which are wanting to me, and this want has made me suffer greatly. I find them still, but less frequently than I need, in our society of St. Vincent de Paul. These weekly soirées are one of the greatest consolations that Providence has left me, and particularly my relations, too little multiplied for my taste, with Chaurand, Arthand, la Perrière, recall to me the best days of Paris.

* * * * *

Adieu, my dear Lallier. I have allowed myself to be drawn into an impetuosity which will appear to you perhaps very juvenile in a man whom this past year ought to have much aged. Adieu. I must finish; but I finish not, I assure you, thinking of you, and praying for your happiness Him in whom I am for always,

Your Friend.

To M. Lallier.

Lyons, April 9th, 1838.

My dear Friend,

I had hoped to carry you myself the reply to your last letter; but delays are still multiplied, and not being able to determine in a precise manner the time of my journey, I must write in order not to leave a void in a correspondence which is so dear to us.

And first receive my very lively thanks for the good offices which you have rendered me. The Municipal Council cannot make its presentation of candidates till after the budget of the town, approved at Paris, shall be returned, bringing implicitly the approbation of the Government for the establishment of the Chair of Commercial Law. I hope much, seeing in this something providential: the most difficult is accomplished, and I cannot be sufficiently astonished that a poor fellow like myself should have arrived at causing a chair to be created. It remains to take care not to add a fifth verse to the "*Sic vos non vobis*" of Virgil. If, nevertheless, it should happen thus, after all human means which can be imagined have been employed in my favour, I would still acknowledge in it a will of God, and I would easily console myself for it. All this affair is for me a question of vocation: I wait the solution of it with respect, and I hope to receive it calmly, whatever it may be. It is, however, true, that a considerable temporal interest is involved in it, for I experience, like you, the disquietudes of the "*Res angusta domi;*" and, what is worse, this disquietude is not confined to myself alone, it extends to my little brother and to my mother, whose needs augment in proportion as her health becomes feebler. And I, who, after so many sacrifices made by my father for my education, ought to be able to replace him to-day and to become the support of my family, I am, on the contrary, but one charge more. A lesson of law that I give every day is the most positive of my revenues. My law connection leaves me large leisure. With the exception of two assize matters which have served me to make a little noise and no money; two processes which I have reconciled; one which I pleaded at the Tribunal of Commerce last week, a tolerably considerable memoir which I have drawn up in a contest between tradesmen; a certain number, lastly, of gratuitous consultations—this is all the occupation which for five months has been given to me by this worthy profession of advocate, one of those in which the best fortune is made in the end, if one is not dead of hunger at the beginning. And yet I will confess to you, that these so rare preoccupations weigh upon me. I cannot acclimatize myself in the atmosphere of chicanery: the discussions of pecuniary interests are painful to me. There is no cause so good that there are not reciprocal wrongs; there is no plea so loyal that some weak points must not be hidden. There exist habits of hyperbole and reticence of which the most respectable members of the bar give the example, and to which one must submit one's self; all the figures of rhetoric are reduced into action before the tribunals which only understand this language. It is agreed that one must ask two hundred francs damages when one desires fifty; that the client cannot fail to be right in all his allegations, and that the adversary is a fool. Explain yourself in terms more reasonable, you pass for having made concessions;

-you have avowed yourself vanquished; your colleagues reproach you with it; your client pretends himself betrayed; and if you meet in the world one of the judges who have sat in the affair, he will accost you with saying "My dear, you are too timid."

But it seems to me that I return to a chapter that you have always had reason to find long in my letters: that of my troubles. I had much of them to say to you; always the same sadnesses around me, and my mother nearly blind; always the same sadnesses in me, and the discontents which my incorrigible nature gives me. At this moment I suffer from an evil which will appear singular to you in a town where I have so many relations and friends—I mean isolation. For on one side I cannot confide to my mother, whose extreme sensibility renders emotion very dangerous, all that I have of care and afflicting thought. I cannot pour them into the heart of my brother, who is almost always absent, and whom I see scarcely ever alone. If I spoke of them to other relations, it would be to ask counsels, which on their part would be orders. My friends, happier than I, have no longer need to go out of their families: they remain habitually shut up there. There exists no more between us that necessity for a mutual drawing together which we experienced at Paris.

*　　*　　*　　*　　*

One distraction remains to me in literary labours to which I can still give myself, but with interruptions so numerous, and such a difficulty of execution, that I often fear being attached by self-love alone to an ungrateful pen, which it would, perhaps, be better to break. I have, however, a service to ask from you. In about three weeks I shall have finished copying my thesis on Dante, which is become a volume. Will you permit me to address it to you, and to beg you, after having read it, to carry it to M. le Clerc, Dean of the Faculty of Letters, to whose examination it should be submitted? Thus I shall at least lessen the delays that I shall have to suffer on arriving at Paris.

The Society of St. Vincent de Paul also owes you thanks for the promptitude with which you have sent her the last report. This poor Society, indeed, has her tribulations too. She has them on the part of her members, whose inexactitude has often made her languish; she has them, above all, from without, whence there cease not to be renewed aggressions whose authors it is difficult to recognise. I need, indeed, an energy and liberty of spirit which my temperament and my affairs leave me not to make head against all; and yet there are circumstances which hinder me from laying down a presidency so ill filled. Nevertheless, we have consolations of more than one kind. Four joyous reunions have gathered together this winter members of the society around a fraternal table, where the bonds of charity are tightened, whilst those of the purses are relaxed.

* * * * *

To M. Lallier.

Lyons, May 17th, 1838.

My dear Friend,

Your excellent letter of Easter Day has solicited a reply for a long time. The report, and the few lines I have just received from you, would leave no excuse to my silence; or rather the need that I always feel to converse with you awaking more lively in proportion as the subjects of conversation multiply, it must needs be that the most importunate occupations yield and give place for some hours to the duties of friendship.

For I assure you, Lamache has well said, and you will thank him for it for me, these friendships, formed under the auspices of faith and charity, in a double confraternity of religious disputes and beneficent works, far from growing lukewarm by the effects of a prolonged absence, gather together and condense themselves as it were. They are nourished with the memory; and you know that memory embellishes all things, idealizes realities, purifies images, and preserves more willingly pleasant impressions than painful emotions. Thus all these humble scenes of our student life, when they come back to me in the twilight of the past, have for me an inexpressible charm : the evening reunions at M. Gerbet's Conferences, which had a little the prestige of mystery, and in which we first met each other; the historic philosophic struggles, in which we engaged with so pure an ardour, and the successes of which were so willingly allowed to be common property; the little assemblies of the street of Petit Bourbon Saint Sulpice;*
. . . and that famous soirée when we assisted at the farewells of the Academy de Saint Hyacinth, and came back to draw up on the spot the petition to Mgr. de Quelen; and the improvised visit which we paid trembling, in which we sustained so hard a shock, whence we came out so much moved; and the first beginnings of Lacordaire

* Society of Saint Vincent de Paul.

at Stanislas, and his triumphs at Notre Dame, which we made a little our own; and the editing of the *Revue Européenne* in M. Bailly's salon; and the vicissitudes of the Society of St. Vincent de Paul, the famous sitting of the last December, 1834, where a division was discussed, where Letaillandier wept, where la Perrière and I treated each other in such harsh fashion, where we finished by an embrace more friendly than ever, by wishing a good year the next day.

*   *   *   *   *

All this, my dear friend, becomes for me as the background in my ideal picture. All this throws a pleasant and somewhat melancholy light on my present existence, which loses much in comparison. I believe I can really comprehend how history becomes poetry for the human mind, and why nations hold their traditions with so filial an attachment. I have also my age of gold, my time of fables, my mythology, if you will permit it; for fable necessarily mingles with it, if it be only in effacing all the trivial things amongst which those whose memory I have kept were confounded. That which is true, that which is most serious, that which has thrown deepest root not only in the imagination, but also in the depth of my heart, is the foundation of affections formed during this period of life. I have surprised the proof in myself at the time of two recent losses—that of Serre and that of la Noue, which have made me shed more tears than others more capable, according to the general order, of drawing them from me. I gain every day some new assurance, when there comes to me some letter from you, some article of Lamache in a journal, some news of Letaillandier, of Pessonneaux, or other similar things.

This makes me forget all the disturbances of the present time, and if it were not ridiculous to use such an expression at twenty-five years, I should say: This makes me young again.

I feel, indeed, a little aged in every way since the day of our last separation. It was the 15th of May, my dear friend : it is a year. You brought me, knowing the misfortune which I knew not, to the carriage which took me away, a very anxious son, and was to bring me back here an orphan. Since then, have I lived? or rather, have I not been in a long dream? I need not tell you over again all these troubles. You have known them; but they are not yet at their term. The time of Easter—that, alas! of the change of seasons—has been a terrible trial for the health of my mother. I have seen her for a fortnight threatened with an attack of apoplexy. She is now in a much less alarming condition; but we are warned to dread everything for the autumn. The future, which is the commonplace of hope, is for us the point where every fear is gathered up. She often repeats that the success of my endeavours for the professorship would prolong her days, and I know not if this last means of attaching her to life will be given to me.

I thank you for all your good services, and particularly for the hospitality which you will willingly give to this poor Dante. He is constant, as when living, and towards the year of grace 1290 he went to pass some time at Paris; he assisted, even, at the lessons of one named Sigier—the Cousin of that time—in the Street du Fouarre. But it is told me that the capital has changed a little since that time; that, besides, the poet has become very old, and would see badly to guide himself there; add that the Sorbonne of the present time resembles little that of St. Louis, and that Dante would run a risk of presenting himself badly, if he were alone, at the door of M. X——, who is not a St. Thomas of Aquin.

However prolonged it has been by the embarrassment of circumstances, this labour would not have wanted pleasure for me, if the aids which I had at Paris had not here completely failed me. Our library is sufficiently rich, but our living literature is singularly poor; and the small number of learned men which we possess, surrounded with a kind of disfavour in society, obliged to fall back upon themselves, have contracted habits of unsociableness which render them inaccessible. I have not, then, been able to find, except with M. Noirot, our old Professor of Philosophy, the counsels which I needed. For the rest, no more of the drawing on, no trace of the general warmth, of the outside life, which at Paris sustained and carried me on. I believe that, if one were stronger in intellectual constitution, better furnished in studies beforehand, this solitary labour would have its advantage : it would preserve an originality which is lost in the sort of contagion of style to which one is exposed at Paris ; there would be found in it a little more of that austerity of thought, of those conscientious convictions which are broken, or at least are rounded off, are lessened by friction. The mind is better polished amongst you, but it is on condition of being worn away. As to me, I am not yet of temper to labour alone ; I am bad company, as it seems to me, for I am never so weary as with myself. And although the books were placed in tiers, at the end of some hours this dead word wearies me. I need to hear animated voices ; for by them alone is it possible to stir souls profoundly. This prestige goes so far with me, that, the merit being equal, the writings of a living author strike me infinitely more than those of an illustrious dead man.

*　　*　　*　　*　　*

I do not know how it was that my letter only reached you the day after the assembly. You would see that it was written specially for the presumed case of Monseigneur's presence. It was necessary, then, to confine one's self to generalities, and I was not able to insert a certain number of observations which the Council for Direction charged me to transmit to you. I now acquit myself of them :

1st. The charity sermon, whose history you so pleasantly relate to me, has met among us a general repulsion. We have thought that Parisians like you might well perceive the commonplace into which the charity sermon has fallen for some time. A thing little productive because it is too frequent ; little edifying because of the self-love of works, of collectors, of preachers even, which it sets moving ; little convenient, above all, for a society, the friend of obscurity, of simplicity, humble by duty and by necessity of position. If, then, a sermon is preached for the poor of a parish, and M. le Curé entrusts to the conference the distribution of the money, nothing better ; but to make our poor name sound from the height of the Christian pulpit is a thing of which we wish not to hear ; and the name, the history, the merits of the society being common property to all its members, we do not think that a particular conference has a right to dispose of them in despite of the opposition of the others.

* * * * *

3rd. I am charged to tell you that we regret the interruption of a habit introduced the last year, in virtue of which to the report was joined a circular containing instructions on those points most interesting to the society.

* * * * *

4th. The Conferences of Lyons, in losing two of their members, who are gone to live in neighbouring towns, have returned to a thought which had already several times preoccupied them : it is to seek to attach to the centre of association the associates isolated by the fatality of circumstances. The utility of these bonds is incontestable. They would hinder those from falling who have need of being sustained; they would prepare beforehand elements to form later new conferences. Two young people from Paris go to fix themselves at Lisle or Montpellier ; alone, they continue no longer the work of St. Vincent de Paul. The following year two come to join them, and two others the year after. They would be sufficient to associate and work together, if the two first were not cold and relaxed, if some relations with their old colleagues had held them still, if they had continued to consider themselves as joined in intention, prayers, merits, with the others. See, then, you who are at the source, how one might be able to multiply the canals. The want is signalled ; you have to fill it. For us, it has seemed to us that it would be possible to the isolated members, (1) to continue to do some good in the place of their sojourn ; (2) to unite themselves, by thought and by prayer, in reciting once a week the prayer of St. Vincent de Paul ; (3) to write once or several times a year to the Society at Paris to give an account of what they have done.

*   *   *   *   *

Lastly, and here I speak in my personal name, I have just seen announced a petition, which is signed at M. de Lamartine's, against the suppression of the *tours*. This petition, written by M. Guiraud, is Catholic. It has for end the re-establishment of one of the most merciful works of St. Vincent de Paul. Would it not be suitable that all the young advocates who make a part of the society, the young doctors also, competent all of them in this matter, should present themselves to sign the petition? Is there not there a homage to render to the memory of our holy patron at the same time as a good action to do?

Adieu; here is certainly enough. You should know me by my prolixity, by my greediness of new things, by a thousand other defects which I know well, and which I have even the pride to avow, for fear of appearing yet more foolish if I ignore them. My dear friend, who will deliver me from myself, if it is not He to whom we pray to deliver us from evil? Let us ask together, and we shall receive. Ask for me at these approaching feasts, for my mother also, and for all mine, and for my poor father whose mournful anniversary we have just celebrated. Count on a just reciprocity. There are many here who love you.

To M. Lallier.

Lyons, August 11th, 1838.

My dear Friend,

It is at first as President of the Society of St. Vincent de Paul at Lyons that I must write to the

Secretary-General to give him an account of the operations of the Council for Direction. Interpreter of several opinions which I have not always shared, I must be short to remain impartial.

*   *   *   *   *

Now, my dear friend, I would for all the world talk by the living voice with you for two hours, and tell you a thousand of those things which may be said and not written. The real dangers which we may run at Lyons, and those imaginary ones which have perhaps too much occupied us; the *Lamennaisian* distrusts and rancours of some, the ardour somewhat clerical of the others; my middle system displeasing to all, and raising against me every day contrary recriminations, and yet without their allowing me to give in my resignation—my fears consequently, and nevertheless my hopes. For it seems to me that with a strong organization, such as you might easily give us, the work of the regeneration of the student youths would begin to be accomplished by our hands. See, then, to what point we shall be responsible for the evil which we shall not prevent, for the good which we shall have omitted to do! God knows how many ideas pass through my mind, and how much better they would be to obtain their execution could they lodge in yours!

You understand, without doubt, my regrets, dear friend, that our projected interview for the 15th of August is put back. I assure you that for two years I have made a hard apprenticeship to a virtue which was not familiar to me, the abandonment of myself to the Divine Will. My plans are successively overturned, without at the same time being so completely destroyed as to hinder me from setting them up again and still attaching myself to them. This time, for example, after having voted the salary of their professor, the Municipal Council had no more to do than to form the list of their candidates; and now it has stopped there without fixing term. This delay, combined with the advice which you transmit to me on the part of M. le Clerc, and above all, with the little flourishing condition of my health, decides me still to delay my departure till the first days of October. Kindly then, in continuing your good offices, for which I know not how to show you my gratitude, suspend the impression, report my manuscript to M. le Clerc, begging him to be willing to read it, to give me later his advice concerning it.

You will achieve the possession of a right to my endless thanks, if, considering the trouble I have to arrange for my journey, you come to seek me yourself. If at your return from Rouen, after having passed a month in your family, whose affairs you have to regulate, you allowed yourself to descend this beautiful Saone as far as the Isle Barbe, which I have showed to you, there, in a little house which we rent there, would be plenty of room to receive you comfortably, as there is in all my family sufficient friendship to rejoice long at your coming. You know that a little further, where this same river loses its colour and its name, another hospitality, not less ancient would wait for you. Thus balanced, in the gentle current of the waters between our dwelling and our affections, saluted by so many others who love you here, welcomed in our conferences by those even who know you not, you would pass among us some days; and I would conduct you back afterwards, happy to prolong our companionship, even to the capital, which has fascinated you and holds you back in despite of our desires.

After Frederic Ozanam had arranged the affairs of his family, he had hastened—in spite of his repugnance—to inscribe his name on the list of advocates at the bar of Lyons. His letters have mentioned various incidents and impressions. An anecdote of him as a pleader at the bar may be inserted here. According to custom as a beginner, he was charged with the defence of an accused person who was too poor to provide himself with an advocate. The client's poverty was his recommendation. Ozanam undertook his cause with "all the resources of his talent" and "all the emotions of the heart." The advocate who sustained the accusation rallied him, and told him ironically that he needed not to put so much earnestness and vivacity into a part that he played only as a form. But this only roused Ozanam, whose indignant reply, in which he reproached his antagonist for taking him for an actor, astonished the public prosecutor, who did not expect to be taken to task in such a manner by a young man of twenty-four. The judges, however, approved the lesson given to their imprudent colleague; and one of them, after the hearing, came to shake Frederic by the hand, and to congratulate him on the manner in which he had performed his duty. "He was never willing," says his brother, "to consent, as beginners often do, to employ an attorney who might have procured him a large number of clients. He had too much delicacy in respect to the justice of the causes which were proposed to him to engage to plead for the first comer. Therefore, his clients were not very numerous. However, he pleaded several times, either in criminal or civil causes, either before the Tribunal of Commerce or at the Assizes. We remember that at the last he had to defend an unhappy deaf mute charged with a capital crime; and after a long and difficult strife, he had the happiness of seeing him completely acquitted. We remember, also, witnessing the marks of gratitude which this poor man came to express to Frederic immediately upon being set at liberty."

In the midst of all these labours and distractions there was one continual source of pleasure to him—in literary labours, from which nothing could turn him. In the end of 1838, he went to Paris with the desire of taking the degree of Doctor of Letters, and succeeded in passing brilliantly, hastening back to Lyons to rejoice his mother with his success.

To M. Henri Pessonneaux.

Lyons, August 21st, 1838.

My dear Friend,

Be thanked a thousand times, since this contagion of forgetfulness, so common at Paris,—where more than elsewhere the poor absent always have the wrong,—has not taken possession of thy soul, since, amidst so many laborious cares and so many domestic griefs, thou hast preserved a memory and a tear for the friend of thy childhood. Be assured that I paid thee with a just reciprocity, and that among the consolations which must render my departure from Lyons less painful, I put first the pleasure of seeing thee again.

But, on one side, the new delays which my affair has undergone, and on the other, the counsels of M. le Clerc, have decided me yet to delay, till the commencement of October, this fabulous journey. I delude myself, as with a pleasant dream, with the idea of making the journey in thy company, reconducting thee thus to thy house, according to our old Parisian habit. Who knows if this idea will not pass away like so many others? I have learned in a hard manner for eighteen months, or rather I have been put in a position to learn, the science of abnegation, which has always appeared so difficult to me. I, who formerly could not close my eye at night without having sketched for the morrow the detailed plan of my day's work; I, who pleased myself in constructing, outside the narrow limits of the present, the capricious edifice of my future, now uncertainty, like our winter fogs, closes my horizon at four paces. My projects are overturned, like the fantastic figures which the clouds form in the distance. I begin to know what the will of man is worth when circumstances are not at its service. Would to God that I might know as well how to trust in Him as to distrust myself!

For the rest, outside my calculations, in me and around me, few things are changed. If, in reading again one of my old letters, thou wast compassionate over my troubles of that time, perhaps it was one of these marvellous affinities which connect hearts at a distance which interested thee in thy ignorance in my present afflictions. My mother always equally suffering, with the greater chance that sufferings already long give to a terrible catastrophe; my brothers almost always far from me; the embarrassment of an insufficient income;

some friends, but very few, with whom there is complete association of tastes and similarity of habits,—the duties of family and of profession, which divide and isolate, have taken the place of the relations in study which united us. Consequently my literary labours are stripped of encouragements and counsels, and yet there is too little business at the bar to distract me, and to detach me from those preoccupations which have hitherto swayed my youth; with health uncertain, fatiguing endeavours to obtain a nomination that is certainly promised, and for which I am made to wait indefinitely; the contrarieties to which the Conference of St. Vincent de Paul has not ceased to be exposed and which all fall on me as president; lastly, my moral infirmities and the perpetual discontent with myself. Thou seest, my dear friend, it is an old and monotonous history: they are griefs which have not even the commonplace consolation of being able to complain, since they have already done that too much.

I should, however, be unjust not to speak of the temperaments which Divine Providence has been pleased to grant; and, to be brief, I will mention two of these. First, the pleasure of having finished my thesis, or rather my work on the philosophy of Dante; then the stay which I have made for some days in a delicious little house which we have rented in the Isle Barbe for the vacation.... I have spoken enough to thee of myself; I am eager to learn in my turn many things, and thy friendly pages are still far from putting me, as I would be, in possession of thy situation and of thy ideas. We will talk of the history of St. Louis. It is, it seems to me, one of the finest subjects which can be treated, but will six months suffice thee? Believe me, the middle age is a little like those enchanted isles of which the poets speak. One lands on passing, and only for a few hours; but one gathers fruit there, one allays one's thirst there at streams which make one's country—that is the present time—to be forgotten; or, to explain myself in a more simple fashion, we are really captivated there by the charm of facts, manners, traditions; we are detained by the multitude of documents.

For myself, I know that my studies on Dante have made me feel something like my journey to Rome; the sweet and voluntary servitude which enchains the soul among ruins, causes it also to please itself in the midst of memories. And what are memories if not other ruins, sadder and, at the same time, more attaching than those which the ivy and the moss cover? And is it not as pious to make a pause at the legends and traditions of our fathers, as to seat one's self on the ruins of aqueducts and temples with which antiquity has sown our soil?

But to what good is it to express on paper, in phrases in which elaboration always betrays itself, ideas which will escape in a much more lively and spontaneous manner in our approaching conversations? To what good to prolong my solitary watch, when soon, perhaps, we may be able to spend together hours much pleasanter and better filled? The lamp which lights me, warns me, in getting low, to go and take a rest, of which my disorders make me feel the need more strongly.

Adieu, my dear friend. Receive from me the promise, so often renewed, of being all my life

Thy faithful friend and cousin.

At this time Ozanam composed several articles for the reviews, and continued his constant interest in the growing work of the Society of St. Vincent de Paul. While he was yet a student at Paris, one of the first Provincial Conferences was established at Lyons, and he had scarcely settled there when he was unanimously named President-General of the Conferences already founded, and of those which were soon to be founded.

To M. Dufieux.

Paris, November 18th, 1838.

MY DEAR FRIEND,

It is a very unexpected visit, but also a very pleasant one, this of yours, under this sky of Paris, where you have been so seldom seen. You are welcome, then, even when you come with a reproach on your lips. I add that you have not all the wrong in presenting yourself thus, for my sole adieu for you in leaving Lyons has been an embarrassment which I left you. My silence since could not fail to seem reprehensible to you; and yet, if it was possible to you, my dear friend, to transport yourself suddenly into the midst of my occupations and my anxieties, I am sure that to the little grudge which you think you owe me, would succeed a feeling of generous pity. My affairs, which began happily enough, have undergone new complications. The vote of the Municipal Council, which fixed the salary of the future Professor of Commercial Law, has been approved by the Minister of the Interior. Thus far, one cannot complain of delays, and I thank you for your friendly offers in this respect.

And although a part of the good people who wished to support me are not at this moment in Paris, nevertheless I am assured of their favourable dispositions. But the event which disturbs me is the approaching and probable retirement of the Minister of Public Instruction. At the same time, I am disputed for by the cares which are exacted by the printing of my work and the preparation of my theses. The desperate slowness of the workmen causes me a vexatious delay; and, to avoid its prolongation, I must torment them without relaxation. Lastly, friendship itself, which has preserved to me at Paris a sufficiently large number of people who see me with pleasure, has reserved to itself, by that feeling alone, the right to levy a frequent tribute on my hours, and often a half day passes in receiving and paying indispensable visits. I find thus trial and contrariety even in the circumstances which ought to make my consolation and my happiness.

For you, my dear friend, in telling me of your approaching journey, you have singularly saddened for me the perspective of the winter of 1839.

You are going, then, to see my poor Italy! You will tread that glorious land whose memories people to-day my imagination. You will measure with your eye those monuments where my thought has so often taken refuge. We shall then have later the joy of talking of them together: a point of contact the more between our hearts!

You desire the suggestion of a book to enlighten your steps—it is in your heart, above all, that you must read, my friend. Your memory has, without doubt, retained sufficiently the principal details of ancient and modern history for the places to appear to you surrounded by the great things which were accomplished in them. The commonest itinerary will tell you the buildings and collections to visit, and will give you the information necessary to comprehend them. For the rest, you will see, you will judge, you will admire for yourself: you will not refer yourself to the judgments of cicerones and tourists. You will, above all, study independently those institutions, those populations, so calumniated, so unknown.

If I returned into Italy, to charm away the annoyances of the road and to make its pleasures fertile, I would read again, without doubt, Titus Livius, Virgil the lives of some saints, as St. Charles Borromeo, St. Francis of Assisi, St. Gregory VII., St. Gregory the Great, and the *Actes des Martyrs*. Thus I should take this blessed country by the two sides which solicit and dispute our respect and our love.

The work of M. Rio, notwithstanding some defects, is of an extreme importance for making known all that part hitherto neglected, and precisely the Catholic part in the history of the arts. I do not know well if you will be able, without his help, to find and to appreciate in the museums and churches the touching and pure works of the painters who preceded Raphael, and whom their disciple, ungrateful without knowing it, has caused to be forgotten. However that may be, always ask them to show you in the monuments and galleries what they have most ancient, which unhappily they hide, to put into prominence and light the artistic creations of the Renaissance, alone honoured by the commonplace praises of travellers.

But you ask me for information, and I think I find myself giving you counsels! Excuse my presumption by my attachment to this dear Italy, which I fear, above all, to see badly comprehended by good people.

In finishing this letter, permit me a complaint which my friendship has long felt owing to you. Why shroud with so many precautions your requests for services? If your delicacy takes this means to make me forget those which you have rendered to me, she succeeds badly. You humble me deeply with your protestations and your excuses. It is only by the title of Christian fraternity that I have ventured so often to disarrange you for me. Act by the same title and with the same liberty. Do you not see for how many good offices I owe you since my departure alone? I reckon in this number the two visits you have kindly made to my mother, and of which she has shown me her lively gratitude; lastly and above all, the place you keep for me in your heart and in your prayers.

To M. X——.

Lyons, February 21st, 1839.

MY DEAR FRIEND,

The Municipal Council, by a majority of twenty-four voices over thirty-six, has nominated me Professor of Commercial Law. But this nomination must be confirmed by M. the Minister of Public Instruction. In consequence I have written to M. Cousin that, in thanking him for the Chair of Philosophy at Orleans, I found myself, nevertheless, obliged by my family duties to choose the Chair of Law at Lyons.

Tell me what you think of my choice, and what my friends the Parisians think of it. Here I have been almost blamed for it. They agreed in believing that my true interests were on the borders of the Loire. For myself, I confess that I was flattered by the perspective of a career exclusively intellectual, of an existence henceforward undivided, and consequently more peaceful, by the neighbourhood of Paris; but I opposed to this the dependence, the isolation in an unknown town, and, above all, the necessity of abandoning my mother ten months in the year, at peril of receiving one day a letter like that of May 12, 1837, and of undertaking once more one of those melancholy journeys of which your consoling friendship has thrice made the experience.

Besides, there is certainly some pleasure in not breaking with our habits and our past entirely; there is place also in my new situation for the illusions of the future. They talk of the foundation of a school of law in this country, and you will understand that the Municipal Professor would be almost sure to find a chair there; that is to say, fixity of condition, honourable position, and liberty to increase at will the sphere of one's teaching. If God lends me life and spirit, and if He fix me by a definite position in these tranquil functions, I believe I should do well in putting my personal labours in harmony with my public duties, and in occupying myself with a Philosophy and a History of Law, which, treated from the Christian point of view, would seem to me to fill a chasm sufficiently large in science, and would suffice to utilize the years I may have to pass on the earth. The time seems long to me ere I may leave general considerations and enter, as they say, on a speciality. And this of which I speak to you seems to me the most apt to combine the resources of my literary and jurisprudential studies, and to lose nothing of what I have gained. I hold to preserving all, because I feel that it is little. What think you? I have so much the more need of your thoughts, as the recent memory of your conversations has made me feel in a more lively manner the privation of them.

For the moment, shut up in more modest anxieties, I am endeavouring to put the last touch to my work on Dante. Some notes on the passages which in my thesis have undergone reasonable criticism; the translation of several fragments of St. Bonaventure and St. Thomas, which will contribute, I hope, to destroy the prejudice of obscurantism and Catholic servilism; a half-dozen chapters of the philosophical works of Dante for the first time reproduced in French; lastly, notes, explanations, and a dissertation on the poetical antecedents of the *Divine Comédie*; this is enough to occupy both of us. Pardon this forced association which I impose upon you. But you have permitted me to hope that you would superintend the printing of my last leaves, and my author's self-love is too much interested in the matter to hold you quit. If you have heard any judicious observations on my work, if you could know that which Cozalès thinks of it, I should be very happy if you would let me know, in order that I may set it right. Enclosed is a letter for M. Ballanche, in which I ask his advice. Kindly take it to him, if you are curious to talk with that eminent man.

My dear friend, in speaking to you of my interests, I do not forget yours; and I recall to myself the gravity of the cares of which your last letter speaks. I am singularly touched with the trials which you have to suffer.

Indeed they seem to me trials very severe; these uncertainties on a question on which an entire life may depend, and, in such circumstances, the unlimited acceptance of the Divine Will must be singularly meritorious. You are too much imbued with these sentiments for the part which you take not to turn to your happiness and salvation.

However, I keep the hope, which is dear to me, to see you preserve some time longer your liberty, your activity—to see you waiting awhile before engaging yourself to new duties, which would captivate you entirely at this time, and would leave you the leisure neither to learn nor to do. Without doubt the solitary existence which you lead is melancholy and sad; but labour can fill it, and religion console it. God and knowledge, charity and study—is not this, then, enough to enchant your youth? . . . . Have you ever seen, without experiencing a pang of heart, the morrow of a wedding? Be sure that man abdicates much of his dignity the day when he enchains himself to the arms of a wife. Read St. Paul again.

However, would I then preach eternal, universal celibacy? God forbid! But I would that we should wait for the conjugal union the day when it becomes necessary, and when it has ceased to be able to be fatal; the time when the mind has attained its development, when the will has acquired all its energy, when one is compromised by labours, by relations, by antecedents of all sorts, in such a way that one cannot disengage one's self; when one has acquired to one's self some right to family enjoyments by solitary labours; when one can offer something and not receive everything:

the time, in a word, when one is sure of being master of one's self and free without.

You will speak to me of the sweetnesses of domestic life; but, my dear friend, this well-being, material or sentimental, this egoism of two, is it well in season? Is society so happy, religion so honoured, the Christian youth so numerous and so active, those who can work for the general good so much at liberty, that you would be right, with the talent God has given you, with the knowledge and the encouragements with which you are surrounded, with this voice which surely from the bottom of the heart calls you to the work, to withdraw yourself already, as a wearied labourer who has borne the burden and heat of the day? Have you, then, not meant seriously all that you have spoken, written, and done—all that your friends have repeated or attempted with you? Do you despair of the regeneration of the country—of the amendment of thought? Or, rather, do you despair of yourself—that is to say, of God, who has created, redeemed, sanctified you? You have difficulty in finding your place here below!—and who cannot say as much? Is that a reason to justify suicide? And is it not a suicide, when one is what you are, to go to M—— to plant cabbages?

I beg you go to see Montalembert, or, rather, ask of him when he is to be seen. I have reason to think that he will talk to you of projects capable of preoccupying your thoughts, and of tempering a little the intellectual want of employment in which you are. Have you completely abandoned your idea of a *History of the Canon Law?* I should be sorry for it.

Excuse the sermons of a man who only makes them

because he has need of them himself. Lend me as soon as possible the last official report of the Society of St. Vincent de Paul. Do not forget the improvements of which you have dreamed for this poor and dear society. Do not be disturbed by the shortness and disorder of this letter. It is written in bad company; I speak of the headache which has not ceased to assail me this evening. Keep yourself well ; I can appreciate the merit of this counsel, and warrant it to you. Believe me, for life, Your devoted friend.

CHAPTER X.

VISIT TO PARIS—INCREASED ILLNESS OF HIS MOTHER—LACORDAIRE—SILVIO PELLICO—HIS MOTHER'S DEATH—OPENS HIS COURSE AS PROFESSOR OF COMMERCIAL LAW—THE CHAIR OF M. QUINET—M. COUSIN.

AGAIN, in 1839, Frederic Ozanam repaired to Paris for the entire conclusion of his business there. He remained till towards the middle of August. On the very day of his departure for home his mother was taken worse, and when he reached home he found her in bed and suffering greatly. Her eldest son had then just ended a retreat at Autun, which he had been giving to a community, and on receiving the news of his mother's danger he hastened immediately to her, travelling all night. "On the great day of the Assumption," he says, "the three brothers found themselves united at the bedside of their dying mother, for our brother Charles, returned from school, began his holidays. Alas! this day, formerly so joyous, because it was the fête of our excellent mother, was no longer filled for us but with funereal threatenings." One may describe this melancholy period to the mother's death, two months later, in her son Frederic's letters, in which the chief cause of trouble is mixed up also with other perturbations and disquietudes of this distressing time of his life.

To the Abbé Lacordaire.

Lyons, August 26th, 1839.

SIR,
When your letter from *la Quercia* came to inform me of your happy arrival at the term of your pilgrimage, the welcome which you had received into the family of St. Dominic, and the memory which you desired to preserve, amid so many grave occupations, of the associates of St. Vincent de Paul, I hesitated for long between the need of showing my gratitude to you for this unhoped-for honour, and the fear of troubling, by an indiscreet importunity, the laborious repose of your novitiate. But during a journey to Paris, whence I am quite recently returned, I have learned that your friends have not ceased to correspond with you; and since you have not disdained to give me this title, I have believed I might take the liberties which are the consequence of it.

Too few months have passed since you left our great capital for the impressions of a traveller of yesterday to have any interest for you. You know, without having need to hear it still repeated, that the movement to which you gave from the pulpit of Notre Dame so powerful an impulsion, has not ceased to spread among the intelligent multitudes. I have seen, near at hand, these men of Republican Carbonarism become humble believers, I have seen impassioned artists asking for the rules of brotherhood. I have perceived the disorganization, the discredit of the rationalistic school, which has reduced it to powerlessness, and forces its two principal organs—the *Revue Française* and the *Revue des Deux Mondes*—to seek for the collaboration of Catholics, or, as says M. Buloz, of honest men.

At the same time that M. de Montalembert has gathered together in the Chamber of Peers a phalanx disposed to contend for the good, M. de Carné affirms that half-a-hundred voices will soon agree in favour of religious questions in the Chamber of Deputies. On another hand, the little Society of St. Vincent de Paul sees its ranks increasing in a surprising manner. A new Conference is formed of the pupils of the Normal and Polytechnic Schools; fifteen young people, composing about the third of the seminary of the University, have asked, as a favour, to spend two hours each Sunday, their only day of liberty, in occupying themselves with God and the poor. The next year, Paris will count fourteen conferences ; we shall have an equal number in province. They will represent a total of more than a thousand Catholics, impatient to march to the intellectual crusade which you will preach.

*   *   *   *   *

For me, humble witness of so many things full of hope, I am now probably fixed in the post which I had so long desired. I am Professor of Commercial Law, and I rejoice in a function which fixes me near to my poor aged mother, and which, nevertheless, does not tear me from my inclinations—unfortunate without doubt, but obstinate—for philosophic and literary labours. Notwithstanding the extreme difficulty of writing, which holds my pen indefinitely captive on the pages where my eye discovers numerous defects, in despite of all the signs in which I ought, perhaps, to see the contrary will of Providence; the attachments of habit, self-love, the encouragement of some friends, make me return a thousand times to projects a thousand times abjured; and I fear much losing in useless efforts a time which I might employ more modestly and more certainly in my own salvation, and in the service of my neighbour. I feel more than ever the need of a spiritual direction which would aid my weakness and ease me of my responsibility. And, to speak with open heart, seeing my mother's malady make such distressing progress, when the possibility of so terrible a loss presents itself to my mind, I see no longer any reason to hold me in a position which filial duty alone made me solicit, and the uncertainty of my vocation comes back upon me with more disturbing influence than ever. It is this inward trouble from which I have suffered for a long time, that I recommend to your charitable prayers; for if God really willed to call me to Himself, I see no militia in which it would be more pleasant to me to serve than that in which you are engaged. I should even be happy to know beforehand the conditions of it, to help me with the counsel of my confessor, to make up my mind. The Rule of the Preaching-Friars is wanting in our library; could you enlighten me on the means of discovering it? You would oblige anew one of those who have already so many obligations to you.

Receive, with my respects, those of my Lyonnese friends, of whom I am at this moment the envied interpreter.

The Abbé Lacordaire to Frederic Ozanam.

La Quercia, October 2nd, 1839.

VERY DEAR SIR,

My first thought is to congratulate you on the very suitable post to which your merit has promoted you. I am truly happy to know you at Lyons, near to your mother and your friends, in a Church which has so inviolably preserved the greatness of its faith. What you tell me of the modifications which are apparent in the tendencies of the clergy, and in the opinions of several men who had contributed to make for them a false position, appears to me to agree with the more general movement which becomes everywhere visible.

*   *   *   *   *

I have seen the reprinting of your Dante announced in the *Univers*, which we receive. This has given me pleasure. It is necessary to beware of quitting the pen. Without doubt writing is a hard trade, but the press has become too powerful to abandon our post in it. Let us write, not for glory, but for Jesus Christ: let us crucify ourselves to our pen. Although no one should read us more in a hundred years, what matters that? The drop of water on the border of the sea has none the less contributed to make the stream, and the stream dies not. "*He who has been of his own time,*" says Schiller, "*has been of all times.*" He has done his task; he has had his part in the creation of things which are eternal. How many books, lost to-day in libraries, have made, three centuries ago, the revolution which we see with our eyes! Our fathers are unknown to ourselves, but we live by them. Besides, nothing in what you have published need discourage your pen.

You have a style which has a nerve, brilliancy, and an erudition which sustains itself well. I engage you strongly to work; and if I were the director of your conscience, I would impose on you the obligation.

The end of your letter, where you speak to me of the persevering instincts which impel you to serve God, has greatly touched me. The hope of one day seeing you with us would be very dear to me. I cannot tell you where you will find our Rules. It seems to me that a Paris bookseller would procure them for you easily.

For the rest, you would with difficulty collect from them the mechanism of our order. I believe that, in a few words, you would be put better into possession. The end is *preaching*, and *Divine knowledge*. The means: *prayer, mortification of the senses, study*.

* * * * *

Kindly present my respectful homage to madame your mother, and recall me to the remembrance of all our friends of Lyons. I embrace you cordially, with a great desire to call you one day my brother and my father.

FREDERIC OZANAM TO M. LALLIER.

Lyons, October 12th, 1839.

MY DEAR FRIEND,

Since the time when I wrote you a very few lines, promising you to open my heart more at ease another time, there have happened things which have only furnished too much reason for my silence.

Fresh uneasiness about my mother's health reached me several times at Paris. However, nothing spoke of a grave peril; and I remained till the entire conclusion of my business, that is to say, till the 11th of the month of August. This very day, which was that of my departure, my mother had a crisis, which compelled her to go to bed; and the evening of my arrival, eve of the Assumption, I found her shedding tears on account of her excessive suffering, attacked by a burning fever, causing, in a word, lively apprehensions. At the same time, my eldest brother, warned by the doctor, travelled post from Autun, where he had been preaching, still suffering from his throat; and Charles was there, passing a melancholy vacation. How sad this return was! At the end of a week the malady took a turn, and from acute became chronic. We took a little hope. But soon we were forced to acknowledge that the evil made incontestable progress; we sought to delude ourselves, and after some time we were forced to confess that the apparent improvement had been deceitful, and, from deception to deception, we have come, my dear friend, no longer to believe a cure possible. To-day, sunk in a heavy and continual drowsiness, caused by a consuming fever, she no longer hears much; she answers scarcely at all, unless when she is spoken to of her children and of God, towards whom all her thoughts continue to rise without effort. She has received the last sacraments with a calm piety which avoided emotion to spare our sobs; she suffers the most inconvenient and the most painful remedies, resigned, gentle, and almost smiling, not by a moral constraint, of which she is no longer capable, but by the habit of kindliness and charity. Never was her virtue more apparent than in these moments when it has in some sort become instinctive. And it is now when we begin to comprehend and to appreciate her, that our poor mother escapes from us, and leaves us all alone in the world—my little brother, so young and so exposed; myself, so weak and so evil.

There is enough here for you to know my grief; but what you know not how to imagine is the trouble which accompanies it. Forsaken by her who was my guardian angel, it seems to me that she carries with her the little that I had of religion. My heart turns sour, and goes astray in its mourning; I feel as if I shall become less Christian than formerly, if the prayer of my friends comes not to my aid. And that is why, my dear Lallier, I can delay no longer writing to you. I have need, for myself, for my brothers, for my mother, of your intercession, and of that of the Catholic souls by whom you may be surrounded. Do not refuse me a succour so necessary.

As this fatal malady is prolonged for more than two months, it does not release me from the obligation of thinking of my business; and the world, which would excuse me perfectly for shutting myself up for eight days by my mother's bedside, would not permit me to remain there for eight or ten weeks. This is a new and not less cruel trial—the *Propagation de la Foi*, my study, the preparation of my course—so many cares which come to throw themselves across my troubles. And the event with which I am threatened changing all my existence, leaves no more any interest for me in these different occupations. At the moment of choosing a profession, seeing my parents still young, I had accepted, to please them, the profession of the bar. Hardly had I taken my degrees, when my poor father failed me, and could not enjoy the fruit of his sacrifices. I tried then a new career, to assist the pecuniary exigencies of my mother, whom I could not leave; and when, after two years, I obtain my nomination, and settle myself to discharge my new functions, my mother will have no advantage from what has been done for her. In truth, this double and severe disappointment startles me, overturns all my designs, and throws me with regard to my vocation into grievous uncertainties of which I do not perceive the end.

The day before yesterday a letter from the Abbé Lacordaire arrived for me. He is still satisfied with the order of St. Dominic—still filled with magnificent hopes.

Where are you? How has your vacation passed? Does health reign in your new household? Do you hope soon to realize the title of "Father" which our familiarity formerly decreed to you? Are you content with your duties? Answer a little at length; you are sure not to weary me.

SILVIO PELLICO TO FREDERIC OZANAM.

Turin, November 5th, 1839.

SIR,

You will have received by M. Collombet my salutations and my thanks. It is time that I begged you to excuse me for having so long delayed to express to you myself how much I appreciate the kind gift which you have sent me. Your book on Dante pleases me; it is a good book in all ways. What you say of the thorough Catholic philosophy of this great poet is the most exact truth. The unhappy writers contrary to the Church who have tried to make of Dante one of their patriarchs have been pitiably blinded by their prejudices. Your manner of refuting them is triumphant. All Italians should felicitate themselves on the brotherhood which unites you to them, and which has inspired yo with so noble and holy an apology for their cherished poet. You make us forget the infinite number of inexact judgments which have been passed on our literature beyond the Alps. But with regard to Dante, it must be said that, among those who have painted him in false colours, there are many Italians.

I join to my thanks for your book the very particular expression of my gratitude for what you address to me with such extreme kindness in your letter. May God lead you always, and may He sanctify you! You have talent; employ it constantly in His honour, to the honour of His dear Church, our mother, the only depositary of the truth. Write, and above all, act always in a manner to edify friends and enemies. Let us aspire unceasingly to render ourselves better servants and children of our divine model, Jesus.

One of my friends, a Piedmontese, the Count Cesar Balbo, has written a life, also very Catholic, of Dante. This work would please you. He has given me a copy of it for you. I send it you by M. Bonafous.

A thousand affectionate things to M. Collombet! Tell him that I thank him for having brought me near to the good Boethius. Tell him that I love his books.

FREDERIC OZANAM TO M. REVERDY.

Lyons, November 10th, 1839.

MY DEAR FRIEND,

Your consoling letter came to visit me in the country, to which my brothers and I had withdrawn ourselves for a few days for the need of our health and the rest of our spirits. Your words came down upon my solitude like the voice of the angel whom Hagar heard in the desert, for there is something angelic, that is to say, fraternal and superior at the same time, in the accent of a friend like you. To the overflowings of so cordial an affection, you join already the authority of your ministry. Your advice has the beneficent force which constrains the soul to open to receive it, and to let itself be healed.

My mother was very ill the last time I had the happiness to see you. Nevertheless, I looked not for so speedy a catastrophe. I thought to keep her yet all winter, and I held with all the obstinacy of despair to this last illusion. It was then with an inexpressible grief that I saw her escape me, when an access of fever, determined by the stormy temperature of the first days of October, warned us of the approaches of her end. And, nevertheless, the intellectual and moral faculties which the malady had at first pressed down seemed to rise again. Every time anyone spoke to her of God and of her children, she answered by some touching words. She understood all the gravity of her position; and yet she was calm, serene, and during sleep a smile spread over her lips.

Our excellent mother was so pious and so charitable,

so exempt even from the small imperfections of her sex, so proved by griefs and sufferings of every kind, so admirable in her last moments.

* * * * *

Without doubt she rests in the bosom of Him whom she loved, and when from the height of these divine splendours she sees us kneeling still under our funeral veils, and praying to obtain for her the deliverance which she already enjoys, without doubt she pardons us this mourning and this error, and she causes those prayers, useless for her, to fall in beneficent dew on souls less happy. It is in this thought that I come to ask you to join your offerings with ours; they will not be lost.

Besides, we have much need of this spiritual help, we who remain. Our age would seem to render us, my eldest brother and me, more firm and more courageous. But we have so long lived the family life, we found ourselves so happy under our mother's wings, that we had never left the birth-nest without the desire to return. When it was necessary to absent ourselves, the privation made us appreciate in a more lively manner what was wanting to us; and absence had taught us to love it better still. The maladies and infirmities which might have prepared us for a separation only served to render it more cruel to us. The cares which they exacted had finished by taking in our days a place which remains empty, and which nothing can fill in the same manner. Above all, how dark and desolate are my evenings when a friend does not come to distract their sadness! But above all, what a loss for the religious interests of my soul! Gentle exhortations, powerful examples, fervour which warmed my lukewarm heart, encouragements which raised my strength! And then it was she whose first teachings had given me faith; she who was for me as a living image of the holy Church—our mother also; she who seemed to me the most perfect expression of Providence. Thus I think I feel nearly as the disciples must have done after the Ascension of the Saviour. I am as if the Divinity was retired from beside me. It seems to me for a moment—shall I confess it to you?—that the faith escapes me with her who was for me the interpreter of it, and that I remain alone in my nothingness. For a week I have worked much; but work which occupies the mind does nothing for the heart. Oh, ask for me of the Lord that He will send to me as to His disciples, orphans likewise, the Spirit who consoles, the Paraclete! I have not, as they had, an extraordinary mission to fill. I do not desire the miraculous gifts with which they were loaded. I desire only to obtain the strength necessary to finish my pilgrimage of some years, perhaps of some days, and to finish at last as my holy mother has finished.

Adieu, my dear friend. I renew to you, with my lively thanks for you, the prayer to recall me to the memories of our common friends.

Adieu. May your mother long be preserved to you! Adieu once more!

Your devoted brother in our Lord.

To M. Lallier.

Lyons, Christmas, 1839.

My dear Friend,

This fair day shall not pass away without my accomplishing a duty very dear, retarded until now by more imperious obligations, or which perhaps seemed to me such, precisely because they were less pleasant. God permits, without doubt, that in these grand solemnities in which He showers upon us graces from heaven, we should mingle a little of the happiness of the earth ; and what happiness purer than that of Christian friendship?

You are come, then, to visit me in the first days of my mourning, and you have had the courage, so rare, to give me veritable and serious consolations. Alas! what need I had of them! what ravages this death has made in my mind and in my heart! Or rather, I mistake— that which has demoralized me is, first, the long malady whose daily undeniable progress carried away from me one by one my last hopes, and which—shall I say it to you?—seemed to desire to dishonour the sacrifice before consuming it, by extinguishing the intellectual faculties, by deadening the moral feelings. This thought was horrible, but it assailed me always. I imagined I saw the soul die at the same time as the body. Happily, the trial was cut short. In the last moments inward energy revived, and the Christ, in descending for the last time into the heart of his well-beloved servant, left there strength for the last combats.

She remained nearly three days calm, serene, murmuring prayers, or replying by some words of ineffable maternal goodness to our caresses and our cares. At length came the fatal night. It was I who watched. Weeping I suggested to our poor mother the acts of faith, hope, and love, which, as a little child, she had formerly taught me to lisp. Towards one o'clock new symptoms alarmed me. I called my eldest brother, who slept in the neighbouring room. Charles heard us, and rose. The servants ran to us. We knelt about the bed. Alphonse uttered the last heartrending prayers, to which we replied with sobs. All the aids which religion preserves for this last solemn hour . . . lastly, the hopes, already near, of a happy immortality—all these circumstances seemed gathered together to soften the horror, to enlighten the darkness of death. No convulsions nor agony, but a sleep which left her countenance almost smiling, a light breath which grew weaker and weaker. A moment came when it stopped —we rose orphans. How shall I tell you the grief and tears which then burst forth without, and yet the inexpressible, the inexplicable peace which we enjoyed within; and how the feeling of a new beatitude carried away, in spite of ourselves, not alone our hearts, but also those of others the dearest to the family! Then the immense concourse at the funeral, and the tears of the poor, the prayers made from all parts spontaneously, without waiting for our solicitations; and at last, to come back to you, the charitable expressions of friendship, astonished, without doubt, to find us so tranquil in our grief.

Happy the man to whom God gives a holy mother! This dear memory will not abandon us. Even in my present solitude, in the midst of the desolation which often ravages my soul, the thought of this august scene comes back to me to sustain me, to raise me up. Considering how short is life, how little distant without doubt will be the reunion of those whom death separates, I feel the temptations of self-love and the evil instincts of the flesh to vanish away. All my desires are confounded in one alone—to die like my mother.

And you, my dear friend, you must share with me this precious memory, as you share already so many others; and if my pen has had some pain in retouching traits which are for me so many inward wounds, on the other hand your affectionate sympathies, on which I reckon beforehand, will become as a new balm to heal them, or at least to purify them.

How well I feel now the truth of your words! and how happy I am not to have deserted this bed of sorrow and of blessing to run after the doubtful promises of a university advancement! Although, at the price of this light sacrifice, I should only have purchased the privilege of passing beside my mother a few months more, of finding myself present at this last night, I should be already overpaid for it. I have so much regretted not having been able to close the eyes of my poor unfortunate father. May they now find themselves gathered together in the same happiness as they were here below in the same labours and the same afflictions! May I continue with them by thought, by faith, by virtue, an intercourse that nothing shall know how to interrupt, and may there be no change in the family but two saints more! Pray, then, *for us*, my excellent friend—for us all—for me above all, who loved so much this existence sheltered by the paternal roof, who in the midst of my brothers, in the midst of my numerous companions, cannot accustom myself to see no longer those of the preceding generation, and who find myself so lonely!

Work comes a little to my help; the cares of my

course of commercial law take the greatest part of my time. I opened only on the 16th December. The discourse succeeded; it was printed, and in time you will have a copy of it. The two following lessons have been a little injured by the hesitation of speech of which I cannot divest myself. Nevertheless, people are not dissatisfied, and the hall, which contains two hundred and fifty persons, was not large enough. The benches, without doubt, will soon be thinned.

I may obtain the chair of Quinet; it will be vacant at Easter. Lastly, the Abbé Lacordaire will be returning in some months, and then, if old desires change into a real vocation, I shall endeavour to correspond. My perplexity is very great. On all sides they already speak to me of marriage. I do not yet know myself sufficiently to resolve. Give me your counsels: you know the burdens and the consolations of the state; you know my character, and the antecedents of the consulter. Tell him, I pray you, your opinion with the same frankness which he formerly used in regard to you. Do not fear the responsibility; I do not promise you that your advice shall be decisive.

You gave me for Christmas a rendezvous where I have not failed. I have prayed our merciful God, who visited me in the midst of the ruins of my poor family, to visit also the young hearth where yours is forming; to be with you as he was with Joseph and Mary; to bless the first hope of your union. I have formed there, in the sincerity of prayer, the wishes that many will address to you in the language of the world, now and for a few days.

Receive my wishes for a happy year. Kindly present

them to Madame Lallier, as those of one of the most devoted friends her husband can have. My eldest brother embraces you, and I do the same.

Adieu. Answer me, and forget not your old comrade.

M. COUSIN TO FREDERIC OZANAM.

July 6th, 1839.

MY DEAR OZANAM,

I did not reply to you whilst I had nothing distinct to say. To-day I come to tell you that in the council of yesterday it was decided that you should be named to the Chair of Commercial Law.

I should have been much better pleased to have seen you in my regiment; but I do not despair of it, and in any case I am sure that with me or without me you will always love and serve the true philosophy.

Do not forget me too much, for you are sure always to find in me

A friend.

M. COUSIN TO FREDERIC OZANAM.

January 8th, 1840.

MY DEAR OZANAM,

I received some days after your *Dante* the sad note in which you announce to me the death of madame your mother. This news has been truly grievous to me, by all the pain which it must have caused to you, and which I have been able to measure by the sacrifices of more than one kind which I have seen you make to this great affection, to this great duty. You are now more free; when you are able to come back to me, you will find me again.

Tell me what you are doing—your works, your affairs, and the state of the good cause of philosophy at Lyons.

A thousand good wishes from the heart.

CHAPTER XI.

OPENING LECTURE OF THE COURSE OF COMMERCIAL LAW—NOTES OF THE COURSE BY M. FOISSET—WEDDING POEM—M. COUSIN'S DESIRE—SOCIETY OF ST. VINCENT DE PAUL—LITERARY CONTEST AND SUCCESS—ENTRANCE INTO THE SORBONNE—HIS FRIENDS' EFFORTS FOR HIS MARRIAGE—HIS OWN THOUGHTS ON IT—AMELIE SOULACROIX—VISITS GERMANY.

FREDERIC OZANAM'S filial piety had at least this result: it had caused him to fix the cords of his tabernacle so strongly, that when in his perplexity as to his vocation he looked round for providential indications, he found them first in the existence of engagements which he had no right to break. He had been courted from different quarters. Above all, there was the Chair of Law, which he could scarcely throw up now after all his own endeavours and his friends' to procure it. It would, as he felt, be a failure in his duties to others, which only the sternest persuasion that God called him to a "religious life," as it is called, would excuse. This persuasion he never had, although temperament, and sorrow, and Lacordaire's influence, all formed for him at this time attractions to it. "Nothing," says his brother, "detaches us more from temporal interests than the loss of our kindred." Frederic must have felt this doubly in the loneliness he endured, and the complete absence of domestic endearments and duties. He resolved, however, to wait, and not to preoccupy himself with the question of *state of life* till after a certain time. " I owe certainly," he says, "to the memory of my poor mother a year of mourning." On the 16th day of December, 1839, he pronounced the opening discourse in his chair. It was printed immediately, and may be found in his complete works.

FREDERIC OZANAM TO M. HENRI PESSONNEAUX.

Lyons, January 15th, 1840.

MY DEAR FRIEND,

It is very late for a New Year visit, but Parisian etiquette, if I am not mistaken, gives the entire month, and thou wilt permit me to take advantage of it. Nevertheless, be persuaded that I should not have let a reply to thy kind letter wait so long, if my professorial *débuts* had not exacted all my cares till now, leaving me hardly sufficient leisure for the official duties which one must fulfil at the time of New Year. Excuse me then, and—let us embrace.

As to me, I walk a day at a time by the ways that Providence indicates to me, without allowing me to see the end. The course of Commercial Law seems to succeed. An immense crowd assisted at the opening discourse; they broke doors and window-panes; and thy dear cousin Louis, to say it in passing, was one of those who committed the misdeed. Since then, the hall has not ceased to be filled, although it contains more than two hundred and fifty people. Nevertheless, I have allowed myself all the digressions—philosophic, historic—that these matters would allow of. I have not even shrunk from severe truths; but no more have I refused an occasion to call up a smile to the lips of the auditors. And, as says de Maistre, the needle makes way for the thread to pass. The Rector, delighted with the success, presses on strongly for my nomination for Quinet's place. . . . The marriage of M—— is an accomplished fact. He has passed the line—" this fine young man who would make so good a husband," according to thy happy expression. The fêtes have been magnificent. This joy, solemn and gentle, which presides at the union of two Christian families, has something singularly touching. No dances; verses, music, animated conversations; tears of emotion in the eyes of the two papas, and the heroes of the ceremony perfectly decorous. Only the bride had the air of being a little learned, and, what is worse, of knowing it. The expression of her face is that of a will a little manly; but she will find to whom she speaks, we need have no fear.

The eve of this brilliant wedding we saw poor Alfred Rieussec die. What contrasts and what reflections on the vanity of human previsions! And thou, my dear friend, what art thou doing? Will the days newly rising upon thee be better for thee? Do thy projects appear likely to be realized; and does the newly acquired acquaintance of Ampère continue to be useful to thee? Write to me—write to me at length; it is a consolation which becomes more necessary to me than ever. My brother, who has not yet lost his throat affection, leaves after to-morrow for Italy, where the doctors' sentence exiles him for three months. Many would envy the favour of such a banishment, but he is sad at leaving me alone. But I shall not be alone; the affection of so many excellent young men has formed around me as a new family. Absence even does not break the bonds; it only renders more pleasant the memory of moments passed together.

* * * * *

He taught in the Chair for the school year of 1840. The course reckoned forty-seven lessons. The notes which remain were published by the care of M. Foisset, Counsellor at the Court of Appeal at Dijon. He says:

"Ozanam is not known altogether if he is not known as jurist.

* * * * *

"The Law for him was not only that which is practised at the palace*; it was not only the application of judicial texts to the affairs of every day. The law was, before all, a branch of philosophy; it was a portion of history; it was even a side of literature.

"When in 1839 a Municipal Chair of Commercial Law was created in favour of Ozanam in his native town, he came into this Chair at twenty-six years, prepared on all sides on the philosophy as on the history, and on the positive theory of the portion of the science which it was his duty to teach.

"Deeply penetrated with the true mission of the Professor, he did not endeavour to accumulate in his course judicial problems. He never lost himself in exhaustless discussions of particular controverted cases.

* Palais de Justice.

He loved better to teach principles than doubts, to inculcate the rules of law, and to point out wisdom from them, than to initiate his auditors—these are his terms —'into the double scandal of the obscurity of the laws and of the contrariety of judgments.'

"But he was ready on the jurisprudence of decrees as on all the rest. One may judge by the notes he had prepared for the first half of this course, too soon interrupted.

"We publish them with confidence. They are only notes, excepting short and rare fragments, which detach themselves, as M. Ampère has so well said, as figures finished before the rest in the sketch of a master. They are only notes, and, nevertheless, what breadth! what light! There are only the great lines of the subject, but they are all there. And the more naked they are, the better they discover the scope and the principal divisions of the vast horizon which they embrace. Thus, apart from all accessory, they define and bring out the outlines with a clearness of delineation full of relief and vigour.

* * * * *

"I would dare to say that we here find Ozanam entire, his erudition so trustworthy, his spirit so broadly open, and so penetrating, his heart so upright, and even some flashes of his eloquence."—Foisset, Preface to the "Notes of a Course of Commercial Law," Ozanam's Complete Works, vol. viii.

By historical and economical considerations Ozanam put life into the teaching, which would seem so dry, of a code of laws, and his mode of teaching appears to have been very attractive. "It was wonderful," says his brother, "to see a young man of twenty-six years inspiring merchants, for the most part much older than himself, with the love and respect of their profession, and consequently the observance of the duties which it imposed, and obtaining their applause, notwithstanding the sometimes severe truths which he believed himself obliged to address to them."

To M. Lallier.

Lyons, February 15th, 1840.

My dear Friend,

What has become of you? And, in the first place, ought we not to salute you seriously with this title of Father, which was formerly bestowed upon you as a happy surname? Has God granted you the ineffable consolation of seeing your youth renewed in the features of childhood in the person of a son? Happy the first-born of an early marriage! He will enjoy his parents in their spring-time; he will not see them whiten until the time when he himself shall have ripened, and the adieu of the tomb will be for a nearer rendezvous. And you also, you will have the leisure to contemplate your accomplished work. After the education of youth, you will accompany your child to the laborious beginnings of manhood, and in the social career which he will enter before you have left it, he will find still recent and recognisable the trace which you have left. If the responsibility of paternal obligations frightens you, the moment is still far off when they will present any difficulty, and until then it is not a burden which God gives you; it is a little angel, whose presence sanctifies your house, renders virtue more amiable to you, and life happier.

For life, with its actual necessities, with its conventional proprieties, with the unholy friction of men and things, must often be burdensome to you; above all, your functions constantly bring before your eyes the least attractive side of humanity. You probably have united the odiousness of the criminal and the wearisomeness of the civil causes; and, if I mistake not, you alternate between the virtuous indignation of the public prosecutor and the incorruptible impartiality of the judge.

On the other side, we seek to keep up the sacred fire of Christian fraternity which you formerly lighted with us. The little Society of St. Vincent de Paul subsists and develops; the extraordinary wants of this winter have roused the activity of our alms. We make progress in the art of plundering the rich for the profit of the poor. Many among ours have offered their services for the patronage of young *libérés*, and the excellent la Perrière is occupied with founding a preventive patronage. But how little is all this, my friend, in presence of a population of sixty thousand workpeople, demoralized by want, and by the propagation of bad doctrines! Freemasonry and Republicanism take advantage of the troubles and the passions of this suffering multitude, and God knows what future awaits us if Catholic charity does not interpose to arrest the slave-war which is at our doors!

Unhappily, more than one void is made in our ranks: several departures, one death. This death, you know without doubt, and you are associated in our mourning: it is that of Alfred Ricussec. His talent, rapidly developed in the struggles of the Bar, promised him the honours of a great public speaker, at the same time that his fortune opened to him a probable access to high political functions. In the midst of such flattering hopes, and among the seductions of a world which always courts rising greatness, he had preserved his simplicity, his goodness a little too calm, his faith, and his habits of religious regularity. He belonged to us, by an assistance still frequent, by the generosity of his offerings, and by the frankness of his affections. A malady which seemed to disappear for a moment before striking the last blow came to snatch him from us in his bloom, and the tears which accompanied him to his last resting-place told sufficiently how we felt his loss. Pray for him!

While this poor friend took the road to eternity, another attached himself to the earth by casting in the gilded anchor of a good and rich marriage. You understand that I speak of Chaurand. God has recompensed him for many virtues by granting him at once all which makes happiness here below. This wedding, celebrated between two respectable and really Christian families, has been very touching. Nothing of the tumultuous joy of a worldly feast, but sweet feeling, and, as it were, a memory of Isaac and of Tobias, a picture of Cana. Myself, in the midst of my troubles, found myself so strongly impressed, that it became possible for me to translate into verse an idea which a long time ago came to me at the marriage of my friends, and which by turns I would fain have expressed for Dufieux, for Arthaud, and for you. It is a symbol common to all pious unions; it is your history as theirs, and this is why I cannot resist the desire to send you the piece here enclosed. And then, these verses are the last outcome of my defunct poetism, and I have for them something of the weakness which accompanies the fatherhood of old men. However incorrect the form may be, the thought pleases me; and, not wishing to profane it by a publicity, which, besides, it would not bear, I reserve it for communications of the closest friendship.

By the same post you will receive the opening discourse of my course. As you will see, it is less a work of art than a business. For the rest, the prospectus has not succeeded badly, to judge by the result. Now that the influx of amateurs and curious have retired, there is left to me a serious auditory of about a hundred and sixty persons, who completely fill the lecture-hall, and sufficiently crowd the lobbies to give a semblance of overflow.

You see me from below, arrayed in the ordinary costume of professors of law (so the Academy has desired), haranguing with a self-possession which astonishes me, and beginning to think I dream, when I remember that yesterday I was still upon the benches. I am endeavouring to put life into the teaching of the letter of the Codes, by their spirit, by historic and economic considerations. I encroach even upon social economy, your old domain. I endeavour to inspire my auditors with the love and respect of their profession, and consequently the observance of the duties which it imposes. I tell them severe truths, and their benevolence willingly gives me the right to do so. Many take notes; I have letters addressed to me; there is zeal and labour. Thus God, who "tempers the wind to the shorn sheep," seems to open a better perspective to my temporal future. Why is it that those whose solicitude prepared it can no more enjoy it?

Would it not be possible for you to find an evening of leisure, and to write me four or five of your good pages? You would do me in that a kindness so much the greater that the visits of friends are not too many now. While my little brother remains this year at school, only leaving it twice in ten months, my eldest brother, on the day I write to you, is, without doubt, at Naples. I begin to know the disorder which you have known so well, *ennui*. Ask for me from the Sovereign Guardian of souls that He would save me from the dangers of isolation—that he would give me light to know His designs upon me, energy to accomplish them. May His will be done on earth as in heaven; that is to say, with faith, with love!

Adieu, my dear friend. Count always on my lively and fraternal affection, and preserve me yours, in order that the hour in which we knew each other may not be an hour lost among those of our life, and that it may be reckoned in the number of those which will be remembered even unto death.

THE TWO GUARDIAN ANGELS.

It was a festal day, the heavens all bright with glory shone,
As kneeling veiled with ivory wings near the eternal throne
Two guardian Angels bended low before the God of grace,
Their voice the only voice whose sound spoke in that holy place.

"Thou knowest, Lord, this multitude of angel forms among
Who sing Thy praises in a hymn of sweet eternal song;
We by a special holy love were first together drawn;
And Thou didst mark with gracious smile in one harmonious tone
Our voices indivisible together sweetly thrown;

And the same ministries we shared where'er for thee we strove,
Living for long beneath thine eyes as brothers in our love.

"When in these later hours we both found ministry on earth ;
The gracious task was given to us, through sorrow and through mirth,
To guide among Thy chosen ones two souls whose separate way
Should in our happy hands unite on one auspicious day.

"Thou knowest, Lord, Thou knowest all the things that since befell,
How in our task we needs must part, who loved each other well.
For one in shelter of her home beside a maiden fair
Took up a place, and watched the flower with guardian earnest care ;
Far from the path where restless men pursue a heedless race,
She bloomed and gave her perfume sweet of virtue and of grace.

"A ruder task the other had committed to his hand,
He by a Christian stood amid an ardent studious band,
Where Reason, with a thoughtless hand, hath unaware let fall
In Learning's pure and generous cup a poison drop of gall:
Where often from the giddy round the thoughtless youth arise,
And find their homes again to draw hot tears from mother's eyes :
Him with grave thoughts he fenced around, and nourished in his heart
The faith which keeps the spirit pure, from error's winds apart.
Ardent, and still in virtue true, he carried home his soul,
A lamp whose steady light no wind of tempest could control.

"And now, Lord, if Thy hand once more, Thy kindly leading will,
Hath brought us both with ready feet to this same city back,
It is that Thou for us to-day shouldst in Thy love fulfil
Thy promise made so long ago—in one bright steady track,
Unite these paths that we so long in hope and faith have guarded,
And, our fond care and love at last with all success rewarded,
  Shouldst join that no man may divide
  These virtuous souls in one sweet band ;
  O'er them our brother wings spread wide,
  And each in clasp of other's hand

Shall strive new virtues to unfold,
Shall strew, with more than gems or gold,
The path they tread,—the poor shall bless
And still—of growing happiness
Their children, good as we, and fair
Among all men the seeds shall bear."
They ceased, and God pronounced the word,
" I bless you, well-beloved ; your prayer is heard !"*

To M. Henri Pessonneaux.

Lyons, April 13th, 1840.

My dear Friend,

Pardon me if thy last letter has remained three weeks without reply. In seeing thy brother again, in prolonging friendly conversations with him, I found myself in some sort in thy company. I forgot the weariness of separation, and the privations of absence. I felt no longer so much, as in the past, the need of the incomplete effusions which fatigue the pen without being able to suffice the overflow of the heart. And also the extreme goodness of my relations and friends, who have sought to enliven my solitude in inviting me to their family fêtes, has thrown a little disorder into the employ of my days. Repasts and soirées carry away many hours from work, and do not even permit the mind to recollect itself as seriously as its custom is, when one returns to the silence of the study. Although the circle of these pleasures, a little worldly, is limited for me to a small number of intimate friendships, the only ones which it would suit me to frequent: nevertheless I am not sorry to see it close up, and give place to the strict habits of Lent. My duties are better filled in this way, and better filled my leisures. To my distant

* This rough translation may, perhaps, be admitted, as, to use Ozanam's expression, it gives the idea, whatever the form may be.

comrades I shall devote a little of the time that I should lose with present friends. Writing is not a profane enjoyment; and our correspondence may refresh itself during the pious quarantine without infringing its claims.

And first, I am eager to satisfy a desire which I feel in a very lively manner, by telling thee how much I have found Mark like himself, that is to say, like thee—that is to say, still a serious Christian, an excellent friend, artist by his tastes, ripened nevertheless by trouble which has not cast him down. His conversation pleases me much; and I intend to have the pleasure of it often, and to tighten our bonds, at least if circumstances will allow it; thou canst not be ignorant that the future is for him filled with uncertainty; and we know not yet to which side this breath of God, which we call vocation, will impel him. If it fix him here, it would be, perhaps, one reason more to bring thee back here from time to time. In this we should find an account in a double manner. *We*, for I have the very pleasant habit of identifying myself with my friends, of making myself through them a second family, of surrounding myself with them to fill the voids which misfortune has made in my path. In proportion as the generation which preceded us, and which so to speak covered us, begins to fall, and leaves us face to face with the enemy, new men, we have need to draw our ranks together; seeing ourselves strongly supported by each other, we shall attack in front with more courage the obstacles and the perils of life. This is felt in so lively a manner, in the difficult days in which we are, that the ordinary engagements of marriage and of fatherhood are no longer sufficient for souls of a little generosity; and outside of the domestic sanctuary, where they gather together for enjoyment and prayer, they continue to seek in associations of another nature the strength to combat. Thus we see with pleasure Arthaud, Chaurand, and yet others, persevering in their old affections : they are not lost ; neither for us, nor for the poor, nor for the great work of the regeneration of French society.

As for me, I observe without any concealed thought, resolute as I am not to occupy myself with the question of *condition* before the end of the approaching vacation. I owe certainly to the memory of my poor mother a year of mourning.

* * * * *

At the same time I begin to prepare for the examination for the fellowship, of which the long and difficult subjects often discourage me. However it may be, I am very glad to be obliged to resume, once for all, my literary studies, and to gather into a complete framework knowledge hitherto gathered by chance in handfuls. It is for me a little the fable of the labourer and his children : if strength fails me, and I am not able to present myself at the competition, or if I fail completely there, at least the study will remain with me ; the treasure will not be found, but the field will be stirred up. It is trying that the time given is so short. If it were not for this, what pleasure to see, one after the other, all these fine and good geniuses from Homer and Plato, to Dante and Tasso, Calderon and Shakespeare, Racine and Schiller ! Unfortunately haste is required, and all these grand figures pass so rapidly before me that they have the effect of a round of phantoms, and it seems to me I hear, always applying it to these illustrious dead, the refrain of the German ballad, "The dead pass quickly! the dead pass quickly!"

The Abbé Maret's book reached me a few days ago; I have read it with a lively satisfaction. This work has the rare merit of treating a subject which is at the same time present and eternal, of seizing the ever-living point of religious polemics, that by which they interest contemporaneous minds, at the same time that it touches all the wanderings of humanity. Pantheism is the intellectual temptation of all ages, and of all civilizations; it is this which under idolatrous forms rallies in the East a hundred millions of Buddhists, resists for three centuries all the efforts of Christian proselytism, and bathes in their blood the missions of Tonquin and Cochin China, as it formerly stifled in the flames of an immense funeral pile the infant churches of Japan. It is this also which, taking the mask of philosophy, threatens Europe to bring her back, in the name of progress, to the doctrines of Alexandria or of Elea.

A learning which is never pedantic, a dialectic which is never insolent, a style gently animated, not at all pretentious, renders the work of M. Maret accessible and acceptable to all intelligent minds who have some thought of the grand problems on which depend the salvation of man and the future of nations. One might desire more energy and a little of that oratorical power which twenty years ago made the prodigious success of the *Essai sur l'Indifférence.* A thousand thanks on my part to the author, and protestation of my efforts to propagate his excellent writings.*

* *Essai sur le Panthéisme dans les Sociétés modernes.*

We have here Mgr. Dupuch, Bishop of Algiers; he will come this evening to an assembly of the Society of St. Vincent de Paul. Without doubt he will there speak to us some of those burning words of charity which can set on fire the souls even of unbelievers. Yesterday in a short audience with which he honoured us, la Perrière and me, he spoke to us much of Clavé, whom he infinitely loves. Give me news of this dear traveller, and let me know when I may offer him the bed and table of hospitality.

Adieu then, my good Henri; for a week I have been suffering a little. Do not be surprised then if more than one passage of this letter betrays the absence of common-sense. Nevertheless, I continue my course, which, to my great consolation, continues to bring together a very suitable auditory.

A thousand things to all ours; to thyself above all the inviolable affection of thy cousin.

TO M. LE COMTE DE MONTALEMBERT.

Lyons, August 27th, 1839, and May, 1840.

MONSIEUR LE COMTE,

My hasty departure from Paris has left me the regret of not being able according to my desire to see you again, and to express to you how deeply your welcome touched me. It is only given to our Divine cause thus to bring together the most unequal destinies, and to efface all the distance between them to form one only family, where faith and charity take place of rank. It is, above all, when the sweet surrounding which Nature had given us begins to fall, breach by breach, under the blows of death; it is then that we feel happy to be able to take refuge in this second enclosure which Christian friendship prepares for us. Thus I have never appreciated its consolations in a more lively manner than during this too short passage among our friends. I went out of it refreshed, strengthened, reanimated, comprehending better than before this word of the Saviour, which is sometimes accomplished by the ministry of His true disciples—*Ego reficiam vos*. According to the energy of this common expression, I believe myself truly re-made and freed for a long time from the hesitations of my character, and the discouraging influences of provincial life. . . . . I shall follow with my eyes the scientific movement of which the term, already near, should be the complete restoration of Catholicism in the convictions; whilst the moral tendencies, each day more powerful, would bring back its influence on the manners. Thus, when a pen which is known to us makes St. Bernard live again; when a loud voice recalls among us the days of St. Dominic, I shall be among the first to hear and to bless God for having reserved to our age, so often decried, so much honour and so much joy. For the rest, the reconciliation of the past and the future, the separation of the religious principle from amongst the political ideas with which it is involved, the work, in a word, to which you have consecrated such generous efforts, begins to be accomplished even in our city, where it might meet more than in any other part with an obstinate resistance.

I am happy to have this occasion to express to you my profound attachment for your person, and the hopes which my young Catholic friends place, as I do, in the elevation of a character crowned with such rare talents.

To M. Lallier.

Lyons, Tuesday, June 21st, 1840.

My dear Friend,

The good fêtes, at the same time that they make us think more seriously of God, make us also remember men more efficaciously. In approaching the holy altar, it is natural to put this privileged hour to profit for one's self, and those whom one loves. To the friend of whom we have made special memory in our morning prayers, we scarcely refrain from writing at night. Thus, although it be very late, I will not lie down without having written a few lines which will come to tell you that you are not forgotten, and which will ask from you as much in return. For this very happy interview of Sens and of Paris is already like a dream for me. Your delightful hospitality of twenty-four hours, of which I would willingly have made twenty-four days to your detriment—your kind visit come so suitably before my departure—all this, to my mind, is no more than a history already told. The time seems very long to me to know what has happened to you since the two months whence dates our last separation. Since, unhappily, Providence does not allow us to walk in the same road, at least, at the distance where we are, let us follow with the eye, and put ourselves in the same step. For me, I should fail in this duty if I did not communicate to you a happy event which will not be without influence on my social position, nor consequently without interest for your friendship. One moment! Think not that it is a question of marriage. In this respect, I enjoy still the most entire liberty, a liberty sometimes inconvenient in the sense that it is exposed to the matrimonial speculations of others, and that one finds one's self compromised without knowing it, by the most embarrassing advances. Such is not, then, the question. Nevertheless, one may say that it affects a point which is not foreign to it, and a subsidiary point, for it is a question of subsidy. The Chamber of Commerce at Lyons, on the request of M. le Recteur, has in effect voted me additional fees. I receive four thousand francs in all—salary of a Faculty Professor. This decision, interesting from the point of sight of the *pot au feu*, has also its price from the point of sight of public consideration, in a city where the merit of offices and of men is measured above all by pecuniary profit. The course of Commercial Law will in this find a sort of solemn sanction, not without need, in the midst of a desertion of auditors sufficiently considerable, which has afflicted me for some weeks, and which I have the modesty to attribute to the excessive heats, to the country, to journeys, etc.

Also, wishing to secure a double plank under my feet, and in addition to comply with the new instances of M. Cousin, from whom I have received a letter here, I continue to prepare myself for the literary competition, with the perspective of cumulating (does not the word already scandalize you?)—of cumulating, I say, two Chairs, if the chest and the head can support it. Grave personages urge me on, and I devour a notable quantity of Greek and Latin without prejudice to the habitual rations of Commercial Code and of

Commentators. This is enough to tell you how my hours are disputed, and what a risk I run of losing common-sense, if God comes not to my aid. At the same time, the *Propagation of the Faith* could not be neglected, and in the number for July you will find a long piece, often detestable in form, but important at bottom, which I felt called to make to establish as much as it was possible, after certain information, a *Statisque générale des Missions*. I point it out to you as document.

And, since we have returned to religious matters, you will know that Lyons is in all the odour of sanctity these days. We have made our processions, which have been magnificent, and, above all, very well received by the people. We shall re-commence this day week. In the interval, our new archbishop, M. de Bonald, will arrive. It is time, for I cannot tell with what impatience he is expected. They hope much from him for the new institutions, and we in particular for the Society of St. Vincent de Paul. Until then we continue our labours obscurely, through many obstacles. The propagation of good books among the soldiery, and the preventive patronage of the young apprentices, prosper well.

For the rest, with the exception of Rieussec and of Frenet, whom God has called to Himself, the nucleus of the Society is composed of those who are known to you. You have not ceased to be dear to them. I have had difficulty in satisfying the questions of la Perrière, of Arthaud, of Chaurand; all would willingly have been of the excursion. They amuse themselves greatly with your son; they represent him already clothed with paternal gravity. They compliment you on him by my mouth.

Kindly join my wishes for happiness to all those with which I am charged for you, and, excusing the brusqueness of the close which the already advanced hour of the night presses, present my respects to Madame Lallier, and receive once more the assurance of a friendship of which you do not doubt.

At this time M. Quinet was Professor of French Literature at the Faculty of Letters at Lyons. He was about to leave his Chair vacant, and Frederic thought he might possibly obtain it and unite it to his own of Law. The Rector of the Academy of Lyons was of this opinion. He had had frequent relations with Frederic in his endeavours after the Chair of Law, and had formed, as will be seen presently, a very high opinion of him. He was delighted with his success in his present course of lectures, and he lent all his influence to his nomination to the desired post. Frederic therefore left for Paris, and visited M. Cousin, then Minister of Public Instruction, who received him in a manner answering to his former intercourse with him. He made him breakfast at his table, conversed freely with him, and announced his intention to nominate him the following year. But M. Cousin made a condition which led to one of Ozanam's greatest successes, and proved the turning-point and settlement in his life. This was that he should come to Paris to compete in a literary tournament which was to be held some months later for the first time. The question was the gaining of a fellowship in the Sorbonne. "Not, indeed," added the Minister, "that you could hope to be named, for you have redoubtable competitors who have been preparing for more than a year, and you have only five or six months to put yourself into condition for it;" but he desired this first occasion to be a brilliant one, and to bring together men of incontestable talent for the contest.

This engagement entailed an immense amount of study on Frederic, for whom perhaps it would have been better if his successes had come more slowly. He made an immense effort, not so much to succeed, perhaps, in the main point, although that must have been in his mind, but to make a creditable appearance. He told his brother later on that he had taken literally M. Cousin's words, and thought that in no case had he any chance of being named; adding that he believed it had been fortunate for him. Convinced that he had nothing to risk, he had spoken more boldly, consequently with more originality, more especially so far as his religious opinions were concerned, in which he had rather pleased than given offence.

To M. Velay.

Lyons, 1840.

My dear Friend,

*   *   *   *   *

We are entering on a period of which no one can foresee the vicissitudes, but of which it is impossible not to perceive the coming. Nevertheless, it is of happy augury for it that it has commenced by a justice rendered to the past. Filial piety brings happiness. In re-attaching ourselves by the traditional bond to the eternal verities of religion, to the laborious conquests of human experience, we shall follow henceforward with less peril the progressive instinct which should enrich and not repudiate this glorious heritage. The sciences will advance with more rapid step when the ground of first principles is not disputed with them; and talent will no more be squandered by bringing into question, in the nineteenth century of our era, problems of which Christianity had given the definitive solution, after they had vainly exhausted all the forces of genius during four thousand years of ignorance and of doubt.

I have spoken of the *Univers*, and I should probably disappoint thy expectation if I told thee not, what more intimate relations have caused me to think of the worth and the destiny of this journal. All the editors are known to me, and they have introduced me during my journey into the situation and resources of their work—a work, and not an enterprise. For a long time the journal was only kept up by the sacrifices of a few generous men, who saw in it the only acceptable organ of our doctrines. Without contradiction, there is still much to desire, and a little to regret, in the foundation and in the form of this journal; but at least it seems to me to offer a general whole the most satisfactory possible for the actual condition of spirits.

The Society of St. Vincent de Paul has not been one of the least subjects of joy and of hope that I have found during my last stay at Paris. The time of one of its solemnities, the second Sunday of Easter, permitted me to see it reunited, and in all the extent of its rapid growth. I have seen gathered together in the amphitheatre of its sittings more than six hundred members, who did not form the whole of those belonging to it at Paris; the mass composed of poor students, but relieved in some sort by the accession of the highest social positions. I have elbowed there a peer of France, a deputy, a councillor of State, several generals, distinguished writers. I have reckoned there twenty-five pupils of the Normal School (of seventy-five that it contains), ten of the Polytechnic School, one or two of the School d'Etat Major. In the morning, more than a hundred and fifty associates approached together to the holy table, at the foot of the shrine of the holy patron. Letters were received from more than fifteen towns of France which have already flourishing conferences. A number nearly equal are organized this year. We are nearly two thousand young men engaged in this peaceful crusade of Catholic charity.

We must hope that the strength of association, so unhappily powerful to ruin the faith of our fathers, will know how to do something to raise it up amongst us and our children; and also, in this stormy age in which we are, it is pleasant to see formed, outside of all the political and philosophical systems, a compact group of men determined to use all their rights as citizens, all their influence as men of information, all their professional studies, to honour Catholicism in time of peace, and to defend it in case of strife.

Lastly, when the wave of pauperism finds itself furious and desperate in presence of a moneyed aristocracy whose hearts are hardened, it will be good to have mediators who may be able to prevent a collision of which the horrible disasters cannot be imagined; who may make themselves heard in both camps; who may carry to the one the words of resignation, to the other counsels of mercy; everywhere the word of order, *reconciliation and love.*

That is what we should do, if we were worthy of it. But how far we are from such a beautiful vocation! What cowardly habits to conquer; what narrow ideas to abdicate; what elevation and what purity of character to acquire, to merit to become the instruments of Providence in the execution of its most admirable designs!

But I forgot the news announced in the beginning of my letter, that which ought, nevertheless, to serve me for excuse to thee. Arrived in the capital—style of the provincial—I could not fail to pay my respects to my most honoured patron, M. the Minister of Public Instruction. I received from him the most affable and the most cordial welcome. After having made me breakfast at his Ministerial table, he was pleased to inform himself of my position and of my views; and he expressed to me his intention of allowing me to fill the place of Quinet the next year. But he has put this favour at a price of which he was naturally the master: he has asked that I should come to compete at Paris in the month of September for the Literary Fellowship, a new institution, to the success of which he holds with the affection of an author. He has caused his invitation to be repeated by several friends, then by the Rector, and lastly by a formal letter, in such a manner that it is impossible to withdraw myself from it. And yet the difficulty of the programme, bristling with the most thorny Greek texts, has already several times almost made me despair; and with the occupations which my course gives me, I' have infinite trouble to find the time rigorously indispensable for the most superficial preparation.

Thence, complete disarray in my correspondence, my relations, and even in my business; thence, again, no more hope of being able to realize the pretty journey projected for this autumn, and of which one of the most agreeable episodes would be to meet thee on the shore of the Lake of Geneva. Instead of departing joyously, staff in hand, knapsack on back, light of foot, head in the air, to pass swiftly along these pretty roads of Switzerland, through beautiful green valleys which crown at prodigious heights the tops of the glaciers; instead of going to salute Fribourg, Berne, Thun, Schwitz, Einsiedeln, Constance—of going to visit those marvels of new-born Catholic art which make the honour of Munich, and of descending again afterwards, by the picturesque passages of the Tyrol, to Venice, to Padua, to Verona, to Milan; of realizing at last this fairy pilgrimage dreamed of for six months—there must be an excursion of another nature, through the asperities of Greek literature, among the innumerable creations of Latin, French, foreign letters—an intellectual journey, which would not be without charm if it could be made at leisure, halting at the finest points of view, pausing at the flowering bushes on the route long enough to detach the fresh bud without tearing it from the thorns. But no; one must pass as one goes by all these admirable things; one must gather with a hasty hand, and at the risk of blighting and injuring them, so many poetic beauties; one must make, instead of a crown, a heavy packet, and after must submit them to the profane elaborations of literary chemistry; infuse them, analyze them, pulverize them to the taste of a pedantic criticism; swallow down as a draught the greatest possible quantity of memories, and arrive all saturated with Greek, Latin, German, before the learned University, with a view there to make proof of a knowledge almost universal.

If to these urgent and precipitate studies thou wilt join the preparations of my lessons in Commercial Law; if thou wilt also add the small but numerous exigences of business and of social life, from which nevertheless I am constrained to escape as much as it is possible— thou wilt nearly comprehend, my dear friend, the discomfort, and, if I may say it, the distress of the time in which I find myself.

It needs nothing less than this to call for thy indulgence, not alone for the long delay, but also for the incredible disorder of this letter, written in part during the ordinary time of sleep. I see that I omitted to tell thee that my brother has returned from Rome, bringing me, with a budget of interesting news, a letter from the Abbé Lacordaire. . . . .

That which you tell me of the Franche-Comtoises does not astonish me. The inhabitants of this province were always recommended by their morality and their religion. As for instruction, it would be difficult not to find as much as here.

If the thought of absent friends who keep faith with thee; if the union of heart with those who, drawn together by age, the past, sentiments, beliefs, are far from thee only by the distance of leagues; if these sweet images of a fraternal and Christian affection can sometimes animate and distract thy isolation, deliver thyself without hesitation to these good thoughts—they will not be illusions; for it is indeed true that in our memories, in our conversations, we are often with thee: we ask of thee the same place in thy memory and also in thy prayers.

Meanwhile, while he, in the midst of polyglots and loneliness, was straining himself, another matter was being settled for him in a manner as unexpected as this one. His friends in the time of his solitude rallied round him, and urged him to marry. We have seen occasionally in his letters his ideas and feelings on this point. Nevertheless, he could not entirely prevent his thoughts from answering to his friends' suggestions; and his brother says he sought to prepare himself in case "Providence called him to marriage," and that it was in great part with that idea that he had asked for M. Quinet's Chair. His attempts in this direction had rendered his relations with M. Soulacroix, the Rector of the Academy, more frequent than before. M. Soulacroix had a daughter seven years younger than Frederic—lovely and accomplished, fitted, as it afterwards proved, to make his ideal of a wife a reality. How much or how little Frederic knew of her does not appear, for at this point the Abbé Noirot, who had proved himself so good a friend before, intervened, and, on his own responsibility, proceeded to speak to M. Soulacroix and to suggest a possible marriage between his daughter and Frederic Ozanam. This overture was so well received that the Abbé next proceeded to speak to Frederic himself, who it is said, "was altogether astonished at this overture, which he was far from expecting." "However," proceeds his brother, "believing he saw a mark of the Will of God in this manifestation, which he had not provoked in any manner, he went from that time occasionally to see M. Soulacroix, under divers pretexts, in the hope of having at least a glimpse of her who had been proposed to him as perhaps one day to partake his destiny. By the continued benevolent intervention of his friend, matters were at length satisfactorily arranged. For a man of Frederic's temperament—self-distrustful, nervous, and undecided—this mode of "arranging" a marriage was probably an excellent one; anyhow, it had the happiest results. Meanwhile, however, by day and by night for months, he laboured in preparation for the concourse and when, at length, his brother accompanied him to the conveyance which was to take him to Paris, he was in such a state of excessive agitation from labour and watching, and a conviction that he should not succeed that he might be said to be almost in a fever. However, the excitement of the contest soon began; and while this would rouse and keep up his spirits, the triumphant close served to calm him. The account is given in his own letters. The immediate result was that M. Fauriel, Professor of Foreign Literature at the Sorbonne, asked, and obtained that Frederic should supply in his Chair from the opening of the course, on account of his age and infirmities. The journey which he thereupon felt it his duty to take is described in his letters; and it also would help very much in restoring the needed tone, mental and physical, although, for various reasons, he did not regard it exactly as an excursion of pleasure.

TO M. LALLIER.

Paris, Saturday morning, October 30th, 1840.

MY DEAR FRIEND,

I would not leave you to learn by the newspaper the good success which has just come to me. After the long tests in which your friendship has been interested for me, I have been named the first in the competition. In consequence, I am offered immediate entry to the Sorbonne, with supply for M. Fauriel.

These events, which have overpassed all my hopes, still embarrass me a little, for I am in the alternative, either of neglecting a future providentially opened, or of breaking with habits and affections very deep founded. I pray God that He will enlighten me. Join yourself to me, and be sure that, on my side, in communicating to-morrow, I will not forget in my feeble prayers to fulfil your friendly intentions.

I use so much in regard to you of friendly want of ceremony as to tell you that, on Tuesday in next week (*l'autre semaine*), I shall again profit twenty-four hours by your hospitality, to talk heart to heart as I have need. Then, better than at present, I shall be able to tell you how I have been touched by the solicitude you have showed towards me; and in thinking of our friends, of our common hopes, and of our duties, we will gather up a little courage for the arduous matters which the present situation of the country and of the Church imposes upon the weakest of their children.

It will be interesting for the reader to find here an extract of the report addressed to the Minister of Public Instruction by M. Victor le Clerc, Dean of the Faculty of Letters, and president of the competition for the fellowship:

"October 3rd, 1840.

"MONSIEUR LE MINISTRE,

* * * * * *

"Three competitors have appeared to take from the first, in these various tests, a superiority which has been sometimes keenly disputed, but which they have, nevertheless, almost always preserved.

"M. Ozanam, already known, as his two rivals whose names follow, by the most honourable proofs before our Faculty, has seemed to the judges to merit the first rank, less by his classical knowledge—very extensive no doubt, but equal, perhaps, among the others—than by his large and firm manner of conceiving an author or a subject, by the breadth of his comments and his surveys, by his bold and just views, and by a language which, joining originality to reason, and imagination to gravity, appears to be eminently suitable for public teaching. Alone of the candidates, he has made proof a grammatical and literary study of the four foreign languages indicated in the programme—Italian, Spanish, German and English.

"M. Egger—whom a prize gained at the Academy of Inscriptions and of Belles-Lettres, and distinguished services in the Colleges of Paris, had pointed out more clearly to our attention—is, before all, a very learned and a very clever philologist; but the rapidity of his thought, the vivacity of his speech, and the immense advantage which he has obtained in French composition, which has made a part of this contest, prove that he is called to join to the merit of great knowledge the talent of being listened to.

"M. Berger, a mind more calm and dispassionate, as incapable of committing a fault in taste as of being deceived in the interpretation of a difficult text, carries to a singular degree purity and precision of language. It is impossible to apply to letters, with more art and elegance, the rigour of philosophic studies.

"It is thus that the contest which has begun under your auspices a new era for the Faculties, will not, perhaps, be surpassed for long."

*   *   *   *   *

TO M. LALLIER.

Paris, October 10th, 1840.

MY DEAR FRIEND,

I am obliged to refuse myself a pleasure, which would have been as grateful as it was desired—that of seeing you on my journey. Charged to supply for M. Fauriel, and to make a course of German literature in the middle age, to begin by the *Nibelungen* and the *Livre des Héros,* I have thought it necessary, for the wants of my imagination and for the satisfaction of my conscience, to see at least in a hasty visit the shores of the Rhine, theatre of all this poetry, barbaric, Germanic, Frank, to the study of which I must devote myself.

I shall return to Lyons by Strasbourg; and after five weeks of business and of work, I shall return to Paris to settle there, and to become your neighbour. In the earlier days of December I will stop at your house in passing; then I shall be able to tell you better than in this hasty moment how good and useful your little letter has been to me; how your friendly suffrage has strengthened my resolutions, which the advice of my family afterwards ratified.

This is an event very grave and solemn for me: the entrance on a new and perilous career; a life to begin anew, a vocation at length! Although I may not have to make a sacrifice of the nature which you seem to suspect, there are, however, others. There are sorrowful separations, and even difficulties of business and of interests; there are dangers of all sorts which await me on my installation; in a word, there is more than needs to be to alarm a mind of mediocre energy. Happy if this feeling of weakness causes the eyes to be raised to Him who gives strength. Until now I have asked of Him light to know His will; now that He seems to have manifested it to me by signs reasonably to be known, it remains to grant me the courage to accomplish it. . . .

To M. LALLIER.
Mayence, Tuesday, October 14th, 1840.

MY DEAR FRIEND,

The journey which I am making is not for the sake of pleasure, not even for health; it is a case of literary conscience. But after having made the effort which duty exacted, of throwing myself into a carriage for Brussels, nature took the upper hand, and during more than twenty-four hours I gave myself up to an access of black melancholy in thinking of the two great enjoyments which I sacrificed, that of seeing my brothers a week sooner, and that of passing a day with you. The heart, without doubt, entered greatly into this; but perhaps also there entered a little of that loquacious instinct with which I am endowed, and which in my moments of charity towards myself I call "a need of opening my heart." Whatever it may be, I promised myself then to replace my day at Sens by a long letter, and thus to fill up one of those long evenings to which the season, already too advanced, subjects travellers. My overweening has reached even to thinking that you would bear me no malice for my indiscretion; that you would receive willingly the first-fruits of the impressions of a novice-tourist on the borders of the Rhine, and that perhaps also your friendship would be a little impatient to have the news of the competition, of which the results still seem to me like a dream.

The sixth day has hardly passed over since my departure, and here I am already more than half-way. This kind of excursion on birds' wing has its inconveniences, without doubt, but perhaps also its advantages. If one perceives no detail, one is more struck in the mass; if one sees less near, one sees higher; the instruction is less real, the impression stronger; and, provided that one does not afterwards make a book of his impressions . . . . the thing has its value, and one obtains to some degree that renewal of the imagination and of the memory, that refreshment of the spirit, that fertility of the soul, which is always produced by the first view of a new world.

Thus nothing has seemed to me more curious, more interesting, than the little kingdom of Belgium, passed through first on my route. In four days it is traversed in every sense, with all the time necessary to visit reasonably Brussels, Antwerp, Ostend, Ghent, and Liége. I felt as if transported into the Empire of Lilliput. And then this miniature of a nation is itself but the reduced portrait of three other nations: a triple copy of France, of England, and of Germany. Imitation everywhere; in the manners, in the costume, in the architecture, even in the language. The people speak Walloon and Flemish; that is to say, a patois of Romanic origin, and another of Germanic origin, but both detestable. The official French of the Government and of the journals is worth little more. The productions of literary growth are distinguished by a taste of the soil. In everything reigns a certain awkwardness, which always accompanies imitation when it is not sure of itself. One trembles at every moment lest this poor *Lion Belge* should show the tip of his ear.

However, after a first good-humoured sally, very pardonable in the presence of so many pretentious and amusing contrasts, we must make room for more serious reflections. And, first, take heed that the shortness of distances, the drawing together of the frontiers, about which we jested a moment ago, was only an admirable illusion, a miracle of labour. If the kingdom is traversed in a half day, it is that in a half-day the car which the steam carries measures fifty leagues. Iron and fire trace on this fertile soil a perpetual furrow. Commerce by the rapidity of transport attains a prosperity of which we have not even an idea—we, artless admirers of the railroad from Paris to Versailles. Friday, in three-quarters of an hour, I found myself transported from Brussels to Louvain. There, in a long conversation with M. Mœlher, Professor at the Catholic University, after a detailed visit to this beautiful establishment, I began to understand what there was of excellence in the Belgic institutions and character.

* * * * *

When I shall have seen Mayence,—where I arrive this evening,—Frankfort and Worms, the Germany of the middle age will have passed under my eyes. For . . . it was at Cologne and at Aix-la-Chapelle that the emperors were crowned and deposed, that the Diets were held, that the Crusades were organized. The names of Charlemagne, of Otho, of Henry, of Frederic, reappear everywhere where an historic stone is set up; and there is not a stone, not a rock, which has not its history, its tradition, or its fable.

To-day finishes for me that which is called "the tour along the Rhine;" for the picturesque or memorable sites are nearly all enclosed in the space which I have run through in two days, and never more grand images were enclosed in a richer frame. My thought, which had often visited this part, had never conceived anything approaching to the truth. A nature altogether different from France, Switzerland, or Italy; a sky where the October clouds yet suffered the rays of the sun to play, and to produce at each instant new effects of light; the stream broad, deep, clear, and yet of a beautiful sea-green. On the borders mountains, which did not form a continuous wall, but which seemed almost all to come from farther inwards, and to form themselves as the efflorescence of innumerable little chains, sometimes leaving between them magnificent openings of view over the neighbouring landscapes. Everywhere odd stratifications, colonnades of basalt, continual traces of volcanic convulsions. This bony framework covered with a mantle of verdure, in which all shades of colour are mingled, from the fresh turf to the dead leaves which are already swept by autumn. Woods of oak at every moment. A colouring oftenest sombre, but sometimes lively; deceitful perspectives; waters with the play of different colours upon them, something of a fascination which pleases and troubles you, and which seems to play with you.

   *   *   *   *   *

Our rapid course hardly permitted us to salute these interesting apparitions of the past; nevertheless, I have promised them not to forget them. These memories will go to join others which were not less precious to me, and which already begin to pass away. This is for me one of the troubles of a journey. There is not a corner on my route from Florence to Fribourg, and from Brussels here, where my affections were not for a moment caught hold of; not an adieu which has not cost me something. I would, at least, have desired to carry away by the thought that which the looks have left; but my memory holds not the figure of places. The shadow of them floats there for some time, and often finishes by disappearing. But at least, for these scenes of the material world, there remains the power, and consequently the hope, of renewing their image in going to seek them, where we know them to be. Why is it that it should not be the same for other memories otherwise dear; that it is no more possible to return on our steps along the roads of life, and to find again those whom we have left there?

Such are, my dear friend, the meditations of this solitary, and by consequence pensive, journey. It is the first time that I have left France without my brother, having, besides, no companions on the road, surrounded by foreign conversation, in English, or in German dialects more or less corrupted, consequently placed in the most favourable circumstance to attain my end— that is, to gather up in one week the largest number of impressions possible. There is no harm in this extreme urgency which presses me on. Forced activity is a good hygiene for idle spirits; there is inspiration in constraint. May it be thus!

But at other moments, my excursion seems to me a folly—the rashness of a journalist who goes away to *discover* Germany; or rather a paltry satisfaction given to my scruples, a kind of subterfuge, to say to my auditors this winter: " Gentlemen, I have seen this!" In the same way as, when I was little, I dipped the ends of my fingers in water, in order to be able to answer mamma without an untruth—" I am washed." Lastly, and to return to great comparisons, it seems to me that I do a little as Caligula, who went as far as the Rhine, gathered pebbles, and came to Rome to receive with the honours of a triumph the name of Germanic!

Apropos of a triumph, I must really tell you something of the one which they say I obtained, now about three weeks ago, and which seems to me still a dream.— I arrived sincerely much frightened, convinced that my candidature, in losing for me the little consideration which I might have enjoyed in the mind of the professors, would play me a bad turn. At last, the day came. We were gathered seven in a hall of the Sorbonne, and there, under key, we had before us eight hours for a Latin dissertation on *" The Causes which arrested the Development of Tragedy among the Romans."*

I found I knew the question, but, not at all accustomed to compose quickly, I was hard up when the fatal hour struck, and I was obliged to give in a fragment of a rough copy, badly written out. The same adventure the third day for the French dissertation on *"The Historic Value of the Funeral Orations of Bossuet."* The auspices were not favourable, and without some encouraging indiscretions of one of the judges who gave me to understand that my compositions had succeeded, I should have retired from the competition.

There came afterwards three distinct argumentations for different days, and about three hours each, on Greek, Latin and French texts, given twenty-four hours in advance. In Greek, I had to explain a chorus of the *Helen* of Euripides, a fragment of the *Rhetoric* of Halicarnassus; little of philology, as you will think, and many phrases—Helen considered as poetic character and religious myth; history of the art of oratory at Athens and at Rome. In Latin, a fragment of Lucan, and a theological chapter of Pliny; discussion on the rôle of César and on the revolutions of religious doctrines among the Romans. In French, *Philemon and Baucis* of la Fontaine, and the Dialogue of Sylla and Eucrate by Montesquieu. Here, some conjectures a little bold on the causes of Sylla's abdication, and a comparison more rash still of Montesquieu, as publicist, with St. Thomas of Aquin. This rather lively sally of Catholicism, as well as two or three others which I allowed myself on the occasion, displeased neither the auditory nor the jury; and some reminiscences of Roman law, come apropos to interpret two or three passages difficult to be understood without them, were not less favourably received. At the close of this test came the interrogation on the four foreign literatures. There, I stumbled in Dante, of whom I believed myself sure.* The Spanish, of which I had taken ten lessons, succeeded marvellously. I extricated myself from Shakespeare; and as I had the happiness to fall on one of the finest and most pious passages of Klopstock, the emotion with which I translated it had an excellent effect.

There remained two lessons on subjects different for each competitor, and chosen by lot, one twenty-four hours, the other one hour, in advance. The subject of ancient literature was for me: the history of *the Scoliasts, Greek and Latin*. This seemed an irony of fate; and they knew so well that I was not at all up in this philologic specialty, that the reading of the billet was received by a general malicious laugh, and perhaps a little revenge, by the numerous members of the University who composed the public. I believed myself lost, and, notwithstanding one of my rivals, M. Egger, with much generosity had passed me some excellent books, yet, after a night of watching and a day of alarm, I arrived, more dead than alive, at the moment of speaking. The despair of myself caused me to make an act of hope in God, such as I had never before made so earnestly, and never, either, had I found myself better. In brief, your friend spoke on the Scoliasts for seven quarters of an hour, with an assurance, a liberty, that astonished himself. He was able to interest, even to move, to captivate, not alone the judges, but the auditory, and he retired with all the honours of war, having put the laughers on his side.

* Perhaps this should rather be "flung myself into Dante, because I was sure of him;" "*bronché pour Dante*" is the expression.

Finally, the last sitting was easier. I had to speak of the literary criticism of the age of Louis XIV. I took then my ease, and gave myself scope on the subject of the fatal influence exercised by the Jansenist school on French poetry, and found means to signalize the success rendered to the language by St. Francis de Sales. I feared I had broken my windows, but all was taken in good part. The definitive scrutiny, made after the average of ranks obtained in the different tests, made me come out the first; and, to my extreme astonishment, in this result it was not necessary to take account of the foreign literatures.

* * * * *

If, then, all this is not a dream, or an impertinent play of chance, one can only justify it in one manner. God gave me grace to bring into this struggle a faith which, even when it does not endeavour to produce itself outwardly, animates the thought, keeps up harmony in the intelligence, heat and life in the discourse. Thus I may say, "*In hoc vici;*" and this idea, which perhaps at first seems proud, is nevertheless that which humbles me, and at the same time reassures me.

A success so marvellously providential confounds me. I seem to see in it that which yourself have seen in it: an indication of a design of God upon me; a veritable vocation—that which my prayers have sought for so many years. My eldest brother is of this advice, and I am treading, with a step still very trembling, but nevertheless calmer, in the new career open before me by this singular event.

There is a limit to all, even to your patience. I finish, then, in pointing out to your friendly gratitude the constant kindness which my judges have shown to me, and, above all, MM. le Clerc, Fauriel, and Ampère: you understand how the presence of this last has been a service to me.

I shall not post this till Strasbourg. Reply to me, if you are not weary with my indiscretion, and allow me to embrace you as your devoted friend.

CHAPTER XII.

RETURN HOME—ENTRANCE ON HIS DUTIES AT THE SORBONNE—MARRIAGE.

AFTER this enforced absence, Ozanam returned to his congratulating friends. Nevertheless, his triumph and happiness were not unmixed. Lyons was his home, had been his home ever since he could remember; his friends —many of them—lived here; here his parents had lived and died; it was breaking many ties of affection, as well as deranging his own plans, to leave Lyons and go to Paris, though it might be to profess at the Sorbonne. Moreover, whatever the value and prestige of a Professorship at the Sorbonne, there were things to be said in comparison of it and his present engagement, to the preference of the latter—it was provisional; being only a supply for another, it might be altered at any time. At Lyons the two chairs would be his own.

His lifelong friend, M. Ampère, who had been one of the judges at the competition, combated his doubts determinedly, telling him that his place was at Paris, and that a brilliant and useful future awaited him there. M. Soulacroix, proud of the successes of his future son-in-law, approved his decision entirely, and placed no obstacle in the way of his speedy marriage with his daughter. The elder brother, in place "of a father and mother whom we still mourned, and who would greatly have approved of this happy alliance," went solemnly to present the younger to his future father-in-law, and Frederic found himself warmly welcomed into a second family circle. The father took them in to his wife and daughter, and after some conversation and mutual congratulations, he took Frederic's hand, and joined it with his daughter's in his own, thus consecrating "the knot which a little later would be tightened for ever."

To M. Lallier.

Lyons, December 6th, 1840.

My dear Friend,

After six weeks of vacation, passed in the midst of great events, it is needful to return to Paris, there to begin my part on the dangerous theatre of the Sorbonne. But I cannot decide to enter on this new and unforeseen phase of my destinies without opening my heart, enlightening and strengthening myself by some talks with the best friend I have in this world. So I propose to myself, in leaving Monday (14th), to stop at Sens Wednesday (16th), and to pass the day with you if you will allow me; this will be a happy indemnification for the privation suffered in the month of October.

How many things to tell you, and how this cruel question of vocation, so long uncertain, is all at once decided! At the same time that Providence calls me back to the slippery ground of the capital, it seems to be willing to give me there an angel guardian to console my solitude; I go away, leaving an alliance concluded which will be solemnized at my return.

I should have had recourse to your counsels if events had not been precipitated with an imperious rapidity. I have recourse now to your prayers. May God preserve to me, during this exile of six months, her whom He seems to have chosen for me, and whose smile is the first ray of happiness which has shone upon my life since the loss of my poor father!

You will find me very tenderly enamoured; but I do not try to hide it, although I cannot sometimes hinder myself from laughing at it. I had believed my heart more bronzed.

You will see me happy: this will compensate for the share you have so often had in my grief.

Adieu, my excellent friend. I feel truly that new affections will never dislodge any of those which were already in the heart, and that it will enlarge that it may lose nothing.

The Abbé Ozanam, looking back forty years on the marriage of his younger brother, recurs with the utmost tenderness to the various details of its arrangements, and even lingers on the softness and gentleness of the name of the bride—Amélie—and its suitability to her who bore it, "who was to make the happiness" of his brother. "A name," he says, "so much the more harmonious to our ears that it was also that of one of our aunts, become in some sort for us a second mother since we had been orphans."

For the few days which remained to Ozanam before his return to Paris, he consoled himself by constant visits to his affianced bride. He did not understand music, but he loved it; and was greatly influenced by it. Amélie Soulacroix was a clever and sweet musician. From her evening witcheries he went out with his whole soul refreshed and inundated with delight. In the beautiful words of Scripture, like Isaac, he "was comforted after his mother's death." In the strength of this refreshment he went alone to Paris. Between the lovers was established a most constant correspondence, in which Frederic laid his muse under contribution "the better to render the hymns which his heart chanted." The letters, however, were far from being sufficient; "for," says the elder brother, "it would be difficult to tell the numerous messages which were then confided to us by the future bride and bridegroom. We delivered ourselves of them," he adds, "so much the more willingly, that besides the happiness which we procured to our two *fiancés*, we had the pleasure of finding again a sister worthy of consoling us to a certain point for her whom we had lost."

This must have been Eliza, who died when Frederic was a mere child, and of whom he says that God "gave him for his first instructress a sister pious and intelligent as the angels whom she went to rejoin;" and whom the Abbé Ozanam thus tenderly recalls to memory. After three months at the Sorbonne, Frederic returned to Lyons for a brief vacation, was compelled to return after a week or two, and comforted and diverted himself in the midst of more serious employment by joining to the preparation of his lessons the interesting of himself in the wedding preparations.

None of the letters of this period are published. But at the end of six months Ozanam thus announces his marriage to the friend to whom so many of his most intimate letters are written, also to M. Ampère and M. de Montalembert.

To M. Lallier.

Château du Vernay, near Lyons,
June 28th, 1841.

My dear Friend,

The great things in which your affection was interested are accomplished. Wednesday last, 23rd June, at ten o'clock in the morning, in the church of St. Nizier, your friend was on his knees. At the altar was his eldest brother, raising his priestly hands, and at the foot his young brother answered to the liturgical prayers. Beside him you would have seen a young girl, white and veiled, pious as an angel, and already—she allows me to say it—tender and affectionate as a friend. Happier than I, her parents surrounded her, and nevertheless, all that heaven has left me of family here had given me the rendezvous; and my old comrades, my brothers of St. Vincent de Paul, and numerous acquaintances filled the choir and peopled the nave. It was beautiful, and strangers whom chance had brought there were deeply moved. As for me, I knew no more where I was. I hardly kept back great but delicious tears, and I felt the divine benediction descend upon me with the consecrated words.

Ah! my dear Lallier, you, the companion of laborious times; you, the consoler of evil days, why were you not there? I would have begged you, you also, like the good Pessonneaux, to give your signature to the act commemorative of this great occasion; you also, I would have presented to the charming bride who was given to me; you also, she would have saluted with the gracious smile which delighted all the world. And afterwards, for five days that we have been together, what calm, what serenity in this soul, that you have known so unquiet, and so ingenious in inflicting suffering on itself!

I allow myself to be happy. I count no more the moments nor the hours. The course of time is no longer for me; what matters the future to me? The happiness of the present, that is eternity—I comprehend heaven.

Help me to be good and grateful. Each day, in discovering to me new merits in her whom I possess, augments my debt towards Providence. What a difference between those days when you saw me so sad at Paris!

I have been half pardoned for having shown you there a certain letter; I shall be altogether pardoned when the pleasure of your acquaintance is realized. You are invited to make yourself at home with us in the month of November.

Adieu. My respects to Madame Lallier; to you a fraternal embrace.

To M. Ampère.

Château du Vernay, near Lyons,
June 29th, 1841.

SIR AND DEAR FRIEND,

Permit me to give you the title of affectionate familiarity that you have taken so many times in sharing my joys and my sorrows. For long a sort of respectful reticence has made me hesitate, but to-day I must take all the liberties which the heart loves; and in my pleasant pride of a bridegroom, I feel myself bolder. It is, then, with a freedom quite brotherly that I come to share my happiness with you. It is very great, it passes all hopes and all dreams; and since Wednesday last, the day on which the benediction of God descended on my head, I have been in a calm, serene, delicious enchantment, of which nothing had given me the idea. The angel who has come to me with so many graces and virtues, is as a new revelation of Providence in my obscure and laborious destiny. I am all lighted up with inward pleasure.

But this light which fills my soul cannot leave in the shade the memories of the past, and above all those which accompany gratitude. Your thought has had its place in the midst of the friends present, whose number pressed to the foot of the altar. And afterwards in the charming conversations in which my new family likes to make me talk of past years, at every moment your name, and that of your venerated father, comes up to be received with the sincerest gratitude. Incapable of ever showing it as I would have wished, I feel, allow me to say so, almost acquitted to you when I hear your praise on those lips so dear, of which a single word thrills me.

I am charged to tell you that to know you in Paris will give great pleasure; and that, even at this time, when the presence of a third party is generally undesired, it would please us if the pilgrimage to Greece should have a station near to us.

Adieu, sir and dear friend; allow me to embrace you with all the overflowing of the day of my departure, and believe in the tender devotedness of all my life. This will be in part your work, and if my actual position is a hope of more in the happy future, you know what part you have taken in it.

To M. DE MONTALEMBERT.

Lyons, July 25th, 1841.

MONSIEUR LE COMTE,

*   *   *   *   *

After having discharged those duties which devolved on me as Secretary, allow me yet a few words in my own name. A design, with which your sympathies were connected, has been accomplished in my behalf. The alliance, already concluded last winter, has been solemnized a few days ago. God, who took from me my poor mother, has been pleased no longer to leave me without an angel guardian. My happiness is great, and whilst I enjoy it in its first sweetness, I remember that you told me of it beforehand. I remember that in leaving you at our last interview, you pressed my hand with kindness, and you told me that intense joys crowned Christian unions here below.

Henceforth in your remembrance, before God, I lay claim to the place you there promised me as Christian husband. St. Elizabeth* has revealed to us the pure joys of conjugal piety; the friendship of her historian may help us to reproduce them.

The happiness which attended his marriage, and the peace of mind which he felt after years of perturbation, had a very favourable effect on his health; but as he was threatened with a weakness of the throat which might affect his ability to take up his duties as Professor, he was advised to try the waters of Allevard, a beautifully situated little village, surrounded

---

* Elizabeth of Hungary.

by pleasant excursions, among which was one to the castle where was born, in 1476, the Chevalier Bayard. Here he was joined by his elder brother, also on account of his throat, and his younger brother, whose vacation it was. Later on, partly for the final cure of his throat, more to instruct himself for his future duties, Frederic and his wife visited Italy. There are no letters published of the former journey; of the latter they will suffice for an account. At Marseilles he made the acquaintance of the relations of his wife's family who resided there. On the 23rd of September they reached Naples.

The following letter to his brothers may close this series.

TO M. L'ABBÉ AND M. CHARLES OZANAM.
Naples, October 3rd, 1841.

MY DEAR BROTHERS,
Here are ten days passed away since our arrival at Naples. To-morrow the steam-boat carries us to Palermo. The short space of time for visiting so many marvels will explain, will justify perhaps, our silence. After having passed the entire day in going over these beautiful places, in interrogating their memories, we return in the evening enchanted, but dead of hunger and fatigue. We dine in haste, and hardly does there rest the time to put in order a few notes, to arrange the plan of the next day's excursion, to regulate the accounts. Eleven o'clock strikes often before we are ready to take a little sleep. At the moment even of taking the pen to-day, I am assailed by such violent temptations to sleep, that I know not whether I speak or dream, and I

shall not be astonished if I write to you in the most fantastic style in the world.

And what more fantastic, indeed, than this long panorama whose scenes succeed each other before us, stirring with them so many thoughts and memories? In the first place the natural world is most beautiful, and surpasses all the conjectures of imagination. The Gulf of Naples, and the two others of Gaeta and of Salerno, all three so well defined, all three displaying majestically the harmonious shapes and roundings of their shores, of their promontories, and of their islands. Everywhere a luxuriant, tropical vegetation ; the green trees and the luxuriant plantations mingling themselves with the thick shadows and the fresh culture of the northern countries. The vines hanging in innumerable festoons from the poplars to give place below to more modest harvests of millet and maize. Woods of orange-trees, with bushes of myrtles and aloes. Then a sky so pure, a light so transparent, that the forms of objects stand out with a perfect clearness, and seem nearer to the deceived eye. On this ever-blue vault a single white cloud floats from the southern side. It is the smoke of Vesuvius, whose imposing mass occupies the first level, whilst far as the eye can reach the horizon is formed by the proud chain of the Apennines.

On this scene so richly adorned, appear in turns the successive civilizations which animated it, beautified it, and sometimes also desolated it. There on the confines of Calabria is the ancient Pestum. Its temples, which we are never weary of seeing, announce by their gigantic proportions, by the grandiose simplicity of their architecture without ornament, the earliest epoch of the Greek colonies. There is still the rudeness of the Etruscans, and there is already the severe art of the Dorians. Above all, there is the work of a people still penetrated with religious sentiment, corrupted as it is, and who do more for their gods than for their magistrates or their actors. Later this will not be the same; and here is Pompeii, where the temples, reduced to the most niggardly dimensions, are effaced before the grandeur and the opulence of particular habitations. This prodigious quantity of marbles, of mosaics, of paintings; this infinite variety of instruments, of utensils, of furniture, of carved ornaments, sculptured with the most extreme delicacy—all this shows at the same time the refinement of an advanced art, and of an insatiable egotism of enjoyments.

The theatre of Herculaneum, so marvellously preserved in its sepulchre of lava, has interested me extremely, by making me comprehend that which I had never properly figured to myself, the arrangement of the ancient tragedies. The beauty of this edifice, and of the amphitheatre of Puteoli, the immense ruins of villas, hot baths, ponds, aqueducts, on the coast of Baiæ, show well the dominant character of the Roman architecture, which was never great except for places of pleasure or works of material utility. The one and the other are found united in the highest degree in the palace of Tiberius at Capri, whence the eye of the tyrant might glance at the same time over the most delicious landscapes in the world, and over all the attempts of his enemies. But these vast constructions, of which so many remains still subsist, and whose stones borne away have sufficed to build the great Church of the Gesù, by what mechanical means have they been able to raise them to this almost inaccessible height? Or rather how many thousands of slaves have toiled and suffered to make this asylum for imperial wickedness? Such was the human destiny at that moment when Redemption was preparing. And indeed, yet a few years, and the Apostle will touch at the port of Puteoli; these places have their page in the Sacred Book. Following after the first bishop, several will go to die one after the other in the arenas, where openings still remaining allow the cages of the ferocious beasts to be seen. We have kissed the soil where the blood of St. Januarius and his companions ran; a few days before we had descended into the Catacombs where their bones were gathered. How we felt our hearts stirred in these sepulchral galleries, as we acknowledged there with a respectful joy the sacred rendezvous of the first faithful, the place of the altar and of the baptistery, and the place whence the voice of the priest made itself heard by the people!

The Church remained not long buried in this funereal darkness. At the first ray of liberty which shone for her, she arrayed herself, she crowned herself, she gave herself rich sanctuaries. It is thus that at St. Januarius we see, in the chapel of St. Restituta, the remains of the ancient cathedral erected on the columns of the temple of Apollo, and the fragments of the mosaics of the seventh century. Later, under the Norman princes, rises the actual basilica, with its Gothic façade, and its nave in ogives. But above all, I have examined there with the greatest interest an oratory situated behind the middle of the edifice, and founded by the family of the Minutoli. There, at the foot of an altar crowned with a daïs richly sculptured, are found the tombs of these old patricians, from the year 1200 to about 1500. Themselves are painted on the wall of the enclosure, kneeling, some with the insignia of the episcopate, others under their armour of knighthood, with joined hands and pious countenance. Above, and as if to console these images of death, one of the old masters of the Neapolitan school has painted the Passion of the Saviour. The artistic and historic merit of this monument has been acknowledged by the enlightened taste of the Cardinal Archbishop, who has caused its restoration to be actively pursued.

How beautiful was this re-born Italy of the ninth to the thirteenth century! What energetic spring of faith, of courage, of genius! At the same time that Naples shook off the odious dependence on the Greek emperors, all the little scattered cities on the coast imitated the example, and became rivals in courage and activity. Then numerous vessels brought the riches of the East to the inhabitants of Amalfi—a powerful republic, which counted amongst its dearest conquests the body of the Apostle St. Andrew. To-day we see it solitary and depopulated, suspended among its picturesque rocks. From the height of the Convent of the Capuchins, under the vault of an immense grotto, we see by moonlight the waves throw their white foam on the shore to which they formerly bore so much glory and treasure. At Salerno, also, we venerated the tomb of Gregory VII., who came there to find a last shelter, when alone he contended for the liberty of Christianity, and the freedom of the Italian Fatherland.

Unfortunately these times were short, and dating from this epoch begin the traces of the foreign invasions and dominations which disputed the two Sicilies. At Capri is the castle of the Emperor Frederic Barbarossa, rivalling that of Tiberius; there, beside the market-place, in the Church of St. Croix, is the block on which the last descendant of the German dynasty, Conradin, perished at sixteen years of age, by the orders of Charles of Anjou, brother of St. Louis. This prince and his successors raised the Château Neuf, whose old feudal towers command the port. The palace of the Queen Jeanne recalls this sanguinary woman, who, murderess of her husband, lost by her crimes the empire of France in Italy. Then begins the ascendancy of Spain; rich foundations in the monasteries, palaces more sumptuous than elegant, the names even of Medina and Toledo, etc., given to the streets of the town, recall the Castilian dynasty. This however, was to end one day, and to give place to our fleurs-de-lis, which are found again with the family of the Bourbons on the Neapolitan throne. These last vicissitudes of history, the sceptre balanced by turns among these rival people, the rending of the country by the arms of the stranger, are so many mysteries which are not yet explained. But those of anterior epochs are so completely unravelled, Providence has so plainly showed its finger in the ancient destinies of this country, that we may be sure to acknowledge it sooner or later in her modern revolutions.

I forget myself in recitals without interest for you. Alphonse has himself just seen all these things; himself can with living voice describe them to Charles better than one knows how to do it by writing. However, I know by experience that we love to hear about that which we have seen, above all when the circumstances are not the same. And now the beauty of the season lends to this country a charm which without doubt was not then there; therefore it is best, is it not, to write you simply my impressions? And as Amelia has told the details of our voyage, there only remains to me the part of generalities. I had much rather talk with you on our affairs, but how can I do it without news? This privation spoils a little the pleasure of our journey; in thinking of the anxieties of one, of the solitude of the other, I reproach myself for not sharing with you these months of repose.

THE END.

Elliot Stock, Paternoster Row, London.

NOTE.

THE translator of this volume originally intended to present to the English reader the whole of Frederic Ozanam's letters. As this has been found impracticable, by reason of their extent, the present volume is issued, as a first series, with the intention of following it by a second, which will contain Ozanam's correspondence from the time of his marriage and settlement in Paris to his death.

www.ingramcontent.com/pod-product-compliance
Lightning Source LLC
Chambersburg PA
CBHW030017240426
43672CB00007B/991